A DEFENCE OF LIBERTY
AGAINST TYRANTS

A

DEFENCE OF LIBERTY
AGAINST TYRANTS

A TRANSLATION OF THE
VINDICIAE CONTRA TYRANNOS

BY

JUNIUS BRUTUS

WITH AN HISTORICAL INTRODUCTION BY

HAROLD J. LASKI

Reader in Political Science in the University of London

GLOUCESTER, MASS.
PETER SMITH
1963

A

DEFENCE OF LIBERTY
AGAINST TYRANTS

A TRANSLATION OF THE
VINDICIAE CONTRA TYRANNOS

BY

JUNIUS BRUTUS

WITH AN HISTORICAL INTRODUCTION BY

HAROLD J. LASKI

Reader in Political Science in the University of London

First Published 1924

Reprinted, 1963
By Permission of
G. BELL & SONS, LTD.

TO

MY COLLEAGUES ON *THE NATION*

H. W. MASSINGHAM, H. W. NEVINSON, H. M. TOMLINSON

J. L. HAMMOND, J. A. HOBSON

" He who sows seed in the minds of men must have
the eye of a hawk to see where it falls, and the vision
of a god to discern whether its fruit be good or evil."

The Nation, April 28, 1923

H. J. L.

NOTE

The *Vindiciae Contra Tyrannos* has been so long a rare book, that it is hoped this reprint of the translation of 1689 will be useful to teachers of political philosophy. One of the great difficulties of the subject is the fact that the writings of all save the most important thinkers are not available outside the great libraries. This volume fills at least a small gap in the need. If it is successful, it is hoped to make it the first of a series of similar reprints. The introduction is intended to supply a quite general background to the theory of the text. Readers who require a fuller treatment should go to G. Weill's excellent *Théories sur le Pouvoir Royal en France pendant les guerres de Religion* (Paris, 1892).

The dedication is a word of thanks on my part for three pleasant years of service in a great fellowship.

H. J. L.

London School of Economics and Political Science.

CONTENTS

HISTORICAL INTRODUCTION

I

All political systems are the natural reflection of their historic environment, and there has been no influential political work that is not, in essence, the autobiography of its time. That does not mean the absence from it of a flavour of universality. Ideas beget a progeny which soon outstrip the narrow concepts of their creator. It means only that the attempt to penetrate the nature of political phenomena has always been coloured by the special experience of the writer. Rousseau is what he is because Geneva retained to the end his ultimate spiritual allegiance; and the federalism of Proudhon bears the marks of one to whom the village of his birth is passionately dear. It is in the competition of the market place that systems receive that correction of the event which gives them their applicability.

This is, in a special degree, true of the Reformation. It was the real starting point of democratic ideas; but, therein, it builded better, or, at least, differently than it knew. In the name of a theory of religious truth, existing ecclesiastical institutions were overthrown; and in the attempt at their reconstruction men were driven to enquire into the nature of obedience. The scale of things underwent a decisive change. European Christianity had previously encountered the notion of reform; it had hardly until the advent of Luther, been compelled to confront the portent of a revolution. The significance of Luther lies in the fact that, all unconsciously, he made the Reformation one of the great turning points in the history of political ideas. From the fall of the Roman empire until his emergence, political thought was always dominated by the notion of a single Christian Commonwealth. Its ultimate sovereignty was the possession of God. Its direction belonged to Pope and Emperor as his viceregents ; and the degree of power allotted to each varied with the affiliations of the given writer. The notion of a Europe divided into self-sufficient and independent states was not completely absent ; but the universality characteristic of the Church, and the closeness of its connection with political life, prevented that notion from attaining its natural results. The prospect, however, of any genuine imperial suzerainty perished with the failure of Lewis of Bavaria ; and when the defeat of the Council of Basle made it clear that any genuine internal purification of Rome was impossible, the way, as Cardinal Cesarini then pointed out, lay open for new political dogmas.

If Luther was not the real author of those dogmas, he was, in a real sense, their efficient cause. Aiming as he did at the reform of the Papacy, conceding, at the outset, the divine character of the Church, it was to a power not less divine in substance that he was compelled to make his appeal. He therefore reasserted the divine character of princely rule ; and he deduced therefrom the right of the ruler to control the religion of his subjects. Put summarily, the result of his effort was simply to endow, within the limits of his territory, the Elector of Saxony with papal attributes ; and had Lutheranism succeeded without opposition, the result might well have been the extinction of political liberty in Europe. For the sixteenth century is, in any case, a centralising time, and the theory of divine right in princely rule added to despotic notions a religious penumbra at once previously absent from, and curiously alien to, the temper of the religion itself. To Luther, no doubt, the dogma was no more than a weapon forged in the smithy of his special needs ; and it had the two obvious merits of attacking the Roman power on the one hand, and

beatifying social order upon the other. Nor was it intended
to be a radical dogma save against Rome ; for Luther,
religious doctrine apart, has a place among the great con-
servatives of history. Yet it was in the discussion of its
true meaning that there were evolved the main principles
of modern political freedom.

For Luther's protest against the degradation of Rome
had synchronised with two other great movements which
lent him the aid of their influence. The growth of nation-
alism in the fifteenth and sixteenth centuries had prepared
the ground for the decentralisation of religious power ; and
the new intellectual atmosphere fostered by the Renaissance
made possible the search for, and acceptance of, new religious
foundations. But religion was then, and, indeed, until
the nineteenth century, too deeply imbedded in the structure
of the state for the discussion of religious dogma to be
possible without, at the same time, involving enquiry into
the validity of political systems. The new religions sought
a place within a state that had been previously part of a
unified system ; and they were prepared to hew their way
to acceptance. Once, therefore, research into their rights
had been undertaken, the unity of the middle ages was
immediately obsolete. Every centre of discontent became
also a centre of novelty. The Christian Commonwealth
which had been one and indivisible was dissolved into a
variety of separate and sovereign states. Men ceased to
think in European terms. The interest of Europe as a
whole, which had, however vaguely, been preserved above
the conflict of nations, was lost before the separate ends of
states which viewed their individual well-being as itself
the highest objective. The loss by the papacy of any
accepted claim to moral leadership was, of course, the main
institutional source of change. The idea of the state as
the end to be preserved found its justification in part from
the renewed contact with Greek political philosophy and in
part from the new and pungent sense of immediate fact
which is the contribution of the Renaissance to the atmosphere
of political discussion. The realism of Aristotle and the
pragmatic analysis of Machiavelli combined to defeat the

incoherent cosmopolitanism of medieval Christianity. The effort was sharpened by religious warfare ; and the new states demanded a new political philosophy for their explanation and safeguard. If they were to be sovereign, they must know the meaning of their sovereignty. Their independence of Rome, on the one hand, and the presence within themselves of dissent, upon the other, made the problem of their internal relationships the main theme of political enquiry.

The sixteenth century is, therefore, nothing so much as one long research into the terms of political obedience. Luther might seek to protect the prince against the anarchy at least in theory implicit in the structure of Protestantism by insisting on the duty of submission to rulers whose power was of God. But that did not bind those to whom his creed was anathema, and, where it brought peace, it was the peace of men who accepted despotism as a relief from war. Yet even then it did not bind those who, coming to full political maturity after the Peace of Augsburg, found themselves outside the narrow boundaries therein laid down for toleration. Had that peace contained some effective measure of protection for the adherents of Calvin, the history of European democracy might have been very different. Dogmas apart, however, temperamental differences between the leaders of Reform made impossible the establishment of a united Protestant front against Rome. The new creed was driven to repeat the belligerent experience of its predecessor.

The result was to throw all political systems once more into the melting pot. Every minority, whether in England or upon the Continent, which struggled against odds for survival, was compelled, by the logic of its situation, to enunciate a theory of the state. It sought to explain its will to live in terms of political right. It challenged the nature of such authority as denied to it a place within the categories of citizenship. Religions which began by protesting that they were entirely innocuous to the existing civil order, continued by insisting that it was the duty of the state to suit its character to the new spiritual dispensation, and they ended by denying the legitimacy of any government which did not admit the merit of toleration. The transformation is well seen in English Protestantism in the movement from Tyndale's *Obedience of a Christian Man*, with its vigorous defence of passive obedience, to Ponet's insistence,[1] a generation later, upon the right to overthrow a *régime* which refuses accommodation. The Scottish Reformation was not less prolific of novelty ; and it is possible that Buchanan's famous Dialogue [2] was the most influential political essay of the century. So soon, also, as Holland raised the standard of revolt, its thinkers stated a theory of politics in which not merely did the right to religious freedom become a natural part of the philosophy of the state, but the denial of it became the definition of tyranny. Even the magistral effort of Althusius is, at bottom, simply an attempt to generalise from a special situation.

Detail excepted, the method is a similar one throughout Europe. The attempt is always, on the one hand, to limit the power of government, and, on the other, to destroy the papal right of interference by showing the sovereign and, therefore, independent character of the state. This destruction of papal power was not, after 1570, the work of religious reformers alone. There came a time when the civil wars produced by religious dissension had wrought a havoc so extensive that even moderate Catholics were willing to deny that the state must perish for conscience sake. Men were then led to see that state and church can be regarded as species of a larger genus, and that neither is dependent upon the other. That vision, indeed, was partial, and had it not lain at the root of Calvinism in its Scottish form, it is possible that the conversion of Henry IV would have prevented it from bearing its natural fruit. For whether men insist on the definitely separate spheres of church and state, as did Melville and the Presbyterians, or admit that toleration, though a *pis aller*, is at a certain point inevitable, as did the Politiques, the way lay open

---

[1] *A short Treatise of Politique Power.*
[2] *De jure Regni Apud Scotos.*

for the emergence of a definitely secular state. But that day still lay in a remote future.

The independent character of the state was reached, immediately, in a somewhat different way. It was accomplished by making the use of power a trust, and giving to the people as a corporate whole the right to judge the character of its exercise. The result, inevitably though not deliberately, is a philosophy of the state that has in it the seeds of democratic institutions. For once it is clear that the prince holds his power upon conditions, it becomes necessary to discover the means through which those conditions may be enforced. The merit of popular sovereignty at once becomes apparent; and to an age still permeated by feudal notions, princely power becomes, at least in part, the result of, and dependent upon, a contract with the people. The purpose is not a democratic one; it is the enforcement of some special desire that the contract has always in view. Nor is any loophole left through which the democracy may catch the vision of its power. For, until the reckless days of the League, and then with some vagueness, the corporate people does not mean the mass of individual citizens. It is taken to mean the representative men of the nation, nobles, magistrates, officials, just as, three centuries later, a French Minister could identify the state with the Chamber of Deputies.[1] The notion of equality had not moved from the religious to the political sphere.

This is, of course, unduly to simplify a complex situation; and it omits the influence of such special views as those of Bodin and his school. Above all, it does not sufficiently emphasise what becomes apparent only from the mass of detail, namely, that the favour accorded to popular sovereignty has always a specifically religious penumbra. All successful political generalisations have been intended to serve a particular end; they give to the " stereotype "[2] of the age a satisfying mythology. So soon as the theory of popular sovereignty had secured for the minority a

[1] Cf. my Authority in the Modern State, p. 367.
[2] Cf. Lippmann, Public Opinion, pp. 79 ff.

toleration which, however grudging, was still toleration, the main root of contemporary political disturbance was removed. The partial toleration so won did not, of course, imply that men had learned to accept the secular nature of the state; it implied only, as the Thirty Years' War was, in its origins, to demonstrate, that the cost of religious warfare necessitated a breathing-space in which they learned the political value of indifference. Nor, in general, did they seek to probe further into the meaning of popular sovereignty. It was not until the French Revolution that Europe as a whole grasped the fact that the theory, with all its possibilities, applied not less to political than to religious needs.

In England, indeed, the transition to the secular state had, at least in part, been made much earlier. The Rebellion and the Revolution transferred the results of the discussion upon the place of religion in the state to the political field a century before Rousseau so depicted them that no man might mistake their meaning. But, even in England, until the emergence of Burke and Bentham, it is the consistently religious background of political speculation that is most striking. Locke could not write a treatise on civil government until, in the *Letter on Toleration*, he had vindicated the self-sufficiency of the state, and its consequent freedom from religious trammels. The implication of the Bangorian controversy was simply, at bottom, that the predominant section of Convocation thought it the duty of the state to persecute in the name of religious truth. Men like Price and Priestley seek so to define the state that they may demonstrate the right of Nonconformists, despite religious difference, to a full citizenship.[1] They and their opponents alike represent the last vestiges of a struggle which goes back to the refusal of Puritan England to accept the system of " Thorough " thrust on it by Laud. But that refusal was not made in the name of toleration, and, in its turn, it takes its form from the long effort to define the nature of a Reformation settlement which refashioned the relationship between state and church. The thought of Tyndale and Ponet, the

[1] *Cf.* my *Political Thought from Locke to Bentham*, pp. 147 ff.

effort of those, Anglican and Catholic alike, who attempted, under Elizabeth and James I, to discover the nature of political allegiance,[1] these are present, at least by implication, not less in the speeches of Eliot and Pym than in the writings of Hobbes and Filmer. The Reformation, in brief, set the perspective of modern political traditions. It was the chief business of later ages, certainly until the Industrial Revolution, to find institutions best fitted to embody its discoveries.

II

The religious wars of France bring out with especial clarity the real nature of the struggle. Not only did they provoke a crisis in which the very notion of royalty was in danger ; they were also a struggle in which political doctrines played a great part in defining and determining the issue. The danger did not come from Calvinism alone. The prospect of a heretic King persuaded the partisans of Rome to the enunciation of dogmas far more extreme than any to which the Hugenots gave adherence. In the shock of conflict, practically every theory of importance in political science until the outbreak of the French Revolution found, in some sort, its expression, with the important and constant exception of egalitarianism. The crisis was, on the whole, unexpected. The firmness of Louis XI, on the one hand, and the easy rule of Louis XII, on the other, seemed to have given the French monarchy a foundation secure beyond all dispute. Yet not only was the succession called into question. The idea of popular election to the throne was mooted. The notion of an inherent, if indirect, right of papal control made itself heard. There were times when the conception of France as a quasi-federation of aristo-cratic republics did not seem impossible. Once, at least, it seemed within prospect that the estates might seek to

---

[1] Cf. C. H. McIlwain, *Political Works of James I.* Introduction.

transform ancient, if dubious, memories into something akin to the form and substance of an English Parliament.

The confusion, of course, did not spring merely from the existence of a Protestant party. It was due, in part, to the economic and social importance of that party's members ; in France, as elsewhere, the connection between Protestant doctrine and commercial development is immediate and significant. In part, also, it was caused by the fact that the nobles seized the opportunity of conflict to reassert claims which the previous half-century had seemed to extinguish ; the age is hardly less a Fronde than a religious struggle. In part, also, the special circumstances of the struggle, the feebleness of the Kings themselves, and the labyrinthine dishonesties of Catharine de' Medici, exasperated men's feelings, and sharpened especially the ambitions of those who, like the Guises, stood within palpable reach of the throne. The hopes of Spain, and the reawakened and reorganised power of Rome undoubtedly contributed to the fashioning of men's thoughts. Yet the existence in France of a powerful body of religious dissent, claiming rights, and with the will to attempt their enforcement in the name of justice, undoubtedly gave to the political ideas of the time a breadth and sharpness of definition they did not have, the work of Buchanan apart, elsewhere. Not indeed that either Catholic or Protestant stood for an unchanging body of coherent doctrine. Each party changed its views with a rapidity that was equalled only by the kaleidoscopic swiftness of events. Protestants who had, under Henry III, embraced the theory of popular sovereignty, had no difficulty, under Henry IV, in proving the virtues of royal absolutism. But ideas have a history more enduring than that of their sponsors. Born of some particular occasion, they live on to become the parent of events far different from what the age of their origin could either have foreseen or desired. The Hugenot who probably sighed with satisfaction when it became unnecessary to test the adequacy of Hotman's history, the Ligueur who, after the Peace of Vervins, looked back upon the feverish democracy of Boucher and Rose as a bad dream, did not realise that they had released forces more powerful by far than the inert quietude they were so thankful to accept.

To Calvin himself only a very limited degree of political novelty can be traced. Rigidly authoritarian in temper, and without an atom of faith in religious tolerance, it was by indirect means only that he opened the way for the developments that ensued. What he preached was obedience to God, and submission, though at one remove, to the magistrate ; and his sense of the importance of authority was clearly shown in his repudiation of Knox to Elizabeth. But he did not clearly recommend any solution when the commands of God and the magistrate were in conflict. The duty of prayer and the acceptance of exile were obvious counsels ; but they hardly suited the energy of a vigorous age, and they had the capital defect of involving ruin for those who accepted them. In part, of course, they originate in Calvin's deep, if gloomy, sense of the natural badness of men, and his consequently natural insistence on the virtue of a strong government which should be fortified against the results of their wickedness. Princes, for him, ruled by the will of God and the right of the people was simply the duty of submission. But there was, alongside the power of the prince, the constituted authority of the magistrates ; and Calvin came to see that when tyranny is in question, they have the right to invoke resistance. It is clear from the general tenor of his writings that by tyranny Calvin meant a *régime* which endangered the existence of the new faith. In that event, resistance was simply obedience to the will of God. He seems to have envisaged a situation in which the general rule is submission, and the call to revolt the result of a confidence on the part of those in authority, without co-operation from the mass, that the safety of religious conviction has reached the extreme point of compromise.

So far, indeed, Calvin might well have claimed that his views were simply traditional to his time. Melancthon had previously emphasised the importance of resisting tyranny ; and until the massacre of Saint Bartholomew not even the growing severity of the Crown tempted any Hugenot theorist to go seriously beyond that point. What Calvin has to say is little different, for example, from Commines' remark, in the previous age, that God sometimes authorises a revolt against a tyrant.[1] The general background of Calvin's politics is, indeed, hardly incompatible with the theory of the state presented in 1519 by so ardent a royalist as Seyssel.[2] But after the death of Louis XII, the despotism depicted by the latter loses its moderation and benevolence, even while the thinkers of the time, and especially the lawyers of the south, continued to insist upon the unlimited nature of royal power. *Quod principi placuit legis habet vigorem* becomes in fact and theory the motto of the French monarchy; and attractive *jeux d'esprit* like the *Contr' Un* of La Boétie would not, before 1572, have provoked any widespread sympathy. A sense of popular right such as the friend of Montaigne depicts is, indeed, as remote from the spirit of the time as the anarchy of Herbert Spencer in an age committed to government interference. The note of all the literature is the unlimited extent of royal power. " The King," said the jurist Vincent de la Loupe in 1551,[3] " can make wars, treaties, and peace when they seem good to him. He can impose taxes, make laws, statutes, and ordinances. He can create such magistrates as he pleases. Whatever he says is accepted as law, and as though it were the oracle of a new Apollo." Nor did the Gallican complexion of French Catholicism do other than emphasise the overwhelming dignity of the King. Du Moulin, for example, did not hesitate, whether as Catholic or Protestant, to admit the royal supremacy over religious matters. When Francis II ascended the French throne, the monarchy seemed securely established in popular acceptance as the pivot of the whole political system. The jurists had given to it the support of legal science. The adherents of either religion had found no discrepancy of importance between dogma and despotism. The change

[1] Bk. IV, c. i. *Cf.* Bk. V, c. xvii-xix.

[2] *La Grande Monarchie de France.*

[3] *Premier et Second Livre des Dignités* (ed. *cf.* 1560), p. 4. This is only one of many similar works on royal authority, of which those of Budé, Brêche, and d'Espence are the best known. Their publication continued right through the civil wars.

of temper which supervened is as remarkable as it is un-expected.

From the mere existence of religious dissent conflict would not necessarily have developed. Calvinism simply gave rein to a wider controversy which is traceable to diverse causes. There was the memory of Statutes which could be interpreted, as Coke and Prynne interpreted the feudalism of Magna Charta, to narrow the boundaries of royal power. The ancient weakness of the Crown could be contrasted with its recent strength to awaken memories of a time when some degree of popular consultation was the avenue to law. The nobility saw itself deprived of power with deep discontent. Under Louis XI it had been almost annihilated. Under his successors it became a court rather than a magistracy. The people were discontented as a result of foreign war; to them princely ambition meant only the growth of taxes. Nor did the municipalities see the invasion of their prerogatives without the sense that the monarchy had used them for its own exaltation without payment for their aid. The Hugenots, therefore, merely precipitated a controversy of which the possibilities were already latent. Once a party was prepared to make protest against oppression, it was inevitable that every cause of discontent should proclaim its presence; for it is impossible to set bounds to a revolution. The consequence was that while the Hugenots were striving to prove that the well-being of the state demanded their toleration, and the Catholics to insist that their religion must not be subordinated to purely temporal considerations, each was in fact compelled to envisage the broader political situation in the hypothesis they presented. The massacre of Saint Bartholomew in one generation, and the accession of a Hugenot King in the next, came to give additional point to the dispute. ‹The central dogma involved was not, at first, the sovereignty of the people, but merely the duties of the Crown to its subjects. But once it was discovered that the real problem was not the duties of the Crown, but their enforcement, the theory of popular sovereignty became the real centre of doctrinal discussion; so much so, that even an abstract essay like that of Bodin is, above all, an attempt at its refutation. Not, of course, that it was a new doctrine. Gregory VII had already appealed to it against the encroachments of the Ghibellines. Thomas Aquinas and Marsiglio of Padua had both estimated its validity. But in the French wars, it became not merely a dogma, but a dogma supported by battalions ; and its analysis was, as a result, something more than academic exercise.

When Francis II ascended the throne, the movement towards popular sovereignty received no direct impetus. Exactly as the early English reformers were almost passionate in their protestations of allegiance, so the Hugenots made a merit of unconditional support to the throne ; and they insisted, at a general synod, on the illegitimacy of rebellion. But events were greater than themselves. They had not yet, in any wholesale fashion, been tried by persecution ; and their demand for toleration was more the desire to forestall difficulties that were approaching than a protest against the concerted oppression of the government. They were, moreover, gaining ground ; Francis Hotman was only the most considerable convert of those won over by the burning of Anne de Bourg. The regency of the Guises united against that disastrous family not merely the nobility, whose pride was affronted by the spectacle of *novi homines* exercising the sovereignty of the state, but also the Hugenots themselves, who were incensed by the increased persecution for which the Guises made themselves responsible. The result was the conspiracy of Amboise ; and thenceforth there was an extending series of outrages until the culmination of all in the massacre of Saint Bartholomew.

But the development of political thought does not take the direct line to its obvious goal. None of the earlier rebels admitted that he was attacking the state. He claimed simply to be protecting the King, during his minority, against the advice of evil counsellors. There is, indeed, some evidence that more radical doctrine was slowly gaining ground, but there was no official avowal of a new outlook. Nor did the Catholics think differently. They simply condemned rebellion out of hand. Whether it derived from motives of religion or politics, it was, in their view, always wrong. To this attack the Hugenots replied not, be it noted, by palliating the rebels, but by insisting that the regency of the Guises was unconstitutional. It destroyed, they urged, the foundations of French government. The estates ought to be convoked, and a council provided for the King. They affirmed with emphasis that they were not defending their religion, but simply protecting the Crown. " That only," says one of their pamphleteers,[1] " that only has armed us—it is false to say that our petition to the King masks a religious purpose." Francis Hotman's famous attack on the Cardinal of Lorraine has no other substance than this. Let the people be consulted, as in ancient days, and the throne will be secure against mischance. The sudden death of Francis II followed the official convocation of the estates ; but not before Coligny had presented a memorial to the council in which, granted a policy of moderation on the part of the Crown, he offered to pay higher taxes than ever before to prove the measure of Hugenot loyalty to the King.

The reign of Francis II showed no marked change in doctrine, but it demonstrated the existence of two formidable possibilities. It had, in the first place, armed Protestants and Catholics alike. If the motives of rebellion were highly confused, that was less significant than the fact of their presence. It had, in the second place, produced from those whom the Guises had excluded from a share in power, the demand that the Crown be put into Commission during a minority. From that position it would be but a short step to demand some system of perpetual limitation upon monarchical power. The Hugenots, moreover, were building upon the assumption that an unfettered King would necessarily desire toleration. That assumption was bound to prove vain. No King in an era such as this could possibly have remained unfettered, nor was toleration as yet a natural standpoint. What, in brief, had been made clear was that persecution would drive the Hugenots to revolt, and that toleration would involve, at least from those Catholics

[1] *Mémoires de Condé*, I, p. 353. *Epistée envoiée au Tigre de la France.*

wedded to the Guises, a grave measure of armed disloyalty. The next years rendered this development inevitable.

For Charles IX was only a child ; and the regent was Catharine de' Medici. She was moved by no purpose save the appetite for power, and she had no policy save that which seemed most likely to maintain her hold upon affairs. For the experiment she embarked upon with Michel de l'Hôpital as chancellor, and toleration as the basis of his government never had any chance of succeeding. Catharine and her minister were swayed by very different motives. She saw in his policy no more than a means of balancing the power of the Guises by the support of the Hugenots, and when the balance broke down, she had no difficulty in moving to a *régime* of persecution. L'Hôpital, indeed, took broader views. As he himself said, he was shocked that Frenchmen of opposing religious views should have less in common than foreigners of the same religion ; and it was to the rebuilding of the national unity of France that he bent his energies. But the ideas of the author of the *Discours de la Réformation de la Justice* could not have been applied until a generation of civil war convinced men of their substance. Frenchmen of all parties were still convinced that force was a solution of their problems ; they had to pay for their ultimate belief in reasonable compromise by years of social misery. What l'Hôpital preached was moderation in terms of royal despotism. With a theory of monarchy hardly different from that of Seyssel, he sought by administrative skill to conciliate alike Hugenots and Catholics. He realised, as Burke realised two centuries later, that the inevitable outcome of repression is revolution. He saw in Spain what the extreme methods of the Counter-Reformation would produce ; and he sought to cut the Gordian knot of metaphysical difference by evading it. He saw that the state could not afford civil war, and his policy was therefore based on the theory that no cause alien from the substance of temporal affairs was sufficient to persuade it to indulgence in such an evil. But the theory of royal power for which he stood was too absolute for a nobility which sought a larger share in government, and a third estate which was prepared to defend the retention of urban franchises which acted as a protection for religious freedom.

Nor were the Hugenots, who counted upon the moderation of his temper, at all wise in the use of their opportunity. For Catharine was the base upon which the pillar of l'Hôpital's conciliation was founded ; and the woman who schooled her children in the precepts of Machiavelli was a foundation which needed the most cautious scrutiny. The true Hugenot policy was silence. But some invited the Queen-Mother to undertake religious reform in time of peace, lest she be driven to attempt it in a time of storm. [1] Others suggested, with more than a hint of threat, that the throne was not hereditary. If these views were exceptional they were important straws in the wind. Nor was this all. The mass of Hugenots were doubtless loyal to the new *régime* ; but some, like Condé, had a conscience whose workings were intimately affiliated to political ambition, and Catharine had learned from her Italian master the proper method with rivals. L'Hôpital could have succeeded only if the results of his policy were not too obvious in the manifest satisfaction of its beneficiaries. The latter were not so wise, and the more extreme Catholics were naturally quick to point out that their own loyalty was affronted by the toleration of heretics. The Chevalier de Villegagnon, for example, was representative of a fairly general temper among his co-religionists when he insisted, in an appeal to Catharine, that the King had sworn to preserve inviolate his religious inheritance, and that to tolerate heresy was to deny his oath. [2] It was hinted abroad that the tolerance of l'Hôpital prepared the way for the conversion of the King ; and the Sorbonne accepted the thesis of a young doctor of theology who maintained the view that the Pope could depose a heretic sovereign. Appeal was even made to Philip of Spain to protect the true faith. The temper of all parties was clearly becoming exacerbated. " They begin," wrote the Venetian ambassador to his government, " by showing contempt for the law. Thence they pass to

[1] *Mémoires de Condé*, II, p. 424.
[2] *Réponse aux Remontrances* (1561).

contempt for the magistrate. They end by proving their contempt for the King himself." [1]

L'Hôpital did not improve matters by attempting, in the Colloquy of Passy, to bring together the two religious parties. Théodore Beza, indeed, who represented the Hugenots, spoke with an unwonted conservatism, and explained that his religion made the prince the representative of God on earth. But the Cardinal of Lorraine, who spoke for the Catholics, significantly demanded persecution when, with much arrogance, he demanded the defence of the established religion. Nor was it from the Church only that hostility developed. The Parliament of Paris asked why, in the face of law, the heresy of the Hugenots went unpunished, and inquired by what right the King gave them a legal status. The reply made by l'Hôpital that the Parliament should not meddle in affairs beyond its competence only increased the number of his enemies. It was obvious that his ideas of pacification went beyond the convictions of his age ; and the growing number of conversions to the reformed faith, a number above all significant in the ranks of the nobility, embittered the Catholics against toleration.

L'Hôpital, indeed, had his defenders ; but the voice of fanaticism was too loud to be resisted. The Catholics began to publish attacks, to this point without justification, upon Hugenot loyalty. Calvin was shown to favour usurpation ; Beza had defended the Conspiracy of Amboise ; Calvinism involved—it was an accusation truer than its proponents could then have understood—a federal system destructive of the French monarchy. When the Duc de Guise was assassinated, though the Hugenots in general sought to clear themselves of complicity some of their leaders, and, most notably, Théodore Beza, spoke in favour of tyrannicide. Catholic indignation grew apace. Exactly as the Hugenots had protested against the persecution of the Guises, so the Catholics protested against the moderation of Catharine and her advisers. They spoke of changing the dynasty, of giving the nobility a larger place in the national councils, of freeing the towns from l'Hôpital's

[1] Tommaseo, *Relations des Ambassadeurs Vénitiens*, I, p. 537.

encroachments. The clergy used their sermons to a similar end ; and it must not be forgotten that the sixteenth-century sermon fulfilled the functions of the modern press. [1] Once the parties had organised civil war was certain, and with the coming of war there is rarely strength of character enough in any people to permit the expression of moderate views. The position was, moreover, complicated by the fact that the strength of Hugenot organisation, both politically and ecclesiastically, was such as to make them regard the prospects of civil war with some confidence. When Condé took charge of the forces of French Calvinism, he ensured the drift of Catharine towards persecution for two reasons. He was, in the first place, controlled by those who elected him to that office ; no happy augury for one who believed in despotism. And Catharine saw in the struggle for religious freedom an avenue through which Condé might seek political power. Her methods, therefore, changed that she might safeguard her position and influence.

The war did not break out without protest ; and some voices were even raised to demand toleration. It was pointed out by one pamphleteer that God had, over Europe as a whole, protected as well Protestants as Catholics and had thereby manifested his will that both should survive. [2] Castellion, as always urgent in the defence of freedom, insisted that the constraining of conscience never secures more than an empty victory. [3] The curiosity of the time is the insistence of each party on the wickedness of sedition and its desire that the position of the Crown should be kept sacred and inviolate. In fact, the struggle was, in its beginnings, less a direct conflict of religions than a fight between opposing factions of the aristocracy for the possession of the government. The problem of reform happened to be there, and, as the war endured, it became more and more the predominant issue. But, at the outset, religious difference simply permitted a classification of the contestants ; it did not define the objects they had in view.

[1] Cf. Labitte, *La Démocratie chez les Prédicateurs de la Ligue,* for the best discussion of their influence.

[2] Cassander, *De officio pii tranquillitatis* (1561).

[3] *Conseil à la France Désolée* (1562).

How true this is becomes clear from Hugenot pamphlets right down to the fatal night of Saint Bartholomew. They are not, they protest, fighting against the King. They merely desire to protect him against the advice of evil counsellors. They wish to protect the ancient laws of France. They are fearful lest liberty be suppressed. They fight, so they affirm, for the corporate people without distinction of religious belief. In the struggle in which they are engaged, says one writer,[1] they are concerned to protect the integrity of the French throne against the usurpations of the Papacy. The Pope has always been the enemy of the House of Capet, and the counsellors of the King must take thought against the danger he represents. The monarch, it is asserted, is losing the affection of the people, and even if he reigns by divine right, he cannot afford to incur that loss. Another pamphlet[2] draws an analogy between the Hugenots and the famous League of Public Safety. Like the latter, it insists, the Hugenots, as in the great days before the crushing despotism of Louis XI, seek to temper the authority of the Crown by the advice of the nobles, and the corporate will of the provinces and towns. It is, in fact, a species of feudal struggle; and the significance of this enthusiasm for the past is that it emphasises those categories of power in which the Hugenots were most strong. Of their religious demands they say almost nothing. Sometimes there escapes a phrase about the patience they have displayed. Sometimes a note of reality appears as in an attack on the influence of the Sorbonne in promoting civil disturbance. A cry like that of the citizens of La Rochelle that a King hostile to God becomes immediately a mere private person was quite exceptional.

The weakness of this attitude is evident enough. It was the protest of a minority not upon the solid ground of right, but upon the shifty basis of administrative error. It did not frankly avow the substance of its claims, while it sought to conceal the real nature of its efforts in an impossible distinction between the King and his advisers. For,

[1] *La Papimanie de France* (1567).
[2] *Mémoires des occasions de la guerre* (1567).

in theory at least, there was little in this statement of the Hugenot position that an antiquarian-minded Catholic might not have been tempted to accept ; and, confronted by the facts as so presented, the Catholic party remained faithful to the Crown. That, indeed, is the substance of its position. Since it was likely to possess the ear of royal authority, its writers devoted themselves to the proof that all rebellion was wrong, and that royal power was absolute by definition. Even a heretic King, said one writer, [1] ought to be obeyed ; a significant claim that had, when Henry of Navarre became King, so obvious an application that the Guises procured from its author an explicit repudiation of the idea. Resignation, it is urged, is the only attitude to be adopted in the face of grievance. What the King wills is of God, and to resist him is, as Charles IX said in a proclamation, to forget all fear of him to whom the royal power is due. Nor should the nobility forget how directly its power is dependent upon that of the King. Let the nobles ally themselves with the third estate against the monarchy, said one pamphleteer, [2] and no property will be safe. A single noble with a handful of servants cannot fight a mob of hundreds ; and the peasants have already begun to attack the estates of the nobility. Let them be once encouraged, as rebellion encourages them, and no one can see the end. Up to the Edict of Longjumeau, the Catholic note is thus moderate, and not unreasonable. If the religious difficulty is largely evaded, that is true also of the Hugenot writers. Astonishment at popular insolence, as with Monluc, [3] insistence that a liberal *régime* would be disastrous because it would give power to that headless monster an ochlocracy are, after all, no more than the staple arguments of conservatism in the face of popular tumult.

But after the Edict of Longjumeau, the atmosphere changes decisively. From the standpoint of Catholic pride, it represented a serious defeat. Catharine saw in it an encroachment by the Hugenots upon her power ; and

[1] *Remontrance salutaire aux dévoyés* (1567).
[2] *Avertissement à la Noblesse* (1568).
[3] *Commentaires*, II, p. 362.

there now developed rapidly that desire to be done with reform which culminated in the plans for the massacre. L'Hôpital, still true to the ideal of moderation, was driven from office. His dismissal, indeed, was marked by the publication of a plea for peace which is not the least noble of his writings. [1] To give way to Condé, he urged, is not to capitulate shamefully to rebellion ; it is to act as any prince would act who recognises that his subjects are free men. If religious toleration is conceded, the cause of war will disappear. And there cannot, in his view, be political freedom without religious toleration. For liberty cannot be enclosed within boundaries so narrow as to exclude therefrom religion and the conscience it controls. " The liberty of serfdom," he said, " is not liberty at all." But l'Hôpital was too late ; Catharine had already made her decision. An edict of September, 1568, announced war in the royal name upon the reformed religion. They seek, said the King, to establish an empire within the empire given to him by God. The pamphleteers took on a new tone. It now became a duty to destroy heresy. The contrast between the conciliatory tone adopted by Beza at Passy, and the fact of rebellion was pointed out. The Hugenots did not change. They still protested their humble obedience to the King. Could religious toleration be accorded to them, they were ready to take an oath of loyalty. But, in reality, their humility was less real than appeared. In worshipping the King, they had not lost sight of the state of which he was the representative. They equated royalty with freedom, and they meant by freedom not merely the assurance of their safety, but also the preservation of ancient franchises into which the experience of the last generation had driven them to pour a new meaning. What they were in reality seeking was the path to a limited monarchy. Already, there were amongst them men who had blessed tyrannicide. Already, they were discussing whether a prince who did not accept the word of God was a prince at all. Nor was the notion of a contract between monarch and people entirely absent.

[1] *Discours sur la Pacification* (1568).

They had, in fact, evolved the foundations of a system incompatible with the ambitions of the court. There lay ready to the hand of Catharine de' Medici a party to which royal absolutism was a dogma unqualified by any limitation. That persecution was right, they did not doubt; that it should be undertaken, they were ready to prove from the implications, as they deemed them, of heresy. France, they urged, was a Catholic Kingdom, and the King ruled it as an absolute monarch. To say that he did not control the consciences of his subjects was to destroy the roots of his power. Were he to be moderate, the experience of Germany would show him the results of such weakness. Such a policy was bound to commend itself to Catharine so soon as it was clear that the aims of l'Hôpital were incapable of success. To that end Spain and the Papacy were alike endeavouring to persuade her. The Hugenot policy in the Netherlands had failed; and she herself suspected both the ambition of the Bourbons, and the ascendancy established by Coligny over the mind of her son. She made her determination; and there was no difficulty in persuading the weak-willed King to sanction the most extreme plans that Rome could have desired. The die was cast; and on the morrow of Saint Bartholomew, Europe awoke to a new epoch in the history of its political doctrines.

III

The change wrought by the news of the massacre is evident immediately. The court had made the holocaust; Charles IX himself had gloried in its success. It was no longer possible to make any distinction between the King and his advisers. It was the person and position of the crown that was now in question. If Kingship existed for the protection of subjects, what were their rights when the very basis of its meaning was taken away? Saint Bartholomew, as Duplessis-Mornay said, [1] destroyed the mutual faith of prince and subjects, and so uprooted the foundations of

---

[1] *Mémoires*, Vol. II (1824), p. 70.

the state. It made necessary the abandonment of the fiction that the powers of the King were not a fit subject for discussion. It became essential to survey the rights of citizenship, to discover whether a royal power so obviously capable of abuse, could be permitted to exist without definite and guaranteed limitations. Men did not dream of over-throwing the notion of monarchy ; but they had no longer any faith either in the theory of absolutism, on the one hand, or its corollary of passive obedience upon the other. Since Protestantism had been derived from the study of the Old Testament, it became possible to remember the names of Joel and Judith and Jehu. The Catholics might urge that David had refused to be responsible for the death of Saul as the anointed of the Lord ; but the Hugenots could retort that at least he had, and with divine sanction, taken up arms against his royal master. The New Testament was ransacked for texts which might seem to justify rebellion ; and all evidence in favour of submission was explained away. Nor did these researches cease with the Bible. France could not fail to remember that Poland had an elective monarchy. The recent revolutions of Denmark and Scotland were used to point their obvious moral. Har-modius and Brutus became popular deities in the Hugenot Valhalla. The revolt against the tyranny of Tarquin became a model and an example to a horror-struck generation. The issue, for the Hugenots, had become a simple choice between their religious faith and their political loyalty. It was fortunate for European liberty that they did not hesitate in their decision.

Most of the writings which owe their origin to Saint Bartholomew are, on the Protestant side, of two kinds. Some are simple narratives of the day's event. The mere horror of what occurred was rightly regarded as likely to carry conviction of its wickedness to all decent-minded men. Others became, as was natural, a definite enquiry into the nature of government, for it had clearly become essential to restate the Hugenot position. The Court had presented two incompatible defences of its action. [1] On

[1] See Lord Acton's magistral article, *The History of Freedom*, p. 161.

the one hand it had depicted the massacre as the untoward result of a factional conflict within the aristocracy ; on the other it had justified, and even boasted of its commission as the necessary consequence of rebellion and a sacrifice offered to the Church. Some Hugenots remained faithful enough to earlier dogma to accept the first explanation. They had then to justify the fact of being in arms ; and this they did by insisting that while they had no grievance against Kingship itself, they could not bow their necks beneath the yoke of intolerable edicts. Such a position was, of course, an impossible one. It accepted absolutism, on the one hand, while it sought to justify occasional revolution on the other. It was, in fact, the coronation of contingent anarchy ; and it did nothing to meet the profounder circumstances of the new situation. It had no philosophy save what had already been condemned by the massacre ; and its justification of rebellion would have had to be made afresh on each occasion, and then not in terms of general right.

One book then existed of which the substance and temper might have satisfied the most extreme of the Hugenots. The *Contr' Un* of La Boétie had probably been written twenty-five years before ; [1] but the problem it envisaged was exactly the tyranny the Hugenots now confronted. But attractive as was the spirit of La Boétie's essay, avowed and academic republicanism was meat too strong for the digestion of the time. Not that La Boétie was entirely without influence ; but he was used as cautiously as an Anglican bishop might, in the sixties, have announced an interest in Darwinism. The pseudo-classicism of the French Renaissance never went so far as a disbelief in monarchy. Much more typical was the treatise, now known to have been written by Théodore Beza, [2] on the *Rights of Magistrates over their Subjects*. The theory of Calvinist politics is here set forth with perfect clarity. To God alone, it urges, does absolute power belong. Magistrates,

[1] On the whole question of the *Contr' Un* see D'Armaingaud : *Montaigne Pamphlétaire*.

[2] On this book and its influence see A. Cartier, in *Bull. Soc. d'Hist. et d'Archéol. de Genève*, II, iv, 1900.

indeed, have wide authority, and they cannot be held to account by the people. Nevertheless, when they command something that is incompatible with true religion, disobedience becomes a duty. And by disobedience, Beza argues, rebellion may, ultimately, be implied. The value of patience and prayer must not be forgotten ; but when the tyranny becomes intolerable, just remedies must be used against it. Not, however, by every member of the state. The ordinary citizen is bound, by the conditions of his citizenship, to submit. The officers of the state, whose business it is to maintain the laws, must secure their authority ; but they must not depose the prince. There are, however, in each state a body of citizens whose function it is to see that the sovereign does his duty ; in France the States-General is a body of such men. They can, if they will, depose the prince. They safeguard the original rights of the people. They may, if they so desire, restore the French monarchy from its present absolutism to a form more consistent with its original and elective foundation. Royalty is, even though divine in nature, essentially dependent upon popular institution. The people has given power to the prince for its own benefit, and, therefore, upon conditions. If the conditions are not fulfilled, it is obvious that the power conferred reverts to the source of its origin. The only thing to be remembered is that the decision of abuse depends upon authorities of a special nature, and cannot be settled by the ordinary citizen.

Though, obviously enough, Beza had French conditions in his mind when he wrote, his book is a purely general treatise. Like most Calvinist pamphlets, it is aristocratic in final texture, and it is wanting in a clear discussion of the exact means whereby the objects Beza had in view could be attained. But it is the first pamphlet published during the civil wars of which the main keynote is the idea of popular sovereignty, and Beza may well claim to be the first in that significant procession of those whom Barclay in the *De Regno* called Monarchomachs. With the Catholic phase of that school we are not, at the moment, concerned, but of the Protestant branch certain general hypotheses may be laid down. In fighting the absolutism of the Reformation State they were concerned to secure religious freedom. None of them valued it as an end in itself. None of them would, had the occasion offered, have conceded freedom to an opponent. But alike in Scotland as with Buchanan, and in France as with Beza and his successors, they were concerned to show the impossibility of an absolute state. They sought to secure certain rights against the possibility of princely encroachment. They had, therefore, to argue, first, that princes are not free to settle as they will the religion of the state, and secondly, that the reason of this limitation lies in the general nature of the state itself. The latter is, for them, practically invariably the result of a contract which, however varied in form, always confers certain rights upon the people. Law is, therefore, never the simple command of an Austinian system, as, for example, that of Bodin, but the attempt to fulfil the purpose of the social contract. If it does not fulfil that purpose, it is not law. Laws, therefore, are the reflection of the law of nature which at once brought into being the social contract and is the purpose and end of political authority.

From the Protestant point of view, the results of this theory are perfectly clear. A law which violates the purpose of the social contract is not a law at all, and may therefore be resisted. Edicts of religious persecution are contrary to that purpose, and the Hugenots, when properly warranted by persons of authority, may take up arms against them. The Monarchomachs had an importance which went far beyond the very limited aim their effort had in view. It was in itself valuable in an age of despotic centralisation so intense as the sixteenth century to have an effective protest against unlimited power. In Scotland, France and Holland the Reformers represented, broadly speaking, a popular movement to which the Crown was hostile ; it consequently became the necessary condition of religious success that the aristocracy of the Crown should be secured or some other form of toleration granted. Even in England it is true to say that the condition upon which Parliament was successful against Charles I was the fact that the Puritans

were prepared to give battle against the finality of the Eliza-
bethan settlement. The development is, of course, most
clear in Holland, where rebellion is not merely successful,
but leads to the formation of a republic of which the prosperity was based on toleration. But the Dutch struggle
is only the most striking of several ; and the whole Monarchomachic movement points the moral that the political liberty
of the seventeenth and eighteenth centuries was the outcome
of the protest against religious intolerance. Had there
not been that protest, the general condition of Europe
would have been similar to that of France under Louis XIV—
an inert people crushed into uniform subjection by a central-
ised and unprogressive despotism.

Nor must another aspect of this effort be neglected. The
sixteenth century is pre-eminently a century of *raison d'état*.
The poison of Machiavelli was in its blood, and, as the
reign of Henry VIII makes evident, a cynical utilitarianism
is its predominant temper. Expediency is a basis of rights ;
it can never become an effective basis of right. It is
to the credit of the Monarchomachs that they moved
the question to higher ground. They were anxious to
make it not merely wise, but also legal, to rebel. In order
to do so, they were compelled to show, as in the work of
Gentillet, [1] the inadequacy of any basis other than ethical
for political institutions. And it is permissible to argue
that no motive save that of religious conviction would have
been strong enough to inspire their effort against the inertia
which made men anxious for any peace, whatever its character. They saw clearly that only by meeting the claims of
the secular state upon the ground of absolute right could
the validity of their plea be accepted. There is no other
way in which the rights of associations can be maintained.
Once utility is admitted as the sole ground of right, the
state can enforce its supremacy as against all other bodies.
It is, of course, true that most of the Monarchomachs were
aiming at a dominance for their own creed not less complete
than that which they denied to the state itself. Undoubtedly
the victory of the state was, on the whole, a necessary victory,

[1] *Discours sur les moyens de bien gouverner* (1579).

but its minimisation by religious bodies was the main guarantee against its abuse.

Beza's book is the beginning of a long tradition which expresses itself in many forms. It was at once applied to purely French conditions in a treatise of 1577. The author of *Whether it is Lawful for the People and the Nobility to take up Arms* is unknown;[1] but it is obvious that he had read Beza's pamphlet to good advantage. Unless, he says, the state of France is remedied, those who love her may well be accused of parricide. They must not confuse the state with the government. The object of the first is the public good; the second may simply seek the welfare of particular persons. With Kingship in particular, it is important to distinguish between the permanent dignity of the office, and the fallible character of some given occupant. If the latter be a tyrant, no one can be so mad as to think resistance to him a crime. Rebellion against tyranny, indeed, is a defence of the real interests of monarchy against those who would destroy it. And the institutions of France have been aptly constructed to this end. The parliaments exercise surveillance over the workings of justice. The chamber of accounts preserves the royal demesne against the danger of excessive alienation. The task of the nobility is to prevent the ruin of the state by enforcing upon the monarch the observance of his coronation oath. Clearly, then, the Hugenots have a right to resist, and when God has made sufficient proof of their endurance, he will not fail to bless their aims.

As a serious defence of the Reformer's position, the pamphlet is at once clear and consistent. Like Beza's essay, it contains within itself the germs of all that was later to be developed into a full and mature theory of the state. Here is set out the notion of a contract between monarch and people, the sense that interference with monarchical power is an ultimate act, for which, however, provision must be made, the conception that power is a trust. The writer is essentially moderate in his outlook. Moved as he obviously was by the spectacle of the massacre,

[1] *Mémoires sur l'état de France sous Charles IX*, II, p. 239.

he yet did not seek to erect the circumstances of a very special act of royal perfidy into a philosophy which viewed it as an ordinary event. Like all the Hugenots, rebellion is for him a detestable thing, and authority is always exalted above the reach of the common people. Other writers, intelligibly enough, were less restrained. Some exhausted themselves in vituperation of the government and sought to show, from the analysis of its members' lives, their complete unfitness to rule. The author of *La France-Turquie*, for example, charges the Crown with seeking to establish a crushing despotism, and in what appears to be the sequel of this pamphlet, [1] he suggests the banishment of Catharine to a convent, the fall of the Chancellor, the exile of the King's counsellors and their replacement by advisers nominated by the provinces, and the dismissal of all foreigners. Until the States-General can be summoned he urges that the towns and provinces of both religions shall form an armed league against tyranny, and refuse to pay taxes. Other writers were deeply anxious for revenge, and demanded any assistance, from within or from without, that might accomplish this end. The author of the *Tocsin*, for example, was not satisfied to call on Condé and Navarre for help against the tyrant; he summons Elizabeth, William of Orange, and the Swiss, to help in the work of liberation. The author of the *Réveille-Matin des Français* went even further, and actually appealed to the Guises, the assassins of Coligny, to expel the House of Valois from the throne, and occupy it themselves.

The *Réveille-Matin* went too far for the vast majority of Hugenots; to embrace the cause of the Guises was only less evil than to see the continuance of the Valois in power. But it is more than a mere *cri de coeur*. Its two dialogues seek to show that Calvinists had been in the history of the previous thirty years devoted to the cause of the Crown, that they had no other object than to assure the well-being of the Kingdom, and the Convocation of the States-General. It speaks with ardent hope of the

---

[1] On this and the following pamphlets see the bibliographical details in H. Hauser, *Les Sources de l'Histoire de France*, VIII, pp. 247 f.

assassination of the tyrant. It depicts a federal organisation of communes which may by rebellion win their freedom. It insists that the estates may limit the power of the prince. It sees in the maintenance of communal immunities the sole effective guarantee against the crushing effects of monarchical despotism. The book is, to some extent, a compilation ; its account of Saint Bartholomew is taken from a widely-read narrative of Hotman's, [1] its theories are often an almost textual reproduction of Beza's essay, and its eloquent picture of the disastrous results of tyranny is taken, in great part, from La Boétie. The compiler is uncertain, though it is possibly that Nicholas Barnaud, the physician, whose violence even Beza condemned. [2] But it had a wide influence. It was many times reprinted, and it was translated both into Dutch and German. Its appeal to the Guises apart, it differs only in its emphatic tone from the bulk of the writings produced after the massacre by the Hugenots.

They have thus a coherent body of doctrine to enunciate. An insistence upon the validity of tyrannicide, a confidence in the results of a guarantee of local liberties, an appeal to the power of the estates, these are the main part of the common stock of ideas upon which the Protestants drew. With their well-organised municipalities, such as La Rochelle and Montauban, with their closely-knit ecclesiastical structure, with their solid power among the nobility and the rich bourgeoisie, they had every reason to hope that the translation of such ideas into the structure of the French state would be the surest guarantee of their safety. These pamphlets, in fact, were not simply published in the void. They attempted the provision of definite institutional channels for the sources of Protestant strength. What was needed was a convincing proof to their generation that they were seeking not daring innovation but genuine reform. If, like Coke and Selden and Prynne in the next century, they could convince their countrymen that the picture they had in their heads was the original institutional pattern of France before the usurpations of Louis XI, they would

[1] *Cf.* Hauser, *op. cit.*, p. 250.   [2] *Ibid.*

immensely increase the power of their appeal. For there is in every generation a large body of men whose zeal for reform is largely dependent upon the degree to which it can be referred to antiquity. If, again, like Locke in the revolution of 1688, they could give to the vague mass of social theory a stability and firmness which made it immediately intelligible to the average citizen, they would become that most deadly of all opponents, a rebellion armed not less with a philosophy than with cannon. So far, the winds of doctrine had blown with equal force on either side. In the next years, and until Henry of Navarre became heir to the throne, the Protestants derived a new strength from their formulation of political doctrine with which the Roman Catholic party was unable to compete.

That strength is not derived entirely from their own resources. Michel de l'Hôpital had seen from the first the vast social loss that would be involved in conflict ; once it was apparent that civil war was not destined to be a mere interlude, the majority of decent-minded Catholics swung round to the support of his ideas. The Politiques, as they are called, are not purely a Catholic party, for Hotman, in his *Brutum Fulmen*, adopted ideas essentially theirs, and the complicated intrigues of which de la Noue was the centre had as their object the union of Protestants and Catholics on the basis of common effort for a peace of moderation. The importance of the Politiques can hardly be overestimated. It is not merely that their ideas eventually prevailed. Their plea for religious toleration was the root of the settlement worked out in the seventeenth century. Their theory of the relation between church and state was, practically speaking, that through which the state eventually won its freedom from the trammels of medievalism. Their emphasis upon passive obedience and indefeasible hereditary right links them up with the Anglican party of seventeenth-century England. Their literary work is of enduring significance, and though some of it is later in date than the actual struggle in France, all of it has in mind the background of that conflict. The outstanding pamphlets are the *Apologia Catholica* of Du Bellay which defends the hereditary

claims of Henry of Navarre against the attempt to
pervert the succession in favour of the House of Guise ;
the *Satyre Ménipée* which is not merely a great satire, but
a veritable storehouse of political opinions ; the *De Regno*
of Barclay which, while it seeks to overthrow the whole
structure of the Monarchomachs, is not the less fatal to
the extreme Roman claims ; the *Quatre Excellent Discours*
of the Sieur de Fay, the grandson of l'Hôpital, which
perhaps best expresses the general feelings of the party ;
and, above all, the *République* of Bodin which, though in
form a general analysis of political science, is essentially
a defence of the position taken up by the Politiques. The
speeches of l'Hôpital are an enduring monument to the
temper of the movement ; while lesser works like the *Discours*
of La Noue and the *Vindiciae* of Servins are, in a lower
rank, illustrative of the diverse aspects possessed by the party.

Few things are more symptomatic of the changing temper
induced by the Reformation than the rise of the Politiques.
Here is a party to whom religion, however individually
important, is, socially, a secondary consideration. They
made it their business to vindicate the supreme character
of the civil power against the claims of any competing
allegiance whatever. Their effort was to secure the unity
of the state ; and they insist that before the demands of
such unity all other demands must give way. Their outlook
was purely utilitarian. They defend indefeasible hereditary
right and the duty of passive obedience simply on the
ultimate ground that the community cannot afford the loss
that is implied in the issue to them of a challenge. They
favour toleration, not on the ground of right, but because
the cost of suppressing diversity of opinion is too heavy to
be endured. What above all impresses them is the paramount
evil of anarchy ; and they insist on the removal of religion
from the sphere of civil policy on the ground that its retention there breeds an expense that will destroy the state.
What they saw clearly was the fact that religious diversity
had come to stay ; and they therefore rejected an ecclesiastical sanction which had ceased to exercise its earlier
magic. They were thus driven back to the ideal of a

religiously indifferent state as the sole territory on which men could continue to act in concert for the public good. Many, if not most of them, admitted that their ideal was a *pis aller ;* could persecution have been made to pay, it would have been desirable as a basis for deepening political unity. But once that had been proved impossible, they searched for foundations which should secure order, whatever the cost. This it is which explains their acceptance of divine right, and their passionate defence of the Salic Law. They insist on the necessity of monarchy, and they reject, as with Servins, Hotman and Pithou, the notion that the Pope has the right to control princes. What they established was the self-sufficient and autocratic state of the Grand Monarch. If, in a sense, that was the direct high road to 1789, it is probably an adequate reply that the Reformation had so seriously endangered the foundations of order that their object could hardly have been achieved in another way. It is true, of course, that their exaltation of order at the cost of liberty was itself, as with Barclay, a direct attack upon the Monarchomachs. Here, indeed, their relationship to the latter is not unlike that of Burke to Thomas Paine. The attention of the one was concentrated always on the method by which reform was secured ; the attention of the other was directed to the substance of the reform achieved. The Monarchomachs saw only the direct evils of the tyranny beneath which they lived ; the Politiques emphasised the cost of overthrowing that tyranny. But they were at one with their antagonists in the root of the problem which was the removal of the cause which led the Hugenots to resistance. Once that had been effected, there was little ground of difference between the protagonists of either party. For the Hugenots did not defend resistance to tyranny, and therefore liberty, as such. What they defended was their right to worship God in their own way. Once that had been granted, then substantive grievance was removed ; and the enforcement of their general case was left to other causes.

But that case was more powerful than they themselves were aware ; and even when its particular occasion had been removed, the record remained to serve new purposes. Nor is it doubtful that the impression produced by its mere statement was, at the time, overwhelming. The immense effort made to answer the chief Hugenot writers is evidence enough that they wrote for a generation which responded eagerly to their work. The intellectual power engaged upon the Hugenot side was not the least important lever in its hands ; and, in the main, it derived that importance from two works. Much, indeed, of the effort of the Politiques is an attempt to answer them ; and it is hardly too much to say that toleration came largely because the Hugenot plea for resistance was the only possible alternative. Of the two books, the earlier was the *Franco-Gallia* of Hotman. It was the first comprehensive attempt to discover the historical nature of the French monarchy, and therefrom to deduce the rightness of the Hugenot plea for a limitation of royal power. The *Vindiciae contra Tyrannos*, probably by Duplessis-Mornay, though mainly a brilliant summary of ideas already adumbrated by members of his party, surpassed all other essays of the time in the vigour and lucidity with which it restated them.

Neither book has the appearance, or even substance, of a pamphlet with an immediate purpose. That of Hotman, in particular, with its formidable apparatus of texts, its careful survey of juristic opinion, its analysis of the chroniclers, was hardly less an historical work of the first importance, than a *livre de circonstance*. It seeks to show that within a time but little beyond the memory of living men, the monarchy of France was elective and controlled by the estates. The men who built the ancient monarchy, the Franks, were in nature, as in name, free. They had sustained their independence against the attack of Rome. If they created a monarchy, they made of their Kings no more than the guardians of their liberties, and to this end, they made the monarchy elective ; that was at once a safeguard of good conduct in the monarch himself, and an assurance that he would educate his sons to be worthy of succeeding him. But he left to them of right nothing save his personal patrimony. The matter of his succession was decided by the people. Hereditary rule had become a custom ; but it was directly embodied in no statute, and it derived its value solely from popular acquiescence. In later editions, indeed, Hotman went further and explained how novel was the existing system of absolute monarchy ; the title of Majesty, for instance, was accorded to Kings only when they presided over the national assembly. In the edition of 1586, Hotman admits that hereditary succession has become an irrevocable method of royal choice ; but since Henry of Navarre had become heir to the French throne in the interval between that date and the first edition, it is unnecessary to suspect any profound explanation of the new emphasis.

Kingship for Hotman, then, has its roots in popular right. It is made by the people, it exists for them. Popular right is not less ample in the organisation of the kingdom. The best form of government is a mixed constitution. That which enables the nobility to be a balance between the competing forces of King and people best secures a *régime* of liberty. Already, clearly, we have moved far from the facile echoes of Seyssel's theories which had, in the half-century before Bartholomew, satisfied Calvinist writers. This idea of a balance is, in Hotman's view, inherent in the French system through the periodic convocation of the estates. It is to that national assembly that final political control is accorded. It is the guardian of the purpose of the state. Peace and war, the making of laws, nomination to high office, all such matters as these are within its competence. It has regulated the succession. It has prevented the undue alienation of the royal demesne. Without its permission, no King could pardon offenders, or dismiss a high functionary from office. It is, indeed, true that within more recent times the age of popular control has passed, and that of government by lawyers has taken its place. Instead of its national assembly, France is cursed with the Parliament of Paris, a body which is no more than a usurping instrument of the royal will, and, above all, an evil which has come to prominence through the usurping power of Rome. But this is an innovation upon constitutional usage. By right, the national assembly is the guardian of historic French liberties. It was, moreover, supported by the existence of definite and large provincial immunities the protection of which was the purpose of much fundamental law. So, too, with municipal rights. Wherever, in brief, we find the material of popular sovereignty, we find the basis of the French constitution. Its institutions are the channel through which that theory runs ; and, where it is obscured, it is because innovation has thwarted its achievement.

The strength of Hotman's book lies not only in the real learning it displays, but also in the very great ability with which it conceals the true object of its polemic. In appearance, it seems to maintain no more than that French absolutism was an historic novelty, and that the true constitution was far more democratic in its operation. But in the process of its argument it is able to buttress every dogma of the Hugenot creed by proving its origin in the facts of French history. Bad Kings may be deposed ; the nobility has a special place in the political structure ; women are excluded from a share in government by the Salic law—a palpable hit, not only at Catharine de' Medici, but also at contingent Spanish ambitions ; the King must be carefully distinguished from the state that the interest of the people may not be confounded with his personal well-being ; local autonomy is the root of political freedom—especially, as in the instance detailed by Hotman, in Languedoc, where Calvinism was especially strong ; such provincial freedoms are safeguarded by fundamental law. The whole apparatus of the edifice represented a formidable weapon in the hands of Hotman's party. It made their opponents seem the innovators, while they themselves appeared as the defenders of historic constitutionalism.

Nor can the Catholic answers to the book be said to have disturbed its central positions. Papire Masson, the royalist historian, could find no more than invective as a retort to its argument. [1] Matharel, one of the writers whose fortune had been made by abject subservience to Catharine de'

---

[1] *Judicium Papiri Massoni de libello Hotmanni.*

Medici, attempted a refutation point by point; [1] but he lacked the knowledge necessary to his task, and was driven to rely upon abuse of plaintiff's attorney. Zampini did, indeed, make Hotman's intransigent position upon the Salic law appear an overemphasis ; but he was overwhelmed in the ridicule of Hotman's reply. [2] The best answer came from a Paris lawyer, Turrellus ; [3] but he could do little more than demonstrate that Hotman had, in a variety of places, refined unduly. It is not, on the whole, untrue to say that the *Franco-Gallia* remained the classic exposition of early French institutions until, in the second quarter of the nineteenth century, Augustin Thierry began their scientific study. Attacks in which Matharel and others sought to show the evil effects of popular rule were, of course, beside the point ; for Hotman had chosen to occupy different ground.

It was to the question of the validity of popular right that the *Vindiciae contra Tyrannos* was addressed. Immediately, it appears probable that the work of Hotman had more effect ; in the long run, the greater interest of Mornay's pamphlet is as certain as its greater influence. So, similarly, the scholastic involutions of Occam's *Dialogus* had interested his generation far more than the direct brevity of the *Defensor Pacis*. But just as the very width of Marsiglio's generalisations gave them a more permanent influence than the labyrinthine theses of Occam, so because Mornay summarised the result of the conflict with telling simplicity, it was to his arguments that a later age turned.

The *Vindiciae* deals directly with the four great questions of the time. Are subjects bound to obey princes if they command that which is contrary to the law of God ? Is it lawful to resist a prince who infringes the law of God, and ruins the Church, and, if so, who ought to resist him, by what means, and how far should resistance extend ? Is it lawful to resist a prince who ruins the state, and, if so, to whom should the organisation of resistance, its means

---

[1] *Ad Franco-Galliam Responsio* (1575).

[2] *Monitoriale adversus . . . anti francogalliam* (1575).

[3] *Contra Othomani Francogalliam libellus* (1576).

and limits, be confided ?   Are neighbouring princes bound
by law to help the subjects of princes who afflict them either
for the cause of religion or in the practice of tyranny ?

To the first question, the *Vindiciae* responds in the
negative. It is clear from the authority of Scripture and
the example of the martyrs that the commands of God
merit obedience before any orders from an earthly prince.
Nor is this situation altered by the fact that princes claim
to rule by divine right. The earth is the possession of
the Lord, and Kings reign only by his will ; one must then
obey them only to the degree that they obey the commands
of their master. The King is a vassal like any other vassal ;
he is, therefore, bound by a contract. Should he break its
terms, *diffidatio* ensues, as it would in any other case. The
establishment of Kingship, in fact, clearly involves a double
contract. There is a contract between God, on the one
hand, and the King upon the other ; there is a contract
also between the King and the people. Clearly again,
therefore, whatever binds the King binds the people also ;
and should the King fail in his duty, the people must not
forget its obligations. To obey its earthly master in prefer-
ence to obedience from God is to invoke the punishment
of heaven. For when men fail to obey the laws of God
they are expelling him from his Kingdom. The King is
instituted only to secure the better observance of those
laws, and, when he fails, his sin ought not to involve popular
acquiescence. That, indeed, is the true rebellion. It is
as though men obeyed an officer rather than the express
ordinance of the King himself. When subjects refuse to
give their conscience into evil keeping, they obey the true
source of right. For there are, as Cicero said, degrees of
duty, of which the highest belongs to God, and the second
only to one's country ; just as in the civil law treason, though
it be a heinous crime, is inferior in wickedness to wrong-
doing. Nor do the Apostles write otherwise. It is one
thing to refuse obedience to a command which infringes
the will of God. Whether one ought to organise resistance
to a prince who seeks to infringe it and attack the Church
seems, at first sight, a more difficult and complex question.

Yet in appearance only. For the people have, jointly with the prince, made a contract with God. They are like a debtor who has a joint obligation to pay a certain sum ; should the other party fail, the entire debt falls upon the remaining signatory. Just as the Jewish people was bound to God, and was warned by the prophets of its duty whenever Kings strayed from the divine path, so also is the Christian people bound. The contract has always involved a popular obligation. Too much danger was risked in committing the custody of the Church to a single person. A people affected to true religion will, therefore, feel itself driven both to reprove, and, if need be, to repress a prince who would destroy it, for they will know that in neglecting to perform this duty, they make themselves guilty of the same crime, and will merit, as they will receive, the same punishment.

But to say that a whole people must resist does not mean that so many headed a monster as the multitude has the duty of revolt. By the people is meant their chosen magistrates who represent, and mirror within themselves, the will of the nation. It is their business to restrain the encroachments of the prince and, in the last instance, to exercise a final control. Every well-ordered kingdom has an authority of this kind, commissioned to speak in its name. It is composed of the natural heads of the state, and, once they decide to act, whatever they will is good, granted only a worthy object as the purpose of their decision. Nor need they hesitate to act, even when, as in the case of the Maccabees, the whole nation is against them. The contract that binds the whole people binds its parts also, just as in Germany each prince and free city is separately bound in fealty to the empire. When a city or a prince refuses obedience in such a case, it absolves itself from membership of what is, in fact, simply an assembly of brigands rather than of Christian men. For where there is no justice, there is no commonwealth, since justice is the virtue which gives to each his own ; yet here, by definition, the prince is depriving God of his heritage. So the Sorbonne and the Parliament of Paris sanctioned the decision of Philip the Fair to cease connection with the papacy of Boniface VIII when the latter sought unduly to extend his prerogative ; so, also, the Assembly of the French Church refused to obey the schismatic pope, Benedict XIII. It is high treason against the divine authority for men in positions of trust to act otherwise.

But what engages the community as a whole through the persons of its magistrates does not similarly bind the private citizen. Unless he is specifically called by authority to revolt, his allotted task is passive resistance only. For what is required of the whole does not bind each unit of the whole in its private aspect ; what, on the contrary, the Scriptures enjoin upon the private citizen is that he shall put his sword into his scabbard. He must do as the faithful did when Jeroboam abolished the service of the true God, and suffer voluntary exile. It is only when the official call comes that he is permitted to resist by force. If each man were to follow his own conscience, there would result not only confusion, but the fatal deception which comes from man's willingness to mistake his private desire for the will of heaven. When the call does come, the citizen need not fear that the use of arms is unlawful. The number of good princes who have by force of arms defended the service of God against the pagan is infinite. The Apostle himself has told us that the magistrate does not bear the sword in vain ; to what better use could he devote it than to the service of the true faith ? Even more, it is his duty to take to himself every weapon that may fortify the vine of Christ against the wild boar of the forest that seeks to uproot and devour it. It is his business to be armed for virtue.

The case, therefore, is clear, where the interests of God are directly in question. The magistrates may authorise resistance by force to the prince who seeks injury against the true church. Are the same principles applicable when the interests concerned are of a purely temporal character ? Here we meet the central problem of politics—the general nature of the obedience due to princes. The latter are instituted by God. But they owe their power to the people, and they exist only that they may bear upon their shoulders the main burdens of the commonwealth. The choice of a King is a matter everywhere of popular election ; and even though hereditary succession has long been the general custom, the ceremony of the coronation, in particular its oath, remains to show that Kingship rests upon popular choice. The King, therefore, is the delegate of the people for specific functions. The people is greater than the King, and he can have no power save that which it confers upon him in the purpose of his institution. The consent of the people is like the base of the Rhodian Colossus ; when it is withdrawn the statue crashes into the dust. And, as with the prince, so with the officers of the Kingdom. They are the servants, not of the King, but of the people. Their nomination derives from the authority of the state, and they are charged to protect, not the personal interest of the prince, but the public interest of all. Once, indeed, they consulted the whole people ; now they are bound only to obey its representatives. It is true that officials have, in recent times, seemed to possess only the shadow of their former power. But the development of princely absolutism is not effective against popular right ; time cannot confer a prescription against the people.

Popular sovereignty is therefore the basis of royal power. How far does that power extend ? Since an institution is good only to the degree to which it fulfils the purpose of its existence, it is from the scrutiny of the latter that the limits of royal authority may be ascertained. But in so speaking we make absolutism impossible ; for it is with limits that we seek the foundations of power. It is with limits because men are by nature apt to the love of liberty, and it is sufficiently obvious that Kingship is maintained because, and only because, they believe in the benefit it confers. What they sought in its establishment was safety from external attack, on the one hand, and freedom, on the other, from the internal conflict which results from the institution of property. The business of the King is thus to make war, if need be, and to render justice. He must preside over the courts, and see to it that the law is supreme there. The maintenance of the law is the very soul of his function. But he does not create it ; he merely gives it support. Law is the embodiment of reason, and so free from the human passions, to which he is subject. To the law, within which, let it be noted, are comprised the liberties of towns and provinces, every King must give obedience. Should he abrogate the law, it can only be on condition that the people, or their natural leaders, are consulted and acquiesce. He cannot punish, save in accordance with law. He cannot otherwise pardon. He can dispose of the private property of his subjects only as the law permits. Nor, similarly, can he alienate the royal demesne ; he has its usufruct, but he is not its owner. He has its usufruct to maintain the state of his office, just as he has taxes for war and other public needs. He is, in short, merely the administrator of the royal demesne. He has the same power over it as a bishop over the property of his diocese. He is the trustee of a temporary possession, but a trustee who may always be held accountable for an abuse of trust. Accountability, in fact, is inherent in the nature of his function ; for a people which sought safety would not submit itself, in any absolute fashion, to the caprice of a man endowed with the same passions as ordinary humanity. To leave him free to make laws or confiscate private property at will would make his relations to his subjects that of a conqueror to the enemies he has laid low.

Every Kingdom, indeed, bears witness to the truth of this conception ; for in every Kingdom there is some sort of covenant between prince and people. The ancient Kings of Burgundy swore to protect all men in their rights according to law and justice. The ceremony of coronation in Aragon not only implied a higher majesty in the commonwealth than in the crown, but also implied, should the coronation oath be broken, the exemption of the subject from allegiance. But two sorts of tyrants must be distinguished. There is the usurper whose power has no basis in right. He invades the country of his neighbours in the sheer lust for dominion, or he may, by corruption and deceit, worm his way to the throne. Sometimes the usurper has been, like Julius Caesar, a popular general ; sometimes it has been a woman who has intruded her presence into a government from which she is excluded by law. Such a tyrant may be killed by the simple citizen without the authority of the magistrate ; for in combating one who stands by definition outside all categories of law, it is life and liberty in their elementary terms that he is concerned to defend. The second form of tyrant is the prince who, though reigning by legal title, neglects the contract to which he is bound by the terms of his inception. His proper treatment is a more difficult matter than in the first case. We must make allowances for the fact that, being a man, he is likely to err. We must therefore first seek, by reasonable means, to lead him to the path of right. The wisdom of a senate may well enable a naturally weak prince to govern well. But when, of set purpose, the prince is determined to pervert justice and equity, force must be used against him ; and it is the officers and nobles of the Kingdom whose business it then is to exact a remedy. That is the reason for their existence, and if they fail, they share in his crimes. In destroying his tyranny, they act on behalf of the state. They protect the humble who, in this instance, have no function save that of resignation, against the wrongs he would commit. They secure the observance of the contract he has made with the state. As a general council may be summoned to protect the Church from the consequence of papal crime, so must the officers of the Kingdom ever remember that if the King has the first place in the realm, theirs is the second. And they are a second who may become the first, for they are the reserve power of the Commonwealth.

There remains the final question of the prince who sees the citizens of another country oppressed either for religious or political causes. What duty is laid upon him ? In matters of religion, there can be no doubt that he is morally bound to intervene. For there is only one true Church, of which Jesus Christ is the head. Should its members be injured, the whole Church participates in the harm and sorrow which result. And since the care of the Church is recommended to the charge of Christian princes in general, they must not merely amplify and extend its boundaries where they can, but also, and in all places, preserve it against attack. So Josias expelled idolatry from the Kingdom of Israel, even though he was then in subjection to Assyria ; so Constantine executed Licinius for his persecution of the Christians, so Moses bound certain tribes beyond the Jordan to aid the Israelites against their enemies, and pronounced an anathema against them if they should fail. Nor is the case less clear in civil matters. Princes are, after all, men, and the duties of humanity are fit and convenient for them. A private citizen is called upon to help a neighbour who is beset by evil men ; how much more, then, is it incumbent upon a prince to act in similar fashion ? If he finds a commonwealth grovelling upon the floor, let him raise it to its former eminence. It may well be that his private interest persuades him to stand aside ; but nothing so much becomes a man, even more a prince, so to dispose his actions that his private interests give place to public need. No prince would hesitate to give assistance to a brother monarch in distress ; how much the more readily, then, should he aid a whole people, when the affliction of many is so clearly the cause of a greater pity. Charity challenges him to the relief of the oppressed, as justice requires that a tyrant be compelled to reason.

IV

In the sixteenth century there are two main forms of political doctrine, of which the *République* of Bodin and the *Vindiciae* of Duplessis-Mornay are perhaps the best examples. In the one, the main effort is to find a juristic basis for *raison d'état*. The root of political wisdom is therefore an unlimited sovereignty which makes a command into law by the mere supremacy of the person from whom it emanates. The true example of law is therefore that positive enactment which is embodied in legislation. The essential thing is that the command shall be supreme, irresponsible, and unhindered by the scrutiny of conditions. It is true that reference is made by Bodin to laws of nature, of God, and of nations by which the ruler is bound [1]; but, as Hobbes was later to point out, since the prince is the only person who can, in this context, enforce obedience to them, the essence of the theory is the unlimited nature of the sovereign power. The real result is to separate ethics from politics, and thus to complete by theoretical means the division which Machiavelli had effected on practical grounds. The state becomes supreme upon its own territory, and the expression of its will is law. And the attempt to introduce moral limitations upon the exercise of that will becomes clearly impossible. All associations become contingent upon its pleasure; and right is to be defined as that which the sovereign permits. *Jus est quod jussum est* becomes the definition of the state. The characteristic of an organised political community is the existence within it of an authority which is not only habitually obeyed, but is itself beyond the reach of authority. [2] Right becomes, so to speak, pluralised into rights; it is no longer the reflection of a universal good, but a series of privileges to be discovered in the statute-book. The state must be obeyed upon the simple ground that it is a state.

It is easy to understand the attractiveness of this theory to the age which enunciated it. The medieval prince was only a greater noble whose power was limited on every side by the special immunities of church and feudalism. The age of the Renaissance brought changes so swift and catastrophic that men welcomed any authority which guarded, or seemed to guard, the possibility of order against the flood tide of anarchy. Its attractiveness was intensified when, as with Henry VIII, the sovereignty of the state could find its incarnation in a prince whose power was immediate and obvious. Here was something, as Barclay always insisted,

[1] Bodin also refers to a limitation induced by *leges imperii* and refers to the Salic Law as an example of them. These also, he argues, the prince cannot touch. It is difficult to see why; and it is probable that Bodin is merely making an inconsistent concession to the controversies of the moment. See some good remarks in Dunning, *Political Theories from Luther to Montesquieu*, p. 101; also Pollock, *History of the Science of Politics* (1912), p. 54.

[2] *Cf.* my *Foundations of Sovereignty*, Chapter I, esp. pp. 16 f.

which, however evil when it entails tyranny, is nevertheless superior to the evils which insurrection brings in its train. The theory of Bodin may not have meant the realisation of abstract right, any more than the existence of the courts implies the realisation of justice ; but it implied the existence of certainty. Men had learned from the previous age rather to be content with an imperfect good than to seek the texture of that perfect commonwealth upon the substance of which so few of them were agreed.

The doctrine of the *Vindiciae* starts from the antithetic standpoint. It is with the establishment of abstract right that it is throughout concerned. By abstract right it means, at bottom, the will of God ; and everything is illegitimate which transgresses its substance. Where Bodin, therefore, is concerned with the irresponsibility of supreme power, Duplessis-Mornay is concerned with its limitations. Where Bodin seeks to show that rights are the creatures of the sovereign will, rights, in the other view, are the reflection of right and therein is to be found the only true source of sovereign power. To Bodin, therefore, the thing of main importance is simply whether the enacting authority is, in the given instance, competent to act in the way it has acted with the inference that if the authority is the sovereign, it is competent without further scrutiny. To Duplessis-Mornay, on the other hand, the crucial point is not the willer, but the substance of the thing willed ; and if that substance, when it contradicts divine law, is maintained, it must be resisted at all costs. In the strictly political sense, therefore, there is really in the *Vindiciae* no such thing as sovereignty at all. We are given right and power ; and rebellion is interposed to mark the extreme limit of divergence between them. Power does not carry with it any political connotation. It is there because God and the people so will it ; but the people which created it is morally obliged to scrutinise its operation, and they must overthrow it in the event of abuse.

The hold of the *Vindiciae* upon not merely its own, but the later generations which absorbed its substance, was, of course, the fact that it gave an obvious means of resisting what any given group of men might choose to regard as oppression. Revolution was, in that age, the only weapon to oppose to religious intolerance; and to men who were being taught by lawyers and learned men that the fiat of the state was enough, it seemed to place rebellion upon the ground of right. To the Politiques' cry of convenience it replied with a plea of moral duty; and when that plea was surrounded by a religious atmosphere passionately felt, it was sufficient to convince. Nor must it be forgotten that, in the strict realm of theory, Bodin was the innovator and Duplessis-Mornay the guardian of traditional doctrine. For his views of the ground of obedience sprang full-grown from the noble medieval concept of the world as governed by natural law. What he was doing for his readers was to refer the actions of the state to the test of an eternal reason which sprang from God and was instinct with his will; all other laws than this were therefore secondary because they sprang from fallible men. When Bodin and, later, Hobbes were striving to make of law simply the command of a sovereign power, they were running counter, as their opponents at once recognised, to the whole burden of medieval notions. Duplessis-Mornay was insisting that important as is civil society, and not a little of his influence comes from his emphasis upon its importance, there are interests higher than those of the state for which no sacrifice is too much. Government, for him, is thus ultimately a theocracy; and it follows that when the human administrator is in conflict with the divine ruler, the citizen can really have no hesitation as to where his obedience must lie.

It is, of course, easy to criticise the structure upon which the *Vindiciae* depends. It does not explain the origins of the state. Buchanan and Mariana apart, indeed, it is a capital fault in all the Monarchomachs that they assume the existence of the state and then explain its primary assumptions in terms for which they offer no historic warranty. For their dependence upon the theory of a social contract lays them open to all the objections raised since the time of Hume to that disastrous hypothesis. Nor is that all. The whole view of the *Vindiciae* is built upon the assumption that it is the duty of the magistrate to represent the popular idea of right ; but it has nowhere any rigorous examination of the representative principle. The *Vindiciae*, indeed, makes the people sovereign, but in such a fashion as to make its supremacy meaningless save where it is governed by a tyrant who has usurped his power. It is represented by magistrates ; but it is admitted that as a matter of contemporary fact, the magistrate has his commission from the very ruler he is supposed to control. No one, in fact, can read the *Vindiciae* without being impressed by the meagreness of its concessions to the people. The latter is an originating but not an active agency. Duplessis-Mornay shares to the full the characteristic Hugenot contempt for the people. He is like a whig aristocrat of the eighteenth century who welcomes popular support but does not concede to it a share in government. He identifies the people with the state ; but the only purpose of the people is to serve as an agency of origin which justifies the resistance of the aristocracy to what they consider an abuse of power. He is not, like Althusius, writing an ample theory of the state. Clearly, at the back of his mind there is the single problem of religious oppression. He sees that the principles he lays down apply to civil not less than to ecclesiastical problems ; but he is not anxious unduly to enlarge their boundaries. Like all the Hugenots, he uses the Bible as the obvious source of social truths ; and it is not without significance that it is the discussion of civil problems that is least grounded in biblical authority. Probably, indeed, the secular aspect of oppression was for him essentially the derivative of the religious ; and it then becomes clear why Duplessis-Mornay could, on the cessation of the latter, revert like Hotman to a belief in the divine right of Kings.

Yet these limitations and inconsistencies impair neither the impressiveness nor the influence of his book. Eighty years after his death a German publicist could declare that he and Althusius more easily seduced men to bad principles than any other writers. [1] But the more immediate heirs

---

[1] In 1661 Archbishop Bramhall was making a similar attack. See the *Serpent Salve : Collected Works*, III, pp. 288 ff., esp. pp. 301, 325, 395.

to his theories were not his friends, but his opponents, even if democratic government was in a real sense his residuary legatee. For with the death of the Duke of Anjou in 1584 Henry of Navarre became the heir apparent to the French throne ; and the certainty that a Hugenot King offered a greater opportunity to the reformed religion than explorations into the realm of the abstract, turned its adherents into thorough-going supporters of hereditary right and the Salic Law. The defence of radicalism then passed into the hands of the League and the Jesuits. What the former was striving to prove was the theory that no heretic could ever be lawfully King of France ; and it relied for proof upon the doctrines of the *Vindiciae*. Just as the advocates of papal dominion had always admitted that a papal heretic can always be deposed, so do the advocates of the League urge that an heretical King is by definition a tyrant and therefore by definition inacceptable. The literature in defence of this position is more remarkable for its quantity than its quality. The pamphlets of Louis d'Orléans, indeed, have some merit. [1] The sermons of Boucher explore with some eloquence the half-known hinterland of invective. [2] The *Dialogue du Manant et Maheustre* shows that behind the unworthy ambitions of the Guises and the preachers there was, struggling for survival, a notion of theocracy that is not devoid of nobility. [3] Perhaps the most characteristic product of the Catholic Monarchomachs is the *True Power of a Christian State* of Rossaeus. It is usually attributed to that Rose, the fanatic bishop of Senlis, who is so severely handled in the *Satyre Ménippée* ; but, as Labitte has shown, the grounds for any attribution are extremely slender, and it is better, perhaps also kinder, to leave its authorship in the pale realm of anonymity. [4]

How dependent Rossaeus was upon the substance of the *Vindiciae* is apparent from the merest summary of his

---

[1] See especially his *Premier et Second Avertissements* (1586).

[2] *Sermons de la Simulée Conversion* (1594), and compare with these Portais, *Cinq Sermons de la Simulée Conversion* (1594).

[3] *Cf.* Figgis, *From Gerson to Grotius*, Lect. V ; and Tilley, *Studies in the French Renaissance*, p. 315.

[4] *Cf.* Labitte, *op. cit.*, p. 295-304.

teaching. He insists upon the naturalness of civil government, which is inherent in the nature of men. But no
special form of government was established ; the constitution of each society has always been dependent upon the
pleasure of the sovereign people. Where it has established
Kingship, it has always been upon the contractual basis of
retaining ultimate power in its own hands and defining
that conceded to the prince by the purpose he is to serve.
The people can always modify the government which
depends upon its will ; and it can even, if it pleases, abolish
monarchy altogether. The prince has no rights save those
he possesses to fulfil the purpose of his institution ; and if
he plays the tyrant he must be deposed. Consultation of
the people is fundamental, for the people has not parted
with its original freedom. What it has established, it builds
only for the attainment of good ; once the King fails to secure
it, his commission is clearly revoked. But good cannot
be secured without religion. Rossaeus does not mean by
religion any form of protestantism ; either form is worse
than paganism. Any government, therefore, which fails
to establish the Roman Catholic religion is, *ipso facto*, illegitimate. A heretic King may, therefore, be deposed, either
by his own subjects, or by a foreign prince ; for he is by
definition a tyrant since his heresy is incompatible with the
maintenance of virtue.

Nor must the immediate background of Rossaeus be
neglected. The *Vindiciae* had pointed its moral for contemporary events by the implications it contained ; Rossaeus
has no hesitation in saying openly what is in his mind.
Turks and Saracens have more rights than the Hugenots,
who are French only in the sense that a dog is called French.
Henry IV can never be a Christian King. He is the worst
of traitors. As an excommunicate he can take no oath ; and
the toleration he would establish is the first step on the
road that would lead to the recognition of Mahomedanism.
He is a heretic, and all history and scripture testify that it
is legitimate to take up arms against him. He is a tyrant,
and the way to treat him was shown in the noble act of
Jacques Clement when he murdered Henry III in defence

of the Church against the wicked plots of the Politiques. The duty of all Frenchmen is to obey the call of the League. It is supported by Spain ; it has as members the Cardinal of Bourbon, who is the rightful King, and the House of Lorraine. If Henry IV is maintained in power, all property will be unsafe. The nobility will be merged in the populace, and lose all influence and position ; for Calvinism is incompatible with Kingship and aristocracy. Its secret plan, indeed, is to make the government of France like to that of Switzerland. It is already, in its ecclesiastical organisation, an *imperium in imperio ;* should it be tolerated longer, the true France will perish.

Clearly enough, the Catholic and Protestant Monarchomachs approach the same problem from different sides. Each party was hostile to the absolute state in the one case because it presaged, in the other because it denied, religious toleration. Each sought relief from its trammels in considerations of right ; and each sought to defend the maintenance of right by means of a social contract derived from the sovereignty of the people. Each was at bottom entirely indifferent to freedom. The Catholics aimed quite definitely at persecution ; and the real effort of the Hugenots was, as Rossaeus himself pointed out, a desire to found such a Presbyterian tyranny as Calvin established at Geneva or Knox in Scotland. Both, that is to say, failed to grasp, as the Politiques had definitely grasped, the notion of the state as a self-sufficient society of which the ethical roots were to be discovered within and not without itself. With both, of course, the contingent implications are far wider than the conscious purpose. Each of them was really puzzled by the single problem of allegiance. They sought to deny the duty of obedience when it involved results unfavourable to a given religion. To a philosophic theory of the state neither could make pretence. Their weapons were too entirely at the service of their desires for it to be as yet possible for them to attain that degree of obstruction at which a philosophic view alone becomes possible. Yet each was making generalisations which, in other hands, would move towards that end. The Monarchomachs are summed up in Salamonius [1] and Althusius on the one side, and the Society of Jesus on the other. The Monarchomachs may have failed to realise all the profits of their thought, but at least they provided the materials for the next generation.

The real inheritors of their work are, in fact, the Jesuits and the English thinkers of the seventeenth century ; for the thought of the time is hardly national, but European, and the two streams of doctrine blended into a common tradition. The Jesuits, of course, had a different aim in view. As the chief agents of the Counter-Reformation, and, in particular, the Spanish theory of it, they were no more concerned with the roots of freedom than their predecessors. But they were confronted with a Europe that was religiously heterogeneous ; and they used the Presbyterian hint of two societies, religious and secular, with concurrent jurisdictions over the same persons as the clue to their purpose. From this they are able to deduce the view of states as independent, equal, and sovereign which, in the hands of Grotius, made possible the development of international law. The independence, indeed, is never real ; there is always, as in the famous book of Bellarmine, [2] the indirect power of the pope outside to destroy its logical result. But they did, the needs of religion apart, emphasise more completely than any other group of thinkers the fact that civil society is a natural product of men's dispositions, that power is organised to serve its purposes, and that power is, as a consequence, always popular in origin that the purpose of its institution may be preserved. The Jesuits did not get so far as Althusius in their sense of the corporateness of communities, with the personality to which that corporateness gives rise, but they did see that political power is the result of social facts and that it remains the eternal possession of the people. The prince for them is always the mere administrator of those institutions which fulfil the end of civil right, and absolutism is ruled out as *a priori* impossible. They use the notion of a social contract, but

[1] *Patritii Romani de principatus, lib.* VI (1578). See Figgis in *Proc. Roy. Hist. Soc.* (1897), Vol. XI, p. 89.

[2] *De Romano Pontifice ; Tractatus de Potestate Summi Pontificis. Cf.* McIlwain, *op. cit.*, pp. 22 ff.

it has not, with them, as it has in the writings of the Monarchomachs, anything like a primary importance. Their
governing concept is natural law. Power is always regarded
as limited that eternal reason, which popular sovereignty
is held ultimately to embody, may correct the deficiencies
of its exercise.

It is clear that this is in the direct tradition of the *Vindiciae*.
It retains, of course, an ultimate religious perspective, and
the state is made as subservient to the ends of the Roman
Church by the Jesuits as it was made to minister to Hugenot
demands by Beza and his disciples. Its translation into a
predominantly secular theory was mainly the result of the
seventeenth-century struggle between King and Parliament in
England. Of that evolution John Locke supplied a magistral
summary ; and he did little, the theory of toleration apart,
but adapt the teachings of the *Vindiciae* to an English
atmosphere. With him, as with his predecessors, there is
the same suppression of the idea of sovereignty, the same
confinement of the law-making power within a previously
defined area of capacity. Like them, too, Locke thinks
of the state as a human, even an artificial contrivance ; he
cannot believe that man surrendered his rights to it save
in terms of a previously guaranteed return. Power for him
is just as much a trust revocable on abuse, as it is with the
thinkers of the sixteenth century. He has the same dread
of absolutism, the same refusal to make the final nature of
social life depend upon some naturally inherent and co-
ordinating power in the state. The atomism of the *Vindiciae*
is, in fact, as notable in Locke as in the earlier exponents
of the contract theory. And not unnaturally, for with
him also the main purpose of the polemic is to set bounds
to the power of government. The absolutism of the sixteenth
century was attacked because it was found to be incompatible
with freedom of religious belief, the prerogative of the
seventeenth found opponents in those who sought a larger
degree of national self-determination. But both ages
found the defence of their position in the concept of a state
built upon the rights separately surrendered by individuals.
Those rights were a matter of contractual organisation ;

and for the state to step outside the boundaries they defined was to deny the character of its origin.

Practically, this is to say, the theory of the state upon which the *Vindiciae* rests determined the character of political speculation from the end of the sixteenth century until the advent of Rousseau. So long as the aim of political philosophy was to outline the area of an abstract right determined *a priori* as a field subtracted from the rights of individuals, the Monarchomachic tradition exhausted the requirements of a liberal outlook. Prynne and Rutherford [1] both drew their nourishment from this source ; and the ideas of the Levellers rest upon a kindred foundation. Through Locke, it is at the base of the thought of Price and Priestley ; through Locke, also, it supplies the perspective of the American Revolution. And Locke himself derived the substance of his ideas from the French thinkers of the Counter-Reformation. He drew upon Grotius and Puffendorf, who are, in turn, dependent upon the Monarchomachic school. The other great formative influence in Locke is Hooker's *Ecclesiastical Polity ;* and if its eighth book is an attempt at refutation of the *Vindiciae,* [2] that is itself sufficient to show that it is an essential source of early English radicalism.

After Rousseau, the situation changes because the foundation of political thought is different. That new theories had been born did not, of course, involve the disappearance of the tradition embodied in the *Vindiciae ;* but it involved its transformation to new purposes. For the *Social Contract* introduces the notion of an organic state ; the rights of the individual are superseded by the theory of corporate personality. That revival of Platonist doctrine was, in the long run, a death-blow to the atomism of the earlier school. It made the state not, as with the *Vindiciae*, the artificial contrivance of men, but a society which supplied human nature with its essential penumbra. If Rousseau lays excessive emphasis upon the degree to which man must be read in a state-context, that was the natural reaction from the individualism of Locke.

---

[1]   In his *Lex Rex* (1644).
[2]   *Cf. Works*, Vol. II (ed. of 1845), esp. pp. 499 f.

Nor was Rousseau the only corrective that outlook was to receive. With Hume and Bentham theories of abstract right gave place to theories of concrete utility ; and the idea of a social contract did not survive the assault they made upon it. The discovery Bentham owed to Holbach that the creative power of the state lies in legislation—a theory built upon the *Esprit des Lois*—added a substance to the theory of politics which had been previously absent. For legislation meant the possibility of deliberate innovation, and that nation was qualitatively different from the declaration of *a priori* rightness which lies at the bottom of Monarchomachic doctrine. Utilitarianism, in brief, brought in the time-spirit as the permanent and conscious background of political philosophy ; and there is a chasm which cannot be bridged between rights regarded as the product of utility, and rights, as with the *Vindiciae*, that have their basis in an eternal right which escapes the categories of space and time.

This does not, indeed, mean that the Monarchomachs were mistaken in the perception their work enshrines. At the bottom of their argument is an emphasis which no political philosophy can afford to neglect. In part, it is the realisation that every state is built upon the consciences of men. Within each individual mind there are reserves into which no organising power can hope to penetrate. For the *Vindiciae* those reserves were, from the nature of its problem, mainly religious in nature, but the concept is a general one, and it applies to the spiritual outlook of every citizen. In part, also, it is the insistence that the state exists to secure for its members some agreed minimum of civilisation. Wherein that minimum consists will, of course, depend upon the character of each age. What only is certain is that the deprivation of certain things deemed good, will, at some given time, lead to the onset of resistance. Natural rights and a social contract raise, as historic concepts, far more difficulties than they solve. But it is important to bear in mind that they are, at the same time, the reflection of ideas upon which the successful working of every state depends.

They are the attempt, in fact, of men who feel that they are being deprived of that which gives to social life its meaning, to insist upon the remedy of their grievance. The social contract is an effort to provide such an institutional channel as will secure that the consent of the mass, and not the arbitrary will of a few, is the creative factor in the making of social tradition. Natural rights are the demands for the fulfilment of certain conditions without which an important fragment of the state ceases to feel loyalty to its institutions. However we phrase their substance, an answer to the problems they raise is integral to an adequate political philosophy. Nor may we neglect the important sense in which even the atomism of this outlook has its value. For to whatever degree society may absorb its members, it is, in their experience, ultimately interstitial in character. No theory of the state is satisfactory which does not realise that man is a solitary creature not less than social. The problem of allegiance is, therefore, in any final analyses, an individual problem. The law may resolve, and attach sanctions to its resolution ; but the decision that is made takes place, if it is a real decision, separately in the mind of each member of the state. This has, of course, been seen by all men who have, at periods of crisis, been driven to challenge the foundations of a social system. It was true of Luther, it was true of Lamennais, of Dollinger and of Tyrrell. Perhaps, indeed, no better test of institutional adequacy can be found than the degree in which it leaves room for the free play of conscience ; for no world is worth preserving which cannot utilise its Athanasius. Some such conclusion as this is, it is clear, implied in the experience of the sixteenth century. At that time the conscience involved, the rights demanded, were mainly religious in texture. Yet it is rather the emphasis than the nature of the problem that has shifted. The reconciliation of authority with freedom, the decision as to what things a creative freedom must embody, are not less pressing in the twentieth century than they were at the time of the Reformation.

V

The authorship of the *Vindiciae* has been for three centuries a matter of learned dispute ; and it cannot be said that any certainty has been attained in the matter. Until the publication of Bayle's article in the *Dictionnaire Critique*, [1] it was usual to assume that Duplessis-Mornay, the counsellor of Henry IV, was its author, though other attributions, most notably that to Theodore Beza, were not wanting. The latter, indeed, was a very popular theory with English royalist writers of the seventeenth century, since it afforded additional evidence of the natural and inherent disloyalty of the Presbyterians. [2] Bayle did not, indeed, state definitely that Languet was the author of the *Vindiciae ;* but he constructed an able and impressive case against any other attribution. He pointed out that Agrippa d'Aubigné, a contemporary witness, definitely states that Languet was the author ; and that where, in his first edition of 1616, he had been discreet, in the second there is simple affirmation. [3] He quotes also a supposed remark of Goulart, an indefatigable controversialist of the time, to the effect that the work was Languet's ; but this testimony is weakened by the fact that the remark does not come directly from Goulart, but is attributed to him by Tronchin, the author of his funeral sermon. [4] He points out, further, that if Duplessis-Mornay was the author of the book, he wrote at an early age an essay of remarkable ability ; the implication being that its composition seems more suited to the maturity of Languet. Bayle certainly destroys any other possibility than the alternative between Languet and his younger friend. He shows clearly that there is no basis whatever for the belief that the *Vindiciae* was due to Beza, or Hotman, or, as an English tradition suggested, the Jesuit Robert

---

[1] (Edition of 1820) Vol. XV, pp. 124 ff.

[2] *Cf.* for instance *Philanax Anglicus—Showing Plainly that it is impossible to be at the same time Presbyterians and not Rebels.* By T. B., 1663, pp. 15 f.

[3] *Histoire Universelle*, 11, 17, 124 ; 11, 2, 3, p. 670.

[4] Voetius, *Selectarum Disputationum*, 1667, IV, pp. 231-4.

Parsons. [1] This last theory, indeed, can only be based upon the assumption that as Parsons wrote many books anonymously attacking legitimate Kingship, the *Vindiciae* might reasonably be laid also to his charge.

Bayle's tentative view held the field for nearly two centuries. At the end of that time the theory that Duplessis-Mornay was the real author was urged independently both in France and Germany. [2] It was impossible to deny the positive statement of d'Aubigné. But there was the remark of Grotius, who, as Bayle says, " knew almost all that passed in the republic of letters," on the other side. [3] And even d'Aubigné's positive assertion is not beyond doubt, for in the first edition of his work he had ascribed to " a learned gentleman of the Kingdom," a phrase much more applicable to Duplessis-Mornay, who was a French subject, than to Languet, who was the servant of a foreign sovereign. There are, moreover, two pieces of testimony which go to outweigh any other evidence we have. The Academician Conrart knew an acquaintance of Duplessis-Mornay. The latter, it appears, kept among his books a cabinet in which his own writings were preserved ; and the friend had seen the *Vindiciae* among those writings. [4] This can, at the least, be set against the supposed witness of Goulart ; and, as M. Waddington urges, it is difficult to escape the implications of an express statement of Madame Duplessis-Mornay. She wrote her reminiscences, as she tells us, that her son might know what manner of man his father was, and, if her Protestantism is ardent, the value of her evidence is beyond all question. [5] She writes that her husband was the author of an essay on *la puissance légitime d'un prince sur son peuple*, which is practically the title of the translation of the *Vindiciae* issued in French in 1581. [6] There is no

---

[1] See Bayle, *op. cit.*, Vol. XV, p. 145, N. xx.

[2] Waddington in *Revue Historique* (1893), Vol. LI ; Lossen, *Les Vindiciae Contra Tyrannos*, 1887. See also A. Elkan, *Die Publizistik der Bartholomausnacht*, 1904, for a full discussion of the whole matter.

[3] *Opera* (ed. of 1679), V, p. 949.

[4] *Opera*, p. 328.

[5] See Hauser, *Les Sources de l'Histoire de France*, VIII, pp. 59-60.

[6] The exact French title is *De la puissance légitime sur le peuple*. I do not discuss here the vexed question of the date of composition (probably 1574-6), or of publication which Lossen has shown was almost certainly 1579.

other work of Duplessis-Mornay's to which this can refer. There was no special point, at the time when Madame Duplessis-Mornay prepared her reminiscences, in claiming authorship for her husband ; rather, in the circumstances of the period, it was an invitation to calumny if she intended her work to be published. If, still more, she wrote only for the eyes of her son, it is even clearer that she had no motive in not telling the truth. Until, then, evidence of equal weight be produced upon the other side, the balance of probability would appear to lean decisively towards the authorship of Duplessis-Mornay.

Nor can there be any doubt of his literary capacity for the work. His theological writing apart, his statesmanlike insight into the problems of his time made him, Sully apart, the most trusted of Henry IV's advisers. His ability to write under an aspect not his own is shown by his *Exhortation à la Paix* of 1574, written as an appeal by a moderate Catholic to his co-religionists ;[1] and his *Remonstrance aux Estats* of 1576, a plea to the Estates of Blois for peace, was published under a similar guise.[2] He may, indeed, almost be called the professional advocate of Henry IV ; and if the tone of the *Vindiciae* is markedly different from his other writings, it may be suggested that, theology apart, it was the only essay addressed to the Hugenots, and the only one in which his effort was rather to encourage his friends than to persuade his opponents. Evidence of style is notoriously deceptive ; but the stern eloquence of the *Vindiciae* seems to fit, not merely his other polemical works, but also the rugged severity of his character. Nor is it worthless to note that, like much else of his work, the *Vindiciae* displays in quotation a profound acquaintance with Scripture. That is a trait markedly absent from the writings of Languet. The latter's polished Latinity is very different from the simplicity of the *Vindiciae's* diction.

The translation here reprinted was published in London by Robert Baldwin in 1689. It is an anonymous translation,

---

[1] *Cf.* Elkan, *op. cit.*

[2] Reprinted in *Mémoires de Ligue*, 11, 113. Many other pamphlets by him are scattered over the volumes of this collection.

and appears to be an exact reproduction of an earlier one
published in the not less significant year of 1648. Its Latin
dress apart, indeed, the *Vindiciae* has a fairly consecutive
English history which bears testimony to the favour with
which it was received. It was printed entire in 1581 [1]
and 1589; in 1588 the fourth question appeared separately
as *A short Apologie for Christian Soldiers*—obviously as a
defence of English assistance to the Dutch rebels. A
translation appeared in 1622, and a reprint of 1631 appears
as *Vindiciae Religionis*, perhaps as an invitation to English
Puritans to throw off the yoke of Stuart despotism. There
were further editions in 1648, 1660, and 1689. In a century,
that is, the *Vindiciae* was reprinted, either in whole or in
part, no less than eight times; and each year of its appearance
has a special import directly related to its text. No trans-
lator of any of these editions is known. Yet it is perhaps
a service due to a picturesque legend to note that the copy
in the British Museum of the edition of 1648 attributes the
work to one William Walker of Darnel, near Sheffield, who
cut off the head of Charles I. [2] The anonymous commen-
tator was perhaps drawing upon a fervid imagination; but
the destruction of the Stuarts was not unconnected with
the *Vindiciae contra Tyrannos*.

---

[1] This edition seems to have been printed in Amsterdam.

[2] This William Walker seems unknown to any authority; and I cannot
find any trace of him in Yorkshire histories.

Vindiciæ contra Tyrannos :

A

Defence of Liberty againſt Tyrants.

O R,

Of the lawful power of the Prince over the *People*, and of the *People* over the *Prince.*

BEING

A Treatiſe written in *Latin* and *French* by *Junius Brutus,* and Tranſlated out of both into E N G L I S H.

Queſtions diſcuſſed in this Treatiſe.

I. *Whether Subjeċts are bound and ought to obey Princes, if they command that which is againſt the Law of God.*

II. *Whether it be lawful to reſiſt a Prince which doth infring the Law of God, or ruine the Church, by whom, how, and how far it is lawful.*

III. *Whether it be lawful to reſiſt a Prince which doth oppreſs or ruine a publick State , and how far ſuch reſiſtance may be extended, by whom, how, and by what Right, or Law it is permitted.*

IV. *Whether neighbour Princes or Siates may be, or are bound by Law, to give ſuccours to the Subjeċts of other Princes, afflicted for the Cauſe of true Religion, or oppreſſed by manifeſt Tyranny.*

Licenſed and Entered according to Order.

L O N D O N,
Printed for *Richard Baldwin,* in the Year, 1689.

THE

Emperors

THEODOSIAS *and* VALENTINIAN

TO

VOLUSIANUS, Great Provost

of the Empire

It is a Thing well becoming the Majesty of an Emperor, to acknowledge Himself bound to obey the Laws. Our Authority depending on the Authority of the Laws, and in very Deed to submit the Principality to Law, is a greater thing than to bear Rule. We therefore make it known unto all Men, by the Declaration of this our Edict, that We do not allow Ourselves, or repute it Lawful, to do anything contrary to this.

AN EPISTLE

Justin in the Second Book, speaks thus of Lycurgus, Law-giver to the Lacedemonians, He gave Laws to the Spartans which had not any ; and was as much renowned for his diligent Observing of them Himself, as for his discreet Inventing of them. For he made no Laws for Others, to the Obedience whereof he did not first submit Himself : Fashioning the People to obey willingly, and the Prince to Govern uprightly.

A DEFENCE OF LIBERTY AGAINST TYRANTS

THE FIRST QUESTION

*Whether subjects are bound and ought to obey princes,
if they command that which is against the law of God.*

THIS question happily may seem at the first view to be
altogether superfluous and unprofitable, for that it seems to
make a doubt of an axiom always held infallible amongst
Christians, confirmed by many testimonies in Holy Scripture,
divers examples of the histories of all ages, and by the
death of all the holy martyrs. For it may be well demanded
wherefore Christians have endured so many afflictions, but
that they were always persuaded that God must be obeyed
simply and absolutely, and kings with this exception, that
they command not that which is repugnant to the law
of God. Otherways wherefore should the apostles have
answered, that God must rather be obeyed than men,
and also seeing that the only will of God is always just,
and that of men may be, and is, oftentimes unjust, who
can doubt but that we must always obey God's commandments without any exception, and men's ever with
limitation ?

But for so much as there are many princes in these days,
calling themselves Christians, which arrogantly assume an
unlimited power, over which God himself hath no command, and that they have no want of flatterers, which adore
them as gods upon earth, many others also, which for fear,
or by constraint, either seem, or else do believe, that princes

65

ought to be obeyed in all things, and by all men. And withal, seeing the unhappiness of these times is such, that there is nothing so firm, certain, or pure, which is not shaken, disgraced, or polluted ; I fear me that whosoever shall nearly and thoroughly consider these things, will confess this question to be not only most profitable, but also, the times considered, most necessary. For my own part, when I consider the cause of the many calamities wherewith Christendom hath been afflicted for these late years, I cannot but remember that of the prophet Hosea, " the princes of Judah were like them that remove the bounds : wherefore I will pour out myself like water. Ephraim is oppressed, and broken in judgment, because he willingly walked after the commandments." Here you see the sin of the princes and people dispersed in these two words. The princes exceed their bounds, not contenting themselves with that authority which the almighty and all good God hath given them, but seek to usurp that sovereignty, which he hath reserved to himself over all men, being not content to command the bodies and goods of their subjects at their pleasure, but assume licence to themselves to enforce the consciences, which appertains chiefly to Jesus Christ. Holding the earth not great enough for their ambition, they will climb and conquer heaven itself. The people on the other side walk after the commandment, when they yield to the desire of princes, who command them that which is against the law of God, and as it were to burn incense, and adore these earthly gods ; and instead of resisting them, if they have means and occasion, suffer them to usurp the place of God, making no conscience to give that to Cæsar, which belongs properly and only to God.

Now is there any man that sees not this, if a man disobey a prince commanding that which is wicked and unlawful, he shall presently be esteemed a rebel, a traitor, and guilty of high treason. Our Saviour Christ, the apostles and all the Christians of the primitive church were charged with these calumnies. If any, after the example of Ezra and Nehemiah, dispose himself to the building of the temple of the Lord, it will be said he aspires to the crown, hatches innovations, and seeks the ruin of the state. Then you shall presently see a million of these minions and flatterers of princes tickling their ears with an opinion, that if they once suffer this temple to be re-builded, they may bid their kingdom farewell, and never look to raise impost or taxes on these men.

But what a madness is this ! There are no estates which ought to be esteemed firm and stable, but those in whom the temple of God is built, and which are indeed the temple itself, and these we may truly call kings, which reign with God, seeing that it is by him only that Kings reign : On the contrary, what beastly foolishness it is to think that the state and kingdom cannot subsist if God Almighty be not excluded, and his temple demolished. From hence proceeds so many tyrannous enterprises, unhappy and tragic death of kings, and ruins of people. If these sycophants knew what difference there is between God and Cæsar, between the King of Kings, and a simple king, between the lord, and the vassal, and what tributes this lord requires of his subjects, and what authority he gives to kings over those his subjects, certainly so many princes would not strive to trouble the kingdom of God, and we should not see some of them precipitated from their thrones by the just instigation of the Almighty, revenging himself of them, in the midst of their greatest strength, and the people should not be sacked and pillaged and trodden down.

It then belongs to princes to know how far they may extend their authority, and to subjects in what they may obey them, lest the one encroaching on that jurisdiction, which no way belongs to them, and the others obeying him which commandeth further than he ought, they be both chastised, when they shall give an account thereof before another judge. Now the end and scope of the question propounded, whereof the Holy Scripture shall principally give the resolution, is that which followeth. The question is, if subjects be bound to obey kings, in case they command that which is against the law of God : that is to say, to which of the two (God or king) must we rather obey, when the question shall be resolved concerning the king, to whom is attributed absolute power, that concerning other magistrates shall be also determined.

First, the Holy Scripture doth teach, that God reigns by his own proper authority, and kings by derivation, God from himself, kings from God, that God hath a jurisdiction proper, kings are his delegates. It follows then, that the jurisdiction of God hath no limits, that of kings bounded, that the power of God is infinite, that of kings confined, that the kingdom of God extends itself to all places, that of kings is restrained within the confines of certain countries. In like manner God hath created of nothing both heaven and earth ; wherefore by good right He is lord, and true proprietor, both of the one and the other. All the inhabitants of the earth hold of Him that which they have, and are but His tenants and farmers ; all the princes and governors of the world are His stipendiaries and vassals, and are bound to take and acknowledge their investitures from Him. Briefly, God alone is the owner and lord, and all men of what degree or quality soever they be, are His servants, farmers, officers and vassals, and owe account and acknowledgment to Him, according to that which He hath committed to their dispensation ; the higher their place is the greater their account must be, and according to the ranks whereunto God hath raised them, must they make their reckoning before His divine majesty, which the Holy Scriptures teacheth in infinite places, and all the faithful, yea, and the wisest among the heathen have ever acknowledged. The earth is the Lord's, and the fulness thereof (so saith King David). And to the end that men should not sacrifice to their own industry ; the earth yields no increase without the dew of heaven. Wherefore God commanded that His people should offer unto Him the first of their fruits, and the heathens themselves hath consecrated the same unto their gods ; to the end, that God might be acknowledged lord, and they his grangers and vine dressers, the heaven is the throne of the Lord, and the earth His footstool.

And, therefore, seeing all the kings of the world are under his feet, it is no marvel, if God be called the King of Kings, and Lord of Lords ; all kings be termed His ministers established to judge rightly, and govern justly the world in the quality of lieutenants. By me (so saith the divine wisdom) kings reign, and the princes judge the earth. If they do it not he looseth the bonds of kings, and girdeth their loins with a girdle. As if he should say, it is in my power to establish kings in their thrones, or to thrust them out, and from that occasion the throne of kings is called the throne of God. Blessed be the Lord thy God (saith the Queen of Sheba to King Solomon) which delighted in thee to set thee on his throne to be king for the Lord thy God, to do judgment and justice. In like manner we read in another place, that Solomon sat on the throne of the Lord, or on the throne of the Lord's kingdom.

By the same reason the people are always called the Lord's people, and the Lord's inheritance, and the king's governor of this inheritance, and conductor or leader of his people of God, which is the title given to David, to Solomon, to Ezechias and to other good princes; when also the covenant is passed between God and the king, it is upon condition that the people be, and remain always, the people of God, to shew that God will not in any case despoil himself of his property and possession, when he gives to kings the government of the people, but establish them to take charge of, and well use them; no more nor less than he which makes choice of a shepherd to look to his flocks, remains, notwithstanding himself, still master and owner of them.

This was always known to those good kings, David, Solomon, Jehosaphat, and others who acknowledged God to be the Lord of their kingdoms and nations, and yet lost no privilege that justly belongs to real power; yea, they reigned much more happily in that they employed themselves cheerfully in the service of God, and in obedience to his commandments. Nebuchadnezar, although he was a heathen, and a mighty emperor, did yet at the end acknowledge this, for though Daniel called him the king of kings, to whom the King of Heaven had granted power and royal majesty above all others, yet, on the contrary (said he), " Thy God, O Daniel, is truly the God of Gods, and Lord of Lords, giving kingdoms to whom He pleaseth," yea, to the most wretched of the world. For which cause Xenophon said at the coronation of Cyrus, " let us sacrifice to God." And profane writers in many places do magnify God the most mighty and sovereign king. At this day at the inaugurating of kings and Christian princes, they are called the servants of God, destined to govern his people. Seeing then that kings are only the lieutenants of God, established in the Throne of God by the Lord God himself, and the people are the people of God, and that the honour which is done to these lieutenants proceeds from the reverence which is born to those that sent them to this service, it follows of necessity that kings must be obeyed for God's cause, and not against God, and then, when they serve and obey God, and not other ways.

It may be that the flatterers of the court will reply, that God has resigned his power unto kings, reserving heaven for himself, and allowing the earth to them to reign, and govern there according to their own fancies ; briefly that the great ones of the world hold a divided empire with God himself. Behold a discourse proper enough for that impudent villain Cleon the sycophant of Alexander, or for the poet Martial, which was not ashamed to call the edicts of Domitian, the ordinances of the Lord God. This discourse, I say, is worthy of that execrable Domitian who (as Suetonius recites) would be called God and Lord. But altogether unworthy of the ears of a Christian prince, and of the mouth of good subjects, that sentence of God Almighty must always remain irrevocably true, " I will not give My glory to any other," that is, no man shall have such absolute authority, but I will always remain Sovereign.

God does not at any time divest himself of his power; he holds a sceptre in one hand to repress and quell the audacious boldness of those princes who mutiny against him, and in the other a balance to control those who administer not justice with equity as they ought ; than these there cannot be expressed more certain marks of sovereign command. And if the emperor, in creating a king, reserves always to himself the imperial sovereignty, or a king, as he of France, in granting the government or possession of a province to a stranger, or if it be to his brother or son, reserves always to himself appeals, and the knowledge of such things as are the marks of royalty and sovereignty, the which also are always understood of themselves to be excepted, although they were altogether omitted in the grant of investiture and fealty promised ; with much more reason should God have sovereign power and command over all kings being his servants and officers, seeing we read, in so many places of Scripture, that he will call them to an account, and punish them, if they do not faithfully discharge their duties. Then therefore all kings are the vassals of the King of Kings, invested into their office by the sword, which is the cognisance of their royal authority, to the end that with the sword they maintain the law of God, defend the good, and punish the evil. Even as we commonly see, that he who is a sovereign lord puts his vassals into possession of their fee by girding them with a sword, delivering them a buckler and a standard, with condition that they shall fight for them with those arms if occasion shall serve.

Now if we consider what is the duty of vassals, we shall find that what may be said of them, agrees properly to kings. The vassal receives his fee of his lord with right of justice, and charge to serve him in his wars. The king is established by the Lord God, the King of Kings, to the end he should administer justice to his people and defend them against all their enemies. The vassal receives laws and conditions from his sovereign. God commands the king to observe his laws and to have them always before his eyes, promising that he and his successors shall possess long the kingdom, if they be obedient, and on the contrary, that their reign shall be of small continuance, if they prove rebellious to their sovereign king. The vassal obligeth himself by oath unto his lord, and swears that he will be faithful and obedient. In like manner the king promises solemnly to command, according to the express law of God. Briefly, the vassal loses his fee, if he commit a felony, and by law forfeits all his privileges. In the like case the king loses his right, and many times his realm also, if he despise God, if he complot with his enemies, and if he commit felony against that royal majesty. This will appear more clearly by the consideration of the covenant which is contracted between God and the king, for God does that honour to His servants to call them His confederates. Now we read of two sorts of covenants at the inaugurating of kings, the first between God, the king, and the people, that the people might be the people of God. The second, between the king and the people, that the people shall obey faithfully, and the king command justly. We will treat hereafter of the second, and now speak of the first.

When King Joas was crowned, we read that a covenant was contracted between God, the king, and the people : or, as it is said in another place, between Jehoiada the high priest, all the people, and the king, " that God should be their Lord." In like manner we read that Josias and all the

people entered into covenants with the Lord: we may
gather from these testimonies, that in passing these covenants the high priest did covenant in the name of God
in express terms, that the king and the people should take
order that God might be served purely, and according to
His will, throughout the whole kingdom of Judah, that the
king should so reign that the people were suffered to serve
God, and held in obedience to his law. Thus the people
should so obey the king, as their obedience should have
principal relation to God. It appears by this that the king
and the people are jointly bound by promise, and did oblige
themselves by solemn oath to serve God before all things.
And indeed presently after they had sworn the covenant,
Josias and Joas did ruin the idolatry of Baal and re-established
the pure service of God. The principal points of the covenants were chiefly these.

That the king himself, and all the people should be
careful to honour and serve God according to His will revealed in His word, which, if they performed, God would
assist and preserve their estates: as in doing the contrary,
he would abandon, and exterminate them, which does plainly
appear by the conferring of divers passages of holy writ.
Moses, somewhat before his death, propounds these conditions of covenant to all the people, and at the same time
commands that the law, which are those precepts given
by the Lord, should be *in deposito* kept in the ark of the
covenant. After the decease of Moses, Joshua was established captain and conductor of the people of God, and
according as the Lord himself admonished, if he would
have happy success in his affairs, he should not in any sort
estrange himself from the law; Joshua also, for his part,
desiring to make the Israelites understand upon what condition God had given them the country of Canaan, as soon
as they were entered into it, after due sacrifices performed,
he read the law in the presence of all the people, promising
unto them in the Lord's name all good things if they persisted in obedience; and threatening of all evil if they
wilfully connived in disobedience. Summarily, he assures
them all prosperity, if they observed the law; as otherwise, he expressly declared, that in doing the contrary they
should be utterly ruined. Also at all such times as they
left the service of God, they were delivered into the hands

of the Canaanites, and reduced into slavery, under their tyranny. Now this covenant between God and the people in the times of the judges, had vigour also in the times of the kings, and was treated with them. After that Saul had been anointed, chosen, and wholly established king, Samuel speaks unto the people in these terms : " Behold the king whom you have demanded and chosen ; God hath established him king over you ; obey you therefore and serve the Lord, as well as your king which is established over you, otherwise you and your king shall perish." As if he should say, you would have a king, and God has given you this here, notwithstanding, think not that God will suffer any encroachment upon his right, but know that the king is as well bound to observe the law as you, and if he fail therein, his delinquency shall be punished as severely as yours. Briefly, according to your desires Saul is given you for your king, to lead you in the wars, but with this condition annexed, that he himself follow the law of God. After that Saul was rejected, because he kept not his promise ; David was established king on the same condition, so also was his son Solomon, for the Lord said, " If thou keep my law, I will confirm with thee the covenant which I contracted with David." Now concerning this covenant, it is inserted into the second book of the Chronicles, as follows. " There shall not fail thee a man in my sight, to sit upon the throne of Israel : yet so that thy children take heed to their way to walk in my law, as thou hast walked before me. But if they serve idols, I will drive them from the land whereof I have given them possession." And therefore it was that the book of the law was called the book of the covenant of the Lord (who commanded the priests to give it the king), according to which Samuel put it into the hands of Saul, and according to the tenure thereof Josias yields himself feudatory and vassal of the Lord. Also the law which is kept in the ark is called the covenant of the Lord with the children of Israel. Finally, the people delivered from the captivity of Babylon do renew the covenant with God, and do acknowledge throughout the chapter, that they worthily deserved all those punishments for their falsifying their promise to God. It appears, then, that the kings swear as vassals to observe the law of God, whom they confess to be Sovereign Lord over all.

Now, according to that which we have already touched, if they violate their oath, and transgress the law, we say that they have lost their kingdom, as vassals lose their fee by committing felony. We have said that there was the same covenant between God and the kings of Judah, as before, between God and the people in the times of Joshua and the judges. But we see in many places, that when the people has despised the law, or made covenants with Baal, God has delivered them into the hands of Eglon, Jabin, and other kings of the Canaanites. And as it is one and the same covenant, so those who do break it, receive like punishment. Saul is so audacious to sacrifice, infringing thereby the law of God, and presently after saves the life of Agag, king of the Amalekites, against the express commandment of God. For this occasion he is called rebel by Samuel, and finally is chastised for his rebellion. " Thou hast sacrificed," saith he, " but thou hadst done better to obey God, for obedience is more worthy than sacrifice." Thou hast neglected the Lord thy God, He also has rejected thee, that thou reign no more over Israel. This has been so certainly observed by the Lord, that the very children of Saul were deprived of their paternal inheritance, for that he, having committed high treason, did thereby incur the punishment of tyrants, which affect a kingdom that no way appertains unto them. And not only the kings, but also their children and successors, have been deprived of the kingdom by reason of such felony. Solomon revolted from God to worship idols. Incontinently the prophet Ahijah foretells that the kingdom shall be divided under his son Rehoboam. Finally, the word of the Lord is accomplished, and ten tribes, who made the greatest portion of the kingdom, do quit Rehoboam, and adhere to Jereboam his servant.

Wherefore is this ? For so much (saith the Lord) that they have left me to go after Ashteroth, the god of the Sidonians and Chamos, the god of the Moabites, etc. I will also break in pieces their kingdom : as if he should say, they have violated the covenant, and have not kept promise ; I am no more then tied unto them. They will lessen my Majesty, and I will lessen their kingdom. Although they be my servants, yet notwithstanding they will expel me my kingdom. But I will drive them out themselves by

Jeroboam, who is their servant. Furthermore, for so much as this servant, fearing that the ten tribes, for the cause of religion should return to Jerusalem, set up calves in Bethel, and made Israel to sin, withdrawing by this means the people far from God ; what was the punishment of so ungrateful a vassal and wicked traitor towards his Lord ? First, his son died, and, in the end, all his race, even unto the last of the males was taken from the face of the earth by the sword of Baasa, according to the judgment which was pronounced against him by the prophet, because he revolted from the obedience of the Lord God : this, then, is cause sufficient, and oftentimes also propounded, for the which God doth take from the king his fee, when he opposes the law of God, and withdraws himself from Him to follow His enemies, to wit, idols, and as like crimes deserve like punishments, we read in the holy histories that kings of Israel and of Judah who have so far forgotten themselves, have in the end miserably perished.

Now, although the form, both of the church and the Jewish kingdom be changed, for that which was before enclosed within the narrow bounds of Judæa is now dilated throughout the whole world ; notwithstanding the same things may be said of Christian kings, the gospel having succeeded the law, and Christian princes being in the place of those of Jewry. There is the same covenant, the same conditions, the same punishments, and if they fail in the accomplishing, the same God Almighty, revenger of all perfidious disloyalty ; and as the former were bound to keep the law, so the other are obliged to adhere to the doctrine of the Gospel, for the advancement whereof these kings at their anointing and receiving, do promise to employ the utmost of their means.

Herod, fearing Christ, whose reign he should rather have desired, sought to put Him to death, as if He had affected a kingdom in this world, did himself miserably perish, and lost his kingdom. Julian the apostate, did cast off Christ Jesus to cleave unto the impiety and idolatry of the pagans : but within a small time after he fell to his confusion through the force of the arm of Christ, whom in mockery he called the Galilean. Ancient histories are replete with such examples, neither is there any want in those of these times. Of late years divers kings, drunk with the liquor which the whore of Babylon has presented unto them, have taken arms, and for the love of the wolf, and of Antichrist, have made war against the Lamb of God, who is Christ Jesus; and yet at this day some amongst them do continue in the same course. We have seen some of them ruined in the deed, and in the midst of their wickedness; others also carried from their triumphs to their graves. Those who survive and follow them in their courses have little reason to expect a better issue of their wicked practices: this sentence remains always most certain, " That though all the kings of the earth do conjure and conspire against Christ and endeavour to cut in pieces our Lamb, yet in the end they shall yield the place, and maugre their hearts, confess that this Lamb is the King of Kings, and Lord of Lords."

But what shall we say of the heathen kings? Certainly although they be not anointed and sacred of God, yet be they His vassals and have received their power from Him, whether they be chosen by lot or any other means whatsoever. If they have been chosen by the voices of an assembly, we say that God governs the heart of man, and addresses the minds and intentions of all persons whither he pleases. If it be by lot, the lot is cast in the lap, saith the wise man, " but the whole disposing thereof is of the Lord." It is God only that in all ages establishes, and takes away, confirms, and overthrows kings according to His good pleasure. In which regard Isaiah calls Cyrus the anointed of the Lord, and Daniel says that Nebuchadnezar and others have had their kingdoms committed unto them by God: as also Saint Paul maintains that all magistrates have received their authority from Him. For, although that God has not commanded pagans in express terms to obey Him as He has done those who have knowledge of Him; yet, notwithstanding the pagans must needs confess that it is by the sovereign God that they reign, wherefore if they will not yield the tribute that they owe to God in regard of themselves, at the least let them not attempt nor hinder the sovereign to gather that which is due from those people who are in subjection to them; nor that they do not anticipate, nor appropriate to themselves divine jurisdiction over them, which is the crime of high treason and true tyranny, for which occasion the Lord has grievously punished even the pagan kings themselves. It then becomes those princes who will free themselves from so enormous a mischief, carefully to distinguish their jurisdiction from that of Gods, yea, so much the more circumspectly for that God and the prince have their right of authority over one and the same land, over one and the same man, over one and the same thing. Man is composed of body and soul, God has formed the body and infused the soul into him; to Him only then may be attributed and appropriated the commands both over the body and soul of man.

If out of His mere grace and favour He has permitted kings to employ both the bodies and goods of their subjects, yet still with this proviso and charge, that they preserve and defend their subjects, certainly kings ought to think that the use of this authority is in such manner permitted, that notwithstanding the abuse of it is absolutely forbidden. First, those who confess that they hold their souls and lives of God, as they ought to acknowledge, they have then no right to impose any tribute upon souls. The king takes tribute and custom of the body, and of such things as are acquired or gained by the industry and travail of the body. God doth principally exact His right from the soul, which also in part executes her functions by the body. In the tribute of the king are comprehended the fruits of the earth, the contributions of money and other charges, both real and personal; the tribute of God is in prayers, sacraments, predications of the pure Word of God; briefly, all that which is called divine service, as well private as public. These two tributes are in such manner divers and distinguished, that the one nothing hurts the other. The exchequer of God takes nothing from that of Cæsar, but each of them have their right manifestly apart. But to speak in a word, whosoever confounds these things, does heaven and earth together, and endeavours to reduce them into their first chaos, or latter confusion. David hath excellently well distinguished these affairs, ordaining officers to look to the right of God, and others for that of the king. Josephat has followed the same course, establishing certain persons to judge the causes that belonged to the Almighty, and others to look to the justice of the king; the one to maintain the pure service of God, the other to preserve the rights of the king. But if a prince usurp the right of God, and put himself forward, after the manner of the giants to scale the heavens, he is no less guilty of high treason to his sovereign, and commits felony in the same manner, as if one of his vassals should seize on the rights of his crown, and put himself into evident danger to be despoiled of his estates; and that so much the more justly, there being no proportion between God and an earthly king, between the Almighty and a mortal man; whereas yet between the lord and the vassal there is some relation of proportion.

So often, therefore, as any prince shall so much forget himself, as insolently to say in his heart, I will ascend into heaven, I will exalt my throne above the stars of God; I will sit also upon the mount of the congregation in the sides of the north; I will ascend above the heights of the clouds, I will be like the Most High: then on the contrary, will the Almighty say, I will rise up more high, I will set myself against thee; I will erase out thy name and all thy posterity, thy counsels shall vanish into smoke, but that which I have once determined shall remain firm, and never be annihilated. The Lord said unto Pharaoh, " let My people go, that they may serve Me, and offer sacrifice unto Me," and for that this proud man answered, that he knew not the God of the Hebrews: presently after he was miserably destroyed. Nebuchadnezar commanded that his statue should be adored, and would be honoured as God, but within a short time the true God did deservedly chastise his unruly boldness, and desiring to be accounted God, he became a brute beast, wandering through desert places like a wild ass, until (says the Prophet) that he acknowledged the God of Israel to be the sovereign Lord over all: his son Belshaser abused the holy vessels of the temple in Jerusalem, and put them to serve his excess and drunkenness; for that therefore he gave not glory to Him, that held in His hands both his soul and his counsels; he lost his kingdom, and was slain in that very night of feasting.

Alexander the Great took pleasure in the lies of his flatterers, who termed him the son of Jupiter, and not only approved, but procured his adoration, but a sudden death gave a sad period to those triumphs, being blinded through his excess of conquests he began with too much affection to delight in Antiochus, under colour of pacifying and uniting his subjects, commanded all men to forsake the laws of God, and to apply themselves in obedience to his ; he profaned the temple of the Jews, and polluted their altars, but after divers ruins, defeats, and loss of battles, despoiled and disgraced, he dies with grief, confessing that he deservedly suffered those miseries, because he would have constrained the Jews to leave their religion. If we take into our consideration the death of Nero, that inhuman butcherer of Christians, whom he unjustly slandered with the firing of Rome, being the abhorred act of his detested self ; the end of Caligula, which made himself to be adored of Domitian who would be called lord and god ; of Commodus, and divers others who would appropriate to themselves the honours due to God alone, we shall find that they have all and always according to their deceits miserably perished ; when, on the contrary, Trajan, Adrian, Antonius the courteous, and others, have finished their days in peace ; for although they knew not the true God, yet have they permitted the Christians the exercise of their religion.

Briefly, even as those rebellious vassals who endeavour to possess themselves of the kingdom, do commit felony by the testimony of all laws, and deserve to be extirpated ; in like manner those are as really guilty which will not observe the divine law, whereunto all men without exception owe their obedience, or who persecute those who desire to conform themselves thereunto, without hearing them in their just defences : now for that we see that God invests kings into their kingdoms, almost in the same manner that vassals are invested into their fees by their sovereign, we must needs conclude that kings are the vassals of God, and deserve to be deprived of the benefit they receive from their lord if they commit felony, in the same fashion as rebellious vassals are of their estates. These premises being allowed, this question may be easily resolved ; for if God hold the place of sovereign Lord, and the king as vassal, who dare deny but that we must rather obey the sovereign than the vassal ? If God commands one thing, and the king commands the contrary, what is that proud man that would term him a rebel who refuses to obey the king, when else he must disobey God ? But, on the contrary, he should rather be condemned, and held for truly rebellious, who omits to obey God, or who will obey the king, when he forbids him to yield obedience to God.

Briefly, if God calls us on the one side to enrol us in His service, and the king on the other, is any man so void of reason that he will not say we must leave the king, and apply ourselves to God's service : so far be it from us to believe, that we are bound to obey a king, commanding anything contrary to the law of God, that, contrarily, in obeying him we become rebels to God ; no more nor less than we would esteem a countryman a rebel who, for the love he bears to some rich and ancient inferior lord, would bear arms against the sovereign prince, or who had rather obey the writs of an inferior judge than of a superior, the commandments of a lieutenant of a province, than of a prince ; to be brief, the directions of an officer rather than the express ordinances of the king himself. In doing this we justly incur the malediction of the prophet Micah, who does detest and curse, in the name of God, all those who obey the wicked and perverse ordinances of kings. By the law of God we understand the two tables given to Moses, in the which, as in unremovable bounds, the authority of all princes ought to be fixed. The first comprehends that which we owe to God, the second that which we must do to our neighbours ; briefly, they contain piety and justice conjoined with charity, from which the preaching of the gospel does not derogate, but rather authorize and confirm. The first table is esteemed the principal, as well in order as in dignity. If the prince commands to cut the throat of an innocent, to pillage and commit extortion, there is no man (provided he has some feeling of conscience) who would execute such a commandment. If the prince has committed some crime, as adultery, parricide, or some other wickedness, behold amongst the heathen, the learned lawyer Papinian who will reprove Caracalla to his face, and had rather die than obey, when his cruel prince commands him to lie and palliate his offence ; nay, although he threaten him with a terrible death, yet would he not bear false witness. What shall we do then, if the prince command us to be idolaters, if he would have us again crucify Christ Jesus, if he enjoins us to blaspheme and despise God, and to drive Him (if it were possible) out of heaven, is there not yet more reason to disobey him, than to yield obedience to such extravagant commands ? Yet a little farther, seeing it is not sufficient to abstain from evil, but that we must do good, instead of worshipping of idols, we must adore and serve the true God, according as he has commanded us, and instead of bending our knees before Baal, we must render to the Lord the honour and service which He requires of us. For we are bound to serve God for His own sake only ; but we honour our prince, and love our neighbour, because and for the love of God.

Now if it be ill done to offend our neighbour, and if it be a capital crime to rise against our prince, how shall we entitle those who rise in rebellion against the majesty of the sovereign Lord of all mankind. Briefly, as it is a thing much more grievous to offend the creator, than the creature, man, than the image he represents ; and as in the terms of law, he that has wounded the proper person of a king, is much more culpable than another who has only broken the statue erected in his memory, so there is no question but a much more terrible punishment is prepared for them who infringe the first table of the law, than for those who only sin against the second, although the one depend on the other ; whereupon it follows (to speak by comparison) that we must take more careful regard of the observation on the first than of the second.

Furthermore, our progenitors' examples may teach us the rule we must follow in this case. King Ahab, at the instigation of his wife Jezebel, killed all the prophets and servants of God that could be taken, notwithstanding, Abdias, steward of Ahab's house, did both hide and feed in a cave a hundred prophets ; the excuse for this is soon ready ; in obligations, oblige they never so nearly, the Divine Majesty must always be excepted. The same Ahab enjoined all men to sacrifice to Baal. Elias, instead of cooling or relenting, did reprove more freely the king and all the people, convinced the priests of Baal of their impiety, and caused them to be executed. Then, in despite of that wicked and furious Jezebel, and maugre that uxorious king, he does redress and reform with a divine and powerful endeavour the service of the true God. When Ahab reproached him (as the princes of our times do) that he troubled Israel, that

he was rebellious, seditious, titles wherewith they are ordinarily charged, who are no way culpable thereof ; nay,
but it is thou thyself, answered Elias, who, by thy apostasy
has troubled Israel, who has left the Lord, the true God,
to acquaint thyself with strange gods His enemies. In the
same manner and by the leading and direction of the same
spirit did Sidrac, Misack, and Abednego refuse to obey
Nebuchadnezar, Daniel, Darius, Eleazar, Antiochas, and
infinite others. After the coming of Jesus Christ, it being
forbidden the apostles to preach the gospel, Judge ye (said
they), whether it be reasonable as in the sight of God to
obey men, rather than God ; according to this, the apostles,
not regarding either the intendments or designs of the
greatness of the world, addressed themselves readily to
do that which their master, Jesus Christ, had commanded
them.

The Jews themselves would not permit that there should
be set up in the temple at Jerusalem the eagle of silver, nor
the statue of Caligula : what did Ambrose when the Emperor
Valentinian commanded him to give the temple at Milan
to the Arrians ? " Thy counsellors and captains are come
unto me," said he, " to make me speedily deliver the temple,
saying it was done by the authority and command of the
emperor, and that all things are in his power." I answered
to it, " That if he demanded that which is mine, to wit, mine
inheritance, my money, I would not in any sort refuse it
him, although all my goods belong properly to the poor, but
the things divine are not in subjection to the power of the
emperor." What do we think that this holy man would
have answered, if he had been demanded whether the
living temple of the Lord should be enthralled to the
slavery of idols ? These examples, and the constancy of
a million of martyrs, who were glorious in their deaths,
for not yielding obedience in this kind, according as
the Ecclesiastical Histories, which are full of them, do
demonstrate, may sufficiently serve for an express law in
this case.

But for all this we have no want of a law formerly written.
For as often and ever as the apostles admonish Christians
to obey kings and magistrates, they do first exhort, and as
it were by way of advice, admonish every one to subject
himself in like manner to God, and to obey Him before and

against any whatsoever, and there is nowhere to be found, in any of their writings, the least passage for this unlimited obedience, which the flatterers of princes do exact from men of small understandings. " Let every soul," saith Saint Paul, " be subject to the higher powers, for there is no power but of God " : he makes mention of every soul, to the end it may not be thought, that he would exempt any from this subjection ; we may easily gather by divers such speeches, that we must obey God rather than the king. For if we obey the king, because, and for the love of God, certainly this obedience may not be a conspiracy against God. But the apostle will stop the gap to all ambiguity in adding that the prince is the servant of God for our good, to wit, to do justice ; from this necessarily follows that which we come from touching, that we must rather obey God than him who is His servant. This does not yet content Saint Paul, for he adds in the end, " Give tribute, honour, and fear to whom they appertain," as if he should say, that which was alleged by Christ, " Give to Cæsar that which is Cæsar's, and to God that which is God's." To Cæsar tribute, and honour ; to God fear. Saint Peter says the same, " fear God, honour the king ; servants obey your masters, not only the good and kind, but also the rigorous." We must practise these precepts, according to the order they are set down in : to wit, that as servants are not bound to obey their masters if they command anything which is against the laws and ordinances of kings, subjects in like manner owe no obedience to kings which will make them to violate the law of God.

Certain lewd companions object, that even in the things themselves that concern the conscience we must obey kings, and are so shameless as to produce for witness of so wicked an opinion the Apostles Saint Peter and Saint Paul, concluding from hence, that we must yield obedience to all that the king shall ordain, though it be to embrace, without reply, any superstition he shall please to establish. But there is no man so grossly void of sense, that sees not the impiety of these men. We reply that Saint Paul says in express terms, we must be subject to princes, not only for wrath, but also for conscience sake. In opposing conscience to wrath, it is as much as if the apostle had said, that the obedience of which he speaks ought not to proceed for fear of punishment, but from the love of God, and from the reverence which we are bound to bear unto the Word. In the same sense Saint Paul enjoins servants in such manner to obey their masters, that it be not with eye service for fear of stripes, but in singleness of heart, fearing God, not simply to acquire the favour of men, whom they may delude, but to bear the burden laid on their shoulders by Him whom no man can deceive.

In brief there is manifest difference between these two manners of speech: to obey, for conscience sake, and to obey in those things which concern the conscience: otherwise those who had much rather lose their lives with infinite torments than obey princes who command them things contrary to the will of God, would have taught us that which these seek to persuade us to. Neither do they express themselves less impudent in that which they are accustomed to object, to those who are not so well able to answer them. That obedience is better than sacrifice, for there is no text in Holy Writ that does more evidently confound them than this, which is contained in Samuel's reprehension of King Saul, for his disobedience to the commandment of God, in sacrificing unfittingly. If then Saul, although he were a king, ought to obey God, it follows in all good consequence that subjects are not bound to obey their king by offending of God. Briefly those who (after the barbarous manner of the men of Calcut) seek to enthral the service of God with a necessary dependence on the will of a mutable man, and religion of the good pleasure of the king, as if he were some God on earth, they doubtless little value the testimony of Holy Writ. But let them (at the least) yet learn of a heathen orator. " That in every public state, there are certain degrees of duty, for those who converse and live in it, by which may appear wherein the one are obliged to the other. Insomuch that the first part of this duty belongs to the immortal God, the second concerns the country, which is their common mother, the third, those who are of our blood, the other parts leading us step by step to our other neighbours. Now, although the crime of high treason be very heinous, yet, according to the civilians, it always follows after sacrilege, an offence which properly pertains to the Lord God and His service; insomuch that they do confidently affirm that the robbing of a church is, by their rules, esteemed a greater crime than to conspire against the life of a prince." Thus much for this first question, wherein we persuade ourselves, that any man may receive satisfaction, if he be not utterly void of the fear of God.

THE SECOND QUESTION

Whether it be lawful to resist a prince who doth infringe the law of God, or ruin His Church : by whom, how, and how far it is lawful.

THIS question seems at the first view to be of a high and difficult nature, for so much as there being small occasion to speak to princes that fear God. On the contrary, there will be much danger to trouble the ears of those who acknowledge no other sovereign but themselves, for which reason few or none have meddled with it, and if any have at all touched it, it has been but as it were in passing by. The question is, If it be lawful to resist a prince violating the law of God, or ruinating the church, or hindering the restoring of it ? If we hold ourselves to the tenure of the Holy Scripture it will resolve us. For, if in this case it had been lawful to the Jewish people (the which may be easily gathered from the books of the Old Testament), yea, if it had been enjoined them, I believe it will not be denied, that the same must be allowed to the whole people of any Christian kingdom or country whatsoever. In the first place it must be considered, that God having chosen Israel from amongst all the nations of the earth, to be a peculiar people to Him, covenanted with them, that they should be the people of God. This is written in divers places of Deuteronomy : the substance and tenor of this alliance was, " That all should be careful in their several lines, tribes, and families in the land of Canaan, to serve God purely, who would have a church established amongst them for ever," which may be drawn from the testimony of divers places, namely, that which is contained in the twenty-seventh chapter of Deuteronomy; there Moses and the Levites covenanting as in the name of God, assembled all the people, and said unto them : " This day, O Israel, art thou become the people of God, obey you therefore His voice," etc. And Moses said, " When thou hast passed the River of Jordan, thou shalt set six tribes on the mountain of Gerizzim on the one side, and the six others on the mountain of Eball, and then the Levites shall read the law of God, promising the observers all felicity, and threatening woe and destruction to the breakers thereof, and all the people shall answer, Amen." The which was afterwards performed by Joshua, at his entering into the land of Canaan, and some few days before his death. We see by this that all the people is bound to maintain the law of God to perfect His church, and on the contrary to exterminate the idols of the land of Canaan : a covenant which can no ways appertain to particulars, but only to the whole body of the people. To which it also seems the encamping of all the tribes round about the ark of the Lord to have reference ; to the end that all should look to the preservation of that which was committed to the custody of all.

Now for the use and practice of this covenant we may produce examples; the inhabitants of Gabaa of the Tribe of Benjamin ravished the wife of a Levite, who died through their violence. The Levite divided his wife into twelve pieces, and sent them to the twelve tribes, to the end that all the people together might wipe away this so horrible a crime committed in Israel. All the people met together at Mizpah and required the Benjamites to deliver to be punished those who were culpable of this enormous crime, which they refused to perform. Wherefore with the allowance of God Himself, the states of the people with an universal consent renounce and make war against the Benjamites, and by this means the authority of the second Table of the Law was maintained by the detriment and ruin of one entire tribe who had broken it in one of the precepts.

For the first we have an example sufficiently manifest in Joshua. After that the Reubenites, Gadites, and Manassites were returned into their dwellings beyond Jordan, they incontinently built a goodly altar near unto the river ; this seems contrary to the commandment of the Lord, who expressly forbids to sacrifice anywhere but in the land of Canaan only, where it was to be feared lest these men intended to serve idols. This business being communicated to the people, inhabiting on this side Jordan, the place assigned for the meetings of the states was at Silo where the Ark of the Lord was. They all accordingly met, and Phineas the High Priest, the son of Eleazar, was sent to the other to treat with them concerning this offence committed against the law. And to the end they might know all the people had a hand in this business, they sent also the principal men of every tribe to complain that the service of God is corrupted by this device, that God would be provoked by this rebellion, and become an enemy, not only to the guilty, but also to all Israel, as heretofore in Beelphegor. Briefly, that they should denounce open war against them, if they desisted not from this their manner of doing. There must of necessity have followed much mischief, if those tribes beyond Jordan had not protested that they erected that altar only for a memorial that the Israelites both on the one and the other side of Jordan, both did and do profess one and the same religion, and at all times whensoever they have shewed themselves negligent in the maintenance of the service of God, we have seen that they have ever been punished : this is the true cause wherefore they lost two battles against the Benjamites according as it appears in the end of the Book of Judges ; for in so carefully undertaking to punish the rape and outrage done to a particular person, they clearly convinced themselves of much negligent profaneness in the maintenance of God's right, by their continual negligence, omission to punish both corporal and spiritual whoredoms ; there was then in these first times such a covenant between God and the people.

Now after that kings were given unto the people, there was so little purpose of disannulling or disbanding the former contract, that it was renewed and confirmed for ever. We have formerly said at the inaugurating of kings, there was a double covenant treated of, to wit " between God and the king " ; and " between God and the people." The agreement was first passed between " God, the king, and the people." Or between the " high priest, the people " (which is named in the first place in the twenty-third chapter of the

second book of the Chronicles) " and the king." The intention of this was, that the " people should be the people
of God " (which is as much as to say) " that the people should
be the church of God." We have shewed before to what end
God contracted covenants with the king.

Let us now consider wherefore also He allies Himself with
the people. It is a most certain thing, that God has not
done this in vain, and if the people had not " authority to
promise, and to keep promise," it were vainly lost time to contract or covenant with them. It may seem then that God
has done like those creditors, which having to deal with
not very sufficient borrowers, take divers jointly bound for
one and the same sum, insomuch as two or more being
bound one for another and each of them apart, for the entire
payment of the total sum, he may demand his whole debt
of which of them he pleases. There was much danger to
commit the custody of the church to one man alone, and
therefore God did recommend, and put it in trust " to all the
people." The king being raised to so slippery a place might
easily be corrupted : for fear lest the church should stumble
with him, God would have the people also to be respondents
for it. In the covenant of which we speak, God, or (in His
place) the High Priest are stipulators, the king and all the
people, to wit, Israel, do jointly and voluntarily assume,
promise, and oblige themselves for one and the same thing.
The High Priest demands if they promise, that the people
shall be the people of God, that God shall always have His
temple, His church amongst them, where He shall be purely
served. The king is respondent, so also are the people
(the whole body of the people representing, as it were, the
office and place of one man) not severally, but jointly, as
the words themselves make clear, being incontinent, and
not by intermission or distance of time, the one after the
other.

We see here then two undertakers, the king and Israel,
who by consequence are bound one for another and each
for the whole. For as when Caius and Titus have promised
jointly to pay to their creditor Seius a certain sum, each of
them is bound for himself and his companion, and the
creditor may demand the sum of which of them he pleases.
In the like manner the king for himself, and Israel for itself
are bound with all circumspection to see that the church

be not damnified: if either of them be negligent of their covenant, God may justly demand the whole of which of the two He pleases, and the more probably of the people than of the king, and for that many cannot so easily slip away as one, and have better means to discharge the debts than one alone. In like manner, as when two men that are indebted, especially to the public exchequer, the one is in such manner bound for the other, that he can take no benefit of the division granted by the new constitutions of Justinian. So likewise the king and Israel, promising to pay tribute to God, who is the King of Kings, for accomplishment whereof, the one is obliged for the other. And as two covenanters by promise, especially in contracts, the obligation whereof exposes the obligees to forfeitures and hazards, such as this is here, the failings of the one endamages the other : so that if Israel forsake their God, and the king makes no account of it, he is justly guilty of Israel's delinquency. In like manner, if the king follow after strange gods, and not content to be seduced himself, seek also to attract his subjects, endeavouring by all means to ruin the church, if Israel seek not to withdraw him from his rebellion, and contain him within the limits of obedience, they make the fault of their king their own transgression.

Briefly, as when there is danger that one of the debtors by consuming his goods may be disabled to give satisfaction, the other must satisfy the creditors who ought not to be endamaged; though one of his debtors have ill husbanded his estate, this ought not to be doubted in regard of Israel toward their king, and of the king towards Israel in case one of them apply himself to the service of idols, or break their covenant in any other sort, the one of them must pay the forfeiture and be punished for the other. Now that the covenant of which we at this time treat is of this nature, it appears also by other testimonies of Holy Scripture. Saul being established king of Israel, Samuel, priest and prophet of the Lord, speaks in this manner to the people. " Both you and your king which is over you serve the Lord your God, but if you persevere in malice " (he taxes them of malice for that they preferred the government of a man before that of God) " you and your king shall perish." He adds after the reason, " for it has pleased God to choose you for His people." You see here both the parties evidently conjoined in the condition and the punishment. In like manner Asa, king of Judah, by the council of the prophet Assary, assembles all the people at Jerusalem, to wit, Judah and Benjamin, to enter into covenant with God. Thither came also divers of the tribes of Ephraim, Manasses, and Simeon, who were come thither to serve the Lord according to His own ordinance. After the sacrifices were performed according to the law, the covenant was contracted in these terms, " Whosoever shall not call upon the Lord God of Israel, be he the least or the greatest, let him die the death." In making mention of the greatest, you see that the king himself is not excepted from the designed punishment.

But who may punish the king (for here is question of corporal and temporal punishment) if it be not the whole body of the people to whom the king swears and obliges himself, no more nor less, than the people do to the king ? We read also that king Josias, being of the age of twenty-and-five years, together with the whole people, makes a covenant with the Lord, the king and the people promising to keep the laws and ordinances of God ; and even then for the better accomplishing of the tenure of this agreement, the idolatry of Baal was presently destroyed. If any will more exactly turn over the Holy Bible, he may well find other testimonies to this purpose.

But to what purpose should the consent of the people be required ; wherefore should Israel or Judah be expressly bound to observe the law of God ? For what reason should they promise so solemnly to be for ever the people of God ? If it be denied, by the same reason that they had any authority from God, or power to free themselves from perjury, or to hinder the ruin of the church. For to what end should it serve to cause the people to promise to be the people of God, if they must and are bound to endure and suffer the king to draw them after strange gods. If the people be absolutely in bondage, wherefore is it commanded then, to take order that God be purely served ? If it be so that they cannot properly oblige themselves to God, and if it be not lawful for them by all to endeavour the accomplishment of their promise, shall we say that God has made an agreement with them, which had no right neither to promise, nor to keep promise ? But on the contrary, in this business of making a covenant with the people, God would openly and plainly show that the people have right to make, hold, and accomplish their promises and contracts. For, if he be not worthy to be heard in public court that will bargain or contract with a slave, or one that is under tutelage, shall it not be much more shameful to lay this imputation upon the Almighty, that He should contract with those who had no power to perform the conditions covenanted ?

But for this occasion it was, that when the kings had broken their covenants, the prophets always addressed themselves to the House of Judah and Jacob, and to Samaria, to advertise them of their duties. Furthermore, they required the people that they not only withdraw themselves from sacrificing to Baal, but also that they call down his idol, and destroy his priests and service ; yea, even maugre the king himself. For example, Ahab having killed the prophets of God, the prophet Elias assembles the people, and as it were convented the estates, and does there tax, reprehend, and reprove every one of them ; the people at his exhortation take and put to death the priests of Baal. And for so much as the king neglected his duty, it behoved Israel more carefully to discharge theirs without tumult, not rashly, but by public authority ; the estates being assembled, and the equity of the cause orderly debated, and sufficiently cleared before they came to the execution of justice. On the contrary, so often, and always when Israel has failed to oppose their king, which would overthrow the service of God, that which has been formerly said of the two debtors, the inability and ill husbandry of the one does ever prejudice the other, the same happened to them ; for as the king has been punished for his idolatry and disloyalty, the people have also been chastised for their negligence, connivency, and stupidity, and it has commonly happened that the kings have been much more often swayed, and drawn others with them than the people, for so much as ordinarily the great ones mould themselves into the fashion of the king, and the people conform themselves in humours to those who govern them : to be brief, all more usually offend after the example of one, than that one will reform himself as he sees all the rest.

This which we say will, perhaps, appear more plainly by examples. What do we suppose to have been the cause of the defeat and overthrow of the army of Israel with their king Saul? Does God correct the people for the sins of the prince? Is the child beaten instead of the father? It is a discourse not easily to be digested, say the civilians, to maintain that the children should bear the punishments due for the offences of their fathers; the laws do not permit that anyone shall suffer for the wickedness of another. Now God forbid that the judge of all the world (said Abraham) should destroy the innocent with the guilty. On the contrary (saith the Lord) as the life of the father, so the life of the son is in my hands; the fathers shall not be put to death for the children, neither shall the children be put to death for the fathers; every man shall be put to death for his own sin. That overthrow, then, did it not proceed for that the people opposed not Saul when he violated the law of God, but applauded that miserable prince when he wickedly persecuted the best men, as David and the priests of the Lord?

Amongst many other examples let us only produce some few. The same Saul to enlarge the possessions of the tribe of Judah broke the public faith granted to the Gibeonites, at the first entry of the people into the land of Canaan, and put to death as many of the Gibeonites as he could come by. By this execution Saul broke the third commandment, for God had been called to witness this agreement, and the sixth also, in so much as he murdered the innocent; he ought to have maintained the authority of the two Tables of the Law; and thereupon it is said, that Saul and his house have committed this wickedness. In the meantime, after the death of Saul, and David being established king, the Lord being demanded, made answer that it was already the third year that the whole country of Israel was afflicted with famine because of this cruelty, and the hand of the Lord ceased not to strike, until that seven men of the house of Saul were given to the Gibeonites, who put them to death; seeing that every one ought to bear his own burden, and that no man is esteemed the inheritor of another's crime; wherefore they say, that all the whole people of Israel deserved to be punished for Saul, who was already dead, and had (as it might seem) that controversy buried in the same grave with him, but only in regard that the people neglected to oppose a mischief so public and apparent, although they ought and might have done it. Think you it reason, that any should be punished unless they deserve it ? And in what have the people here failed, but in suffering the offence of their king.

In like manner when David commanded Joab and the governors of Israel to number the people, he is taxed to have committed a great fault ; for even as Israel provoked the anger of God in demanding a king, one in whose wisdom they seemed to repose their safety, even so David did much forget himself, in hoping for victory through the multitude of his subjects ; for so much as that is properly (according to the saying of the prophet) to sacrifice unto their net, and burn incense unto their drag, a kind of abominable idolatry ; for the governors, they seeing that it would draw evil on the people, drew back a little at the first ; afterwards, as it were, to be rid of the importunity they made the enrolment : in the mean· season all the people are punished, and not David alone, but also the ancients of Israel, who represented the whole body of the people, put on sack-cloth and ashes, the which, notwithstanding, was not done nor practised when David committed those horrible sins of murder and adultery. Who sees not in this last act, that all had sinned, and that all should repent ; and finally that all were chastised, to wit, David, who had provoked God by so wicked a commandment, the governors (as peers and assessors of the kingdom, ought in the name of all Israel to have opposed the king) by their connivency and over-weak resistance, and all the people also who made their appearance to be enrolled ? God, in this respect, did like a chief commander or general of an army ; he chastised the offence of the whole camp by a sudden alarm given to all, and by the exemplary punishments of some particulars to keep all the rest in better awe and order.

But tell me wherefore after that the King Manasses had polluted the Temple at Jerusalem, do we read that God not only taxed Manasses, but all the people also ? Was it not to advertise Israel, one of the sureties, that if they keep not the king within the limits of his duty, they should all smart for it ; for what meant the prophet Jeremy to say, the house of Judah is in subjection to the Assyrians, because of the impiety and cruelty of Manasses ? but that they were guilty of all his offences, because they made no resistance ; wherefore Saint Austin and Saint Ambrose said Herod and Pilate condemned Jesus Christ, the priests delivered Him to be crucified, the people seem to have some compassion, notwithstanding all are punished. And wherefore so? For so much as they are all guilty of His death, in that they did not deliver Him out of the hands of those wicked judges and governors. There must also be added to this many other proofs drawn from divers authors for the further explication of this point, were it not that the testimonies of holy scripture ought to suffice Christians.

Furthermore, in so much as it is the duty of a good magistrate rather to endeavour to hinder and prevent a mischief than to chastise the delinquents after the offence is committed, as good physicians who prescribe a diet to allay and prevent diseases, as well as medicines to cure them, in like manner a people truly affected to true religion, will not simply consent themselves to reprove and repress a prince who would abolish the law of God, but also will have special regard, that through malice and wickedness he innovate nothing that may hurt the same, or that in tract of time may corrupt the pure service of God; and instead of supporting public offences committed against the Divine Majesty, they will take away all occasions wherewith the offenders might cover their faults; we read that to have been practised by all Israel by a decree of Parliament in the assembly of the whole people, to remonstrate to those beyond Jordan, touching the altar they had built, and by the king Ezechias, who caused the brazen serpent to be broken.

It is then lawful for Israel to resist the king, who would overthrow the law of God and abolish His church; and not only so, but also they ought to know that in neglecting to perform this duty, they make themselves culpable of the same crime, and shall bear the like punishment with their king.

If their assaults be verbal, their defence must be likewise verbal; if the sword be drawn against them, they may also take arms, and fight either with tongue or hand, as occasion is: yea, if they be assailed by surprisals, they may make use both of ambuscades and countermines, there being no rule in lawful war that directs them for the manner, whether it be by open assailing their enemy, or by close surprising; provided always that they carefully distinguish between advantageous stratagems, and perfidious treason, which is always unlawful.

But I see well, here will be an objection made. What will you say ? That a whole people, that beast of many heads, must they run in a mutinous disorder, to order the business of the commonwealth ? What address or direction is there in an unruly and unbridled multitude ? What counsel or wisdom, to manage the affairs of state ?

When we speak of all the people, we understand by that, only those who hold their authority from the people, to wit, the magistrates, who are inferior to the king, and whom the people have substituted, or established, as it were, consorts in the empire, and with a kind of tribunitial authority, to restrain the encroachments of sovereignty, and to represent the whole body of the people. We understand also, the assembly of the estates, which is nothing else but an epitome, or brief collection of the kingdom, to whom all public affairs have special and absolute reference ; such were the seventy ancients in the kingdom of Israel, amongst whom the high priest was as it were president, and they judged all matters of greatest importance, those seventy being first chosen by six out of each tribe, which came out of the land of Egypt, then the heads or governors of provinces. In like manner the judges and provosts of towns, the captains of thousands, the centurions and others who commanded over families, the most valiant, noble, and otherwise notable personages, of whom was composed the body of the states, assembled divers times as it plainly appears by the word of the holy scripture. At the election of the first king, who was Saul, all the ancients of Israel assembled together at Kama. In like manner all Israel was assembled, or all Judah and Benjamin, etc. Now, it is no way probable, that all the people, one by one, met together there. Of this rank there are in every well governed kingdom, the princes, the officers of the crown, the peers, the greatest and most notable lords, the deputies of provinces, of whom the ordinary body of the estate is composed, or the parliament or the diet, or other assembly, according to the different names used in divers countries of the world ; in which assemblies, the principal care is had both for the preventing and reforming either of disorder or detriment in church or commonwealth.

For as the councils of Basil and Constance have decreed (and well decreed) that the universal council is in authority above the bishop of Rome, so in like manner, the whole chapter may over-rule the bishop, the university the rector, the court the president. Briefly, he, whosoever he is, who has received authority from a company, is inferior to that whole company, although he be superior to any of the particular members of it. Also is it without any scruple or doubt, that Israel, who demanded and established a king as governor of the public, must needs be above Saul, established at their request and for Israel's sake, as it shall be more fully proved hereafter. And for so much as an orderly proceeding is necessarily required in all affairs discreetly addressed, and that it is not so probably hopeful that order shall be observed amongst so great a number of people ; yea, and that there oftentimes occur occasions which may not be communicated to a multitude, without manifest danger of the commonwealth : we say, that all that which has been spoken of privileges granted, and right committed to the people, ought to be referred to the officers and deputies of the kingdom : and all that which has been said of Israel, is to be understood of the princes and elders of Israel, to whom these things were granted and committed as the practice also has verified.

The queen Athalia, after the death of her son Ahazia king of Judah, put to death all those of the royal blood, except little Joas, who, being yet in the cradle, was preserved by the piety and wisdom of his aunt Jehoshabeah. Athalia possesses herself of the government, and reigned six years over Judah. It may well be the people murmured between their teeth, and dare not by reason of danger express what they thought in their minds.

Finally, Jehoiada, the high priest, the husband of Jehoshabeah, having secretly made a league and combination with the chief men of the kingdom, did anoint and crown king his nephew Joas, being but seven years old. And he did not content himself to drive the Queen Mother from the royal throne, but he also put her to death, and presently overthrew the idolatry of Baal. This deed of Jehoiada is approved, and by good reason, for he took on him the defence of a good cause, for he assailed the tyranny, and not the kingdom. The tyranny (I say) which had no title, as our modern civilians speak. For by no law were women admitted to the government of the kingdom of Judah. Furthermore, that tyranny was in vigour and practice. For Athalia had with unbounded mischief and cruelty invaded the realm of her nephews, and in the administration of that government committed infinite wickedness, and what was the worst of all, had cast off the service of the living God to adore and compel others with her, to worship the idol of Baal. Therefore then was she justly punished, and by him who had a lawful calling and authority to do it. For Jehoiada was not a private and particular person, but the high priest, to whom the knowledge of civil causes did then belong. And besides, he had for his associates, the principal men of the kingdom, the Levites, and being himself the king's kinsman and ally. Now for so much as he assembled not the estates at Mizpah, according to the accustomed manner, he is not reproved for it, neither for that he consulted and contrived the matter secretly, for that if he had held any other manner of proceeding, the business must probably have failed in the execution and success.

A combination or conjuration is good or ill, according as the end whereunto it is addressed is good or ill ; and perhaps also according as they are affected who are the managers of it. We say then, that the princes of Judah have done well, and that in following any other course they had failed of the right way. For even as the guardian ought to take charge and care that the goods of his pupil fall not into loss and detriment, and if he omit his duty therein, he may be compelled to give an account thereof, in like manner, those to whose custody and tuition the people have committed themselves, and whom they have constituted their tutors and defenders ought to maintain them safe and entire in all their rights and privileges. To be short, as it is lawful for a whole people to resist and oppose tyranny, so likewise the principal persons of the kingdom may as heads, and for the good of the whole body, confederate and associate themselves together ; and as in a public state, that which is done by the greatest part is esteemed and taken as the act of all, so in like manner must it be said to be done, which the better part of the most principal have acted, briefly, that all the people had their hand in it.

But here presents itself another question, the which deserves to be considered, and amply debated in regard of the circumstance of time. Let us put the case that a king seeking to abolish the law of God, or ruin the church, that all the people or the greatest part yield their consent, that all the princes or the greatest number of them make no reckoning; and, notwithstanding, a small handful of people, to wit, some of the princes and magistrates desire to preserve the law of God entirely and inviolably, and to serve the Lord purely: what may it be lawful for them to do if the king seek to compel those men to be idolaters, or will take from them the exercise of true religion? We speak not here of private and particular persons considered one by one, and who in that manner are not held as parts of the entire body, as the planks, the nails, the pegs, are no part of the ship, neither the stones, the rafters, nor the rubbish, are any part of the house. But we speak of some town or province, which makes a portion of a kingdom, as the prow, the poop, the keel, and other parts make a ship: the foundation, the roof, and the walls make a house. We speak also of the magistrate who governs such a city or province.

If we must make our defence with producing of examples, although we have not many ready by reason of the backwardness and carelessness of men when there is question to maintain the service of God: notwithstanding, we have some few to be examined and received according as they deserve. Libna, a town of the priests, withdrew itself from the obedience of Joram, king of Judah, and left that prince, because he had abandoned the God of his fathers, whom those of the town would serve, and it may be they feared also lest in the end they should be compelled to sacrifice to Baal. In like manner when that the king Antiochus commanded that all the Jews should embrace his religion, and should forsake that which the God Almighty had taught them, Mattathias answered, we will not obey, nor will we do anything contrary to our religion: neither did he only speak, but also, being transported with the zeal of Phineas, he killed with his own hands a Jew, who constrained his fellow citizens to sacrifice to idols. Then he took arms and retired into the mountain, gathered troops, and made war against Antiochus, for religion, and for his country, with such success, that he regained Jerusalem, broke and brought to nothing the power of the pagans whom they had gathered to ruin the church, and then re-established the pure service of God. If we will know who this Mattathias was, he was the father of the Machabees of the tribe of Levi; insomuch as it was not lawful for him, according to the received custom and right of his race to restore the kingdom by arms from the tyranny of Antiochus. His followers were such as fled to the mountains together with the inhabitants of Modin, to whom had adjoined themselves divers neighbouring Jews, and other fugitives from sundry quarters of Judæa; all who solicitously desired the re-establishment of the church. Almost all the rest, yea, the principals, obeyed Antiochus, and that after the rout of his army, and his own miserable death. Although there was then a fair occasion to shake off his yoke, yet the Jews sought to the son of Antiochus, and entreated him to take on him the kingdom, promising him fidelity and obedience.

I might here produce the example of Deborah. The Lord God had subjected Israel to Jabin king of Canaan, and they had remained in this servitude the space of twenty years, who might seem in some sort to have gained a right by prescription over the kingdom; and together also, that almost all Israel followed after strange gods. The principal and most powerful tribes, to wit, Reuben, Ephraim, Benjamin, Dan, Asher, and some others, adhered wholly to Jabin. Yet, notwithstanding, the prophetess Deborah who judged Israel, caused the tribes of Zebulon, Nephthalie, and Issachar, or at the least some of all those tribes, to take arms under the conduct of Barak, and they overthrew Sisera the lieutenant of Jabin, and delivered Israel, who had no thought of liberty, and was content to remain in bondage; and having shaken off the yoke of the Canaanites they re-established the pure service of the living God. But for so much as Deborah seems to have an extraordinary vocation, and that the scripture does not approve in express terms the doings of them of Libna, although that in not disallowing of their proceedings, it may seem in some sort to allow them, and for that the history of the Machabees has had no great authority in the ancient church, and for that it is commonly held that an assertion must be proved by laws and testimonies, not by examples, let us examine by the effect, what we ought to judge, according to the right of the matter now in question.

We have formerly said that the king did swear to keep the law of God, and promised to the uttermost of his power to maintain the church ; that the people of Israel considered in one body, covenanting by the high priest, made the same promise to God.   Now, at this present, we say that all the towns and all the magistrates of these towns, which are parts and portions of the kingdom, promise each of them on his own behalf, and in express terms, the which all towns and Christian communalties have also done, although it has been but with a tacit consent.   Joshua, being very old and near to his death, assembled all Israel at Sichem in the presence of God, to wit, before the ark of the covenant, which was there.   It is said that the ancients of the people, the heads of the tribe, the judges and governors, and all who had any public command in the town of Israel, met together there, where they swore to observe and keep the law of the Lord, and did willingly put on the yoke of the Almighty God : whereby, it appears, that these magistrates did oblige themselves in the names of their towns and communalties, who did send them to take order, that God should be served throughout the whole country, according as He had revealed in His law.   And Joshua, for his part, having passed this contract of agreement between God and the people, and enregistered the whole, according as it was done, for a perpetual memorial of the matter he incontinently set up a stone.

If there were occasion to remove the ark of the Lord, the principals of the country and towns, the captains, the centurions, the provosts, and others, were summoned by the decree and commandment of David ; and of the synagogue of Israel, if there be a purpose of building the Lord's temple, the same course is observed.   And to the end it be not supposed, that some alteration has been inserted after the creation of kings.   In the times of Joas and Josias, when there was question of renewing the covenant between God and the people, all the estates met together, and all were bound and obliged particularly.   Also not only the king, but the kingdom, and not only all the kingdom, but also all the pastors of the kingdom, promise each of them for themselves, fidelity and obedience to God.   I say again, that not only the king and the people, but also all the towns of Israel, and their magistrates, oblige themselves to God, and, as homagers to their liege Lord, tie themselves to be His for ever, with and against all men. For further proof of the aforesaid, I would entreat the reader diligently to turn over the Holy Bible, especially in the books of the Kings and the Chronicles. But for a yet more ample explication of this matter, let us produce for example what is in practice at this day.

In the empire of Germany, when the emperor is to be crowned, the electors and princes of the empire, as well secular as ecclesiastical, meet together personally, or else send their ambassadors. The prelates, earls and barons, and all the deputies of the imperial towns, come thither also, or else send special proxies ; then do they their homage to the emperor, either for themselves, or for them whom they represent, with, and under, certain conditions. Now, let us presuppose that one of these who has done homage voluntarily, afterwards endeavours to depose the emperor, and advance himself into his place, and that the princes and barons deny their sovereign the succour and tribute which they owe him, and that they have intelligence with that other who conspired and sought to possess himself of the imperial throne. Think you that they of Straesbourgh or of Nurembergh, who have bound themselves by faith unto the lawful emperor, have not lawful right to repress and exclude this traitorous intruder ? Yea, on the contrary, if they do it not, if they give not succour to the emperor in this his necessity, think you that they have satisfied or per- formed their fealty and promise, seeing that he who has not preserved his governor when he had means to do it, ought to be held as culpable and guilty as he who offered the violence and injury unto him ? If it be so (as every one may sufficiently see it is) is it not then lawful for the men of Libna and of Modin ? and does not their duty enjoin them to do as much as if the other estates of the kingdom have left God, to whose service and pleasure they know and acknowledge themselves to be bound to render obedience ?

Let us imagine then some Joram or Antiochus who abol- ishes true religion, and lifts up himself above God, that Israel connives and is content, what should that town do which desires to serve God purely ? First, they should say with Joshua, for their parts, look whom you desire rather to obey, the living God, or the gods of the Amorites; for our parts, we and our families will serve the Lord. Choose you then, I say, if you will obey in this point him, who, without any right, usurps that power and authority which no way appertains unto him; for my part, happen what may, I will keep my faith to him to whom I promised it. I make no question but that Joshua would have done the uttermost of his endeavour to maintain the pure service of the living God in Thamnathe Serathe, a town of Ephraim, where his house and estate lay; if the Israelites besides had so much forgotten themselves as to have worshipped the god of the Amorites in the land of Canaan.

But if the king should pass yet further, and send his lieutenants to compel us to become idolaters, and if he commands us to drive God and His service from amongst us; shall we not rather shut our gates against the king and his officers, than drive out of our town the Lord who is the King of Kings? Let the burgesses and citizens of towns, let the magistrates and governors of the people of God dwelling in towns, consider with themselves that they have contracted two covenants, and taken two oaths. The first and most ancient with God, to whom the people have sworn to be His people; the second and next following, with the king, to whom the people have promised obedience, as unto him who is the governor and conductor of the people of God. So then, as if a viceroy conspiring against his sovereign, although he had received from him an unlimited authority, if he should summon us to deliver the king whom he held besieged within the enclosure of our walls, we ought not to obey him, but resist with the uttermost of our power and means, according to the tenor of our oath of allegiance. In like manner think we, that it is not a wickedness of all most detestable, if at the pleasure of a prince who is the vassal and servant of God, we should drive God from dwelling amongst us, or deliver Him (as far as in us lieth) into the hands of His enemies.

You will say, it may be that the towns appertain to the prince. And I answer, that the towns consist not of a heap of stones, but of that which we call people, that the people is the people of God, to whom they are first bound by oath; and secondly, to the king. For the towns, although that the kings have power over them, notwithstanding the right of inheritance of the soil belongs to the citizens and owners, for all that which is in a kingdom is indeed under the dominion of the king, but not of his proper patrimony. God in truth is the only Lord proprietor of all things, and it is of Him that the king holds his royalties, and the people their patrimony. This is as much as to say, you will reply, that for the cause of religion it shall be lawful for the subjects to revolt from the obedience of their king. If this be once granted, it will presently open a gap to rebellion ? But, hearken, I pray you patiently, and consider this matter more thoroughly. I might answer in a word, that of two things, if the one must needs be done, it were much better to forsake the king, than God ; or with Saint Augustine in his fourth book, *Of the city of God*, chapter iv, and in the nineteenth book, and chapter xxi, that where there is no justice, there is is no commonwealth ; that there is no justice when he that is a mortal man would pull another man out of the hands of the immortal God, to make him a slave of the devil, seeing that justice is a virtue that gives to every one that which is his own, and that those who draw their necks out of the yoke of such rulers, deliver themselves from the tyranny of wicked spirits, and abandon a multitude of robbers, and not the commonwealth.

But to re-assume this discourse a little higher, those who shall carry themselves as has been formerly said, seem no ways accusable of the crime of revolt. Those are said properly to quit the king or the commonwealth, which, with the heart and purpose of an enemy, withdraw themselves from the obedience of the king or the commonwealth, by means whereof they are justly accounted adversaries, and are oftentimes much more to be feared, than any other enemies. But those of whom we now speak do nothing resemble them. First, they do in no sort refuse to obey, provided that they be commanded that which they may lawfully do, and that it be not against the honour of God.

They pay willingly the taxes, customs, imposts, and ordinary payments, provided that with these they seek not to abolish the tribute which they owe unto God. They obey Cæsar while he commands in the quality of Cæsar ; but when Cæsar passes his bounds, when he usurps that dominion which is none of his own, when he endeavours to assail the

Throne of God, when he wars against the Sovereign Lord, both of himself and the people, they then esteem it reasonable not to obey Cæsar; and yet, after this, to speak properly, they do no acts of hostility. He is properly an enemy who stirs up, who provokes another, who out of military insolency prepares and sets forth parties to war. They have been urged and assailed by open war, and close and treacherous surprisals; when death and destruction environ them round about, then they take arms, and wait their enemies' assaults. You cannot have peace with your enemies when you will; for if you lay down your weapons, if you give over making war, they will not for all that disarm themselves, and lose their advantage. But for these men, desire but peace and you have it; give over but assailing them, and they will lay down their arms; cease to fight against God, and they will presently leave the lists. Will you take their swords out of their hands? Abstain you only then from striking, seeing they are not the assailants, but the defendants; sheathe your sword, and they will presently cast their buckler on the ground, which has been the reason that they have been often surprised by perfidious ambuscades, whereof these our times have afforded over-frequent examples.

Now, as we cannot call that servant stubborn or a fugitive, who puts by the blow which his lord strikes at him with his sword, or who withdraws or hides himself from his master's fury, or shuts his chamber door upon him until his choler and heat be passed over, much less ought we to esteem those seditious, who (holding the name and place of servants and subjects) shut the gates of a city against their prince, transported with anger, being ready to do all his just commandments, after he has recovered his judgment, and related his former indignation. We must place in this rank, David, commander of the army of Israel, under Saul, a furious king. David, oppressed with calumnies and false taxations, watched, and waylaid from all parts, he retired unto, and defended himself in unaccessible mountains, and provided for his defence to oppose the walls of Ceila against the fury of the king; yea, he drew unto his party all those that he could, not to take away Saul's life from him, as it plainly appeared afterwards, but to defend his own cause: see wherefore Jonathan, the son of Saul, made no difficulty, to make alliance with David, and to renew it from time to time, the which is called the alliance of the Almighty. And Abigail says in express words, that David was wrongfully assailed, and that he made the war of God.

We must also place in this rank the Machabees, who, having good means to maintain wars, were content to receive peace from king Demetrius and others, which Antiochus had offered them before, because by it, they should be secured in the free possession and exercise of their religion. We may remember that those who in our times have fought for true religion against Antichrist, both in Germany and France, have laid down arms as soon as it was permitted them to serve God truly according to His ordinance, and oftentimes having fair means and occasion to advance and continue the war to their much advantage: as when the Philistines compelled Saul to cease attack, and Antioch to desist from an assault upon its neighbours; and other occasions when everything favoured further warfare. See then the marks which distinguish and separate sufficiently those of whom we speak from rebels or seditious.

But let us yet see other evident testimonies of the equity of their cause; for their defection is of that nature, that take away but the occasion, if some extreme necessity compel not the contrary, they presently return to their former condition, and then you cannot properly say, they separated themselves from the king, or the commonalty; but that they left Joram, and Antiochus, or if you will, the tyranny and unlawful power of one alone, or if divers particulars, who had no authority nor right to exact obedience in the same manner, as they commanded. The doctors of the Sorbonne have taught us the like sundry times: whereof we will allege some examples.

About the year 1300 Pope Boniface VIII, seeking to appropriate to his See the royalties that belonged to the crown of France, Philip the Fair, the then king, did taunt him somewhat sharply: the tenor of whose tart letters are these:

"Philip by the Grace of God, King of the French, to Boniface, calling himself Sovereign Bishop, little or no health at all.

"Be it known to the great foolishness and unbounded rashness, that in temporal matters we have only God for our superior, and that the vacancy of certain churches belongs to us by royal prerogative, and that appertains to us only to gather the fruits, and we will defend the possession thereof against all opposers with the edge of our swords, accounting them fools, and without brains who hold a contrary opinion."

In those times all men acknowledged the pope for God's vicar on earth, and head of the universal church. Insomuch, that (as it is said) common error went instead of a law, notwithstanding the Sorbonists being assembled, and demanded, made answer, that the king and the kingdom might safely, without blame or danger of schism, exempt themselves from his obedience, and flatly refuse that which the pope demanded ; for so much as it is not the separation but the cause which makes the schism, and if there were schism, it should be only in separating from Boniface, and not from the church, nor from the pope, and that there was no danger nor offence in so remaining until some honest man were chosen pope. Every one knows into what perplexities the consciences of a whole kingdom would fall, which held themselves separated from the church, if this distinction be not true. I would demand now, if it be not yet more lawful to make use of this distinction, when a king invades and encroaches on the jurisdiction of God, and oppresses with hard servitude, the souls dearly bought with the precious blood of Jesus Christ. Let us add another example.

In the year of our Lord 1408, when pope Benedict XIII did oppose the French church by tributes and exactions ; the clergy, assembled by the command of King Charles VI decreed, That the king and inhabitants of the kingdom ought not to obey Benedict, who was an heretic, a schismatic, and altogether unworthy of that dignity : the which the estates of the kingdom approved, and the parliament of Paris confirmed by a decree. The same clergy also ordained that those who had been excommunicated by that pope, as forsakers and enemies of the church, should be presently absolved, nullifying all such excommunications, and this has been practised not in France only, but in other places also, as histories do credibly report. The which gives us just occasion most perspicuously to see and know, that if he who holds the place of a prince do govern ill, there may be a separation from him without incurring justly the blame of revolt ; for that they are things in themselves directly contrary, to leave a bad pope, and forsake the church, a wicked king, and the kingdom. To return to those of Lobna, they seem to have followed this before remembered expedient ; for after the re-establishment of the service of God they presently became again the subjects of king Ezekias. And if this distinction be allowed place, when a pope encroaches on the rights of any prince, which, notwithstanding in some cases acknowledges him for his sovereign, is it not much more allowable, if a prince who is a vassal in that respect, endeavours to assure and appropriate to himself the rights of God ? Let us conclude, then, to end this discourse, that all the people by the authority of those, into whose hands they have committed their power, or divers of them, may, and ought to reprove and repress a prince who commands things against God. In like manner, that all, or at the least, the principals of provinces or towns, under the authority of the chief magistrates, established first by God, and secondly by the prince, may according to law and reason, hinder the entrance of idolatry within the enclosure of their walls, and maintain their true religion : yea, further, they may extend the confines of the church, which is but one, and in failing hereof, if they have means to do it, they justly incur the penalty of high treason against the Divine Majesty.

Whether private men may resist by arms

It remains now that we speak of particulars who are private persons. First, particulars or private persons are not bound to take up arms against the prince who would compel them to become idolaters. The covenant between God and all the people who promise to be the people of God, does not in any sort bind them to that ; for as that which belongs to the whole universal body is in no sort proper to particulars, so, in like manner, that which the body owes and is bound to perform cannot by any sensible reason be required of particular persons : neither does their duty anything oblige them to it ; for every one is bound to serve God in that proper vocation to which he is called. Now private persons, they have no power ; they have no public command, nor any calling to unsheathe the sword of authority ; and therefore as God has not put the sword into the hands of private men, so does He not require in any sort that they should strike with it. It is said to them, " put up thy sword into thy scabbard." On the contrary the apostles say of magistrates, they carry not the sword in vain. If particular men draw it forth they make themselves delinquents. If magistrates be slow and negligent to use it when just occasion is offered, they are likewise justly blameable of negligence in performing their duties, and equally guilty with the former.

But you will say unto me, has not God made a covenant, as well with particular persons as with the generality, with the least as well as the highest ? To what purpose was circumcision and baptism ordained ? What means that frequent repetition of the covenant in so many passages of holy writ ? All this is true, but the consideration hereof is diverse in their several kinds. For as all the subjects of a good and faithful prince, of what degree soever they be, are bound to obey him ; but some of them, notwithstanding, have their particular duty, as magistrates must hold others in obedience ; in like manner all men are bound to serve God ; but some are placed in a higher rank, have received greater authority, in so much as they are account-able for the offences of others, if they attend not the charges of the commonalty carefully.

The kings, the commonalties of the people, the magistrates into whose hands the whole body of the common-wealth has committed the sword of authority, must and ought to take care that the church be maintained and preserved ; particulars ought only to look that they render themselves members of this church. Kings and popular estates are bound to hinder the pollution or ruin of the temple of God, and ought to free and defend it from all corruption within, and all injury from without. Private men must take order, that their bodies, the temples of God, be pure, that they may be fit receptacles for the Holy Ghost to dwell in them. If any man defile the temple of God, saith the apostle, him shall God destroy ; for the temple of God is holy, which temple ye are ; to the former He gives the sword which they bear with authority ; to the other He recommends the sword of the Spirit only, to wit, the word of God, wherewith Saint Paul arms all Christians against the assaults of the devil. What shall then private men do, if the king will constrain them to serve idols ? If the magistrates into whose hands the people have consigned their authority, or if the magistrates of the place, where these particulars dwell, do oppose these proceedings of the king, let them in God's name obey their leaders, and employ all their means (as in the service of God) to aid the holy and commendable enterprises of those who oppose themselves lawfully against his wicked intention. Amongst others they have the examples of the centurions, and men at arms, who readily and cheerfully obeyed the princes of Judah, who, stirred up by Jehoidas, purged the church from all profanation, and delivered the kingdom from the tyranny of Athaliah. But if the princes and magistrates approve the course of an outrageous and irreligious prince, or if they do not resist him, we must lend our ears to the counsel of Jesus Christ, to wit, retire ourselves into some other place. We have the example of the faithful mixed among the ten tribes of Israel, who, seeing the true service of God abolished by Jeroboam, and that none made any account of it, they retired themselves into the territories of Judah, where religion remained in her purity. Let us rather forsake our livelihoods and lives, than God, let us rather be crucified ourselves, than crucify the Lord of Life : fear not them (saith the Lord) who can only kill the body. He Himself, His apostles, and an infinite number of Christian martyrs, have taught us this by their examples ; shall it not then be permitted to any private person to resist by arms ? What shall we say of Moses, who led Israel away in despite of King Pharaoh ? And of Ehud, who, after ten years' servitude, when Israel might seem to belong by right of prescription to him who held the possession thereof, killed Eglon, the king of Moab, and delivered Israel from the yoke of the Moabites : and of Jehu, who put to death his lord the king Joram, extirpated the race of Ahab, and destroyed the priests of Baal. Were not these particulars ? I answer, that if they be considered in themselves, they may well be accounted particular persons, insomuch as they had not any ordinary vocation. But, seeing that we know that they were called extraordinarily, and that God Himself has (if we may so speak) put His sword into their hands, be it far from us to account them particular or private persons : but rather let us esteem them by many degrees, excelling any ordinary magistrates whatsoever.

The calling of Moses is approved by the express word of God, and by most evident miracles : it is said of Ehud, that God stirred him up to kill the tyrant, and deliver Israel : for Jehu, he was anointed by the commandment of the prophet Elizeus, for to root out the race of Ahab, besides, that the principal men saluted him king, before he executed anything. There may as much be said of all the rest, whose examples are propounded in holy writ. But where God Almighty does not speak with His own mouth, nor extraordinarily by His prophets, it is there that we ought to be exceedingly cautious, and to stand upon our guard ; for if any, supposing he is inspired by the Holy Ghost, do attribute to himself the before-mentioned authority, I would entreat him to look that he be not puffed up with vain glory, and lest he make not a God to himself of his own fancy, and sacrifice to his own inventions. Let him not then be conceived with vanity, lest instead of fruit he bring forth deluding lies. Let the people also be advised on their parts, lest in desiring to fight under the banner of Jesus Christ, they run not to their own confusion to follow the army of some Galilean Thendas, or of Barcozba : as it happened to the peasants and Anabaptists of Munster, in Germany, in the year 1323. I will not say, notwithstanding, that the same God who to punish our offences, has sent us in these our days, both Pharaohs and Ahabs, may not sometimes raise up extraordinary deliverances to His people : certainly His justice and His mercy continue to all ages, firm and immutable.

Now, if these visible miracles appear not as in former times, we may yet at the least fall by the effects that God works miraculously in our hearts, which is when we have our minds free from all ambition, a true and earnest zeal, a right knowledge, and conscience ; lest being guided by the spirit of error or ambition, we rather make idols of our own imaginations, than serve and worship the true and living God.

Whether it be lawful to take arms for religion

Furthermore, to take away all scruple, we must necessarily answer those who esteem, or else would that others should think they hold that opinion, that the church ought not to be defended by arms. They say withal that it was not without a great mystery that God did forbid in the law, that the altar should be made or adorned with the help of any tool of iron ; in like manner, that at the building of the temple of Solomon, there was not heard any noise of axe or hammer, or other tools of iron ; from whence they collect the church which is the lively temple of the Lord, ought not to be reformed by arms ; yea, as if the stones of the altar, and of the temple were hewed and taken out of the quarries without any instrument of iron, which the text of the holy scripture doth sufficiently clear.

But if we oppose to this goodly allegory, that which is written in the fourth chapter of the Book of Nehemiah, that one part of the people carried mortar, and another part stood ready with their weapons, that some held in one hand their swords, and with the other carried the materials to the work-men, for the re-building of the temple ; to the end, by this means, to prevent their enemies from ruining their work ; we say also, that the church is neither advanced nor edified by these material weapons ; but by these arms it is war-ranted and preserved from the violence of the enemies, which will not by any means endure the increase of it. Briefly, there has been an infinite number of good kings and princes (as histories do testify) which by arms have maintained and defended the service of God against pagans. They reply readily to this, that wars in this manner were allowable under the law ; but since the time that grace has been offered by Jesus Christ, who would not enter into Jerusalem mounted on a brave horse, but meekly sitting on an ass, this manner of proceeding has had an end. I answer first, that all agree with me in this, that our Saviour Christ, during all the time that He conversed in this world, took not on Him the office of a judge or king ; but rather of a private person, and a delinquent by imputation of our transgressions ;

so that it is an allegation besides the purpose, to say that
He hath not managed arms. ·

But I would willingly demand of such exceptionalists,
whether that they think by the coming of Jesus Christ in
the flesh, that magistrates have lost their right in the sword
of authority ? If they say so, Saint Paul contradicts them,
who says that the magistrates carry not the sword in vain,
and did not refuse their assistance and power against the
violence of those who had conspired his death. And if
they consent to the saying of the apostle, to what purpose
should the magistrates bear the sword, if it be not to serve
God, who has committed it to them, to defend the good
and punish the bad ? Can they do better service than to
preserve the church from the violence of the wicked, and
to deliver the flock of Christ from the swords of murderers ?
I would demand of them, yet, whether they think that all
use of arms is forbidden to Christians ? If this be their
opinion, then would I know of them, wherefore Christ did
grant to the centurion his request ? Wherefore did He give
so excellent a testimony of him ? Wherefore does Saint John
Baptist command the men at arms to content themselves
with their pay, and not to use any extortion, and does not
rather persuade them to leave their calling ? Wherefore did
Saint Peter baptize Cornelius the Centurion, who was the
first-fruits of the Gentiles ? From whence comes it that he
did not in any sort whatsoever counsel him to leave his
charge ?

Now, if to bear arms and to make war be a thing lawful,
can there possibly be found any war more just than that
which is taken in hand by the command of the superior,
for the defence of the church, and the preservation of the
faithful ? Is there any greater tyranny than that which is
exercised over the soul ? Can there be imagined a war more
commendable than that which suppresses such a tyranny ?
For the last point, I would willingly know of these men,
whether it be absolutely prohibited Christians to make
war upon any occasion whatsoever ? If they say that it is
forbidden them, from whence comes it then that the men
at arms, captains and centurions, who had no other employ-
ment, but the managing of arms, were always received into
the church ? Wherefore do the ancient Fathers, and Christian
historians make so horrible mention of certain legions

composed wholly of Christian soldiers, and amongst others of that of Malta, so renowned for the victory which they obtained, and of that of Thebes, of the which Saint Mauritius was general, who suffered martyrdom, together with all his troops, for the confessing of the name of Jesus Christ ? And if it be permitted to make war (as it may be they will confess) to keep the limits and towns of a country, and to repulse an invading enemy, is it not yet a thing much more reasonable to take arms to preserve and defend honest men, to suppress the wicked, and to keep and defend the limits and bounds of the church, which is the kingdom of Jesus Christ ? If it were otherwise, to what purpose should Saint John have foretold that the whore of Babylon shall be finally ruined by the ten kings, whom she has bewitched ? Furthermore, if we hold a contrary opinion, what shall we say of the wars of Constantine, against Maxentius, and Licimius, celebrated by so many public orations, and approved by the testimony of an infinite number of learned men ? What opinion should we hold of the many voyages made by Christian princes against the Turks and Saracens to conquer the Holy Land, who had not, or at the least, ought not to have had, any other end in their designs, but to hinder the enemy from ruining the temple of the land, and to restore the integrity of His service into those countries ?

Although then the church be not increased by arms, notwithstanding it may be justly preserved by the means of arms. I say further, that those that die in so holy a war are no less the martyrs of Jesus Christ than their brethren who were put to death for religion ; nay, they who die in that war seem to have this disadvantage, that with a free will and knowing sufficiently hazard, into which they cast themselves, notwithstanding, do courageously expose their lives to death and danger, whereas the other do only not refuse death, when it behoveth them to suffer. The Turks strive to advance their opinion by the means of arms, and if they do subdue a country, they presently bring in by force the impieties of Mohamet, who in his Alcoran, hath so recommended arms, as they are not ashamed to say it is the ready way to heaven, yet do the Turks constrain no man in matter of conscience. But he who is a much greater adversary to Christ and true religion, with all those kings whom he has enchanted, opposes fire and faggots, to the light of the gospel, tortures the Word of God, compelling by wracking and torments, as much as in him lies, all men to become idolaters, and finally is not ashamed to advance and maintain their faith and law by perfidious disloyalty, and their traditions by continual treasons.

Now on the contrary, those good princes and magistrates are said properly to defend themselves, who environ and fortify by all their means and industry the vine of Christ, already planted, to be planted in places where it has not yet been, lest the wild boar of the forest should spoil or devour it. They do this (I say) in covering with their buckler, and defending with their sword, those who by the preaching of the gospel have been converted to true religion, and in fortifying with their best ability, by ravelins, ditches, and rampers the temple of God built with lively stones, until it have attained the full height, in despite of all the furious assaults of the enemies thereof. We have lengthened out this discourse thus far, to the end we might take away all scruple concerning this question. Set, then, the estates, and all the officers of a kingdom, or the greatest part of them, every one established in authority by the people : know, that if they contain not within his bounds (or at the least, employ not the utmost of their endeavours thereto) a king who seeks to corrupt the law of God, or hinders the re-establishment thereof, that they offend grievously against the Lord, with whom they have contracted covenants upon those conditions. Those of a town, or of a province, making a portion of a kingdom, let them know also, that they draw upon themselves the judgment of God if they drive not impiety out of their walls and confines if the king seek to bring it in, or if they be wanting to preserve by all means, the pure doctrine of the Gospel, although for the defence thereof, they suffer for a time banishment, or any other misery. Finally, more private men must be all advertised, that nothing can excuse them, if they obey any in that which offends God, and that yet they have no right nor warrant, neither may in any sort by their private authority take arms, if it appear not most evidently, that they have extraordinary vocation thereunto, all which our discourse will suppose we have confirmed by pregnant testimonies drawn from holy writ.

THE THIRD QUESTION

Whether it be lawful to resist a prince who doth oppress or ruin a public state, and how far such resistance may be extended: by whom, how, and by what right or law it is permitted.

For so much as we must here dispute of the lawful authority of a lawful prince, I am confident that this question will be the less acceptable to tyrants and wicked princes ; for it is no marvel if those who receive no law, but what their own will and fancy dictate unto them, be deaf unto the voice of that law which is grounded upon reason. But I persuade myself that good princes will willingly entertain this discourse, insomuch as they sufficiently know that all magistrates, be they of never so high a rank, are but an inanimated and speaking law. Neither though anything be pressed home against the bad, can it fall within any inference against the good kings or princes, as also good and bad princes are in a direct diameter opposite and contrary : therefore, that which shall be urged against tyrants, is so far from detracting anything from kings, as on the contrary, the more tyrants are laid open in their proper colours, the more glorious does the true worth and dignity of kings appear ; neither can the vicious imperfections of the one be laid open, but it gives addition of perfections and respect to the honour of the other.

But for tyrants let them say and think what they please, that shall be the least of my care ; for it is not to them, but against them that I write ; for kings I believe that they will readily consent to that which is propounded, for by true proportion of reason they ought as much to hate tyrants and wicked governors, as shepherds hate wolves, physicians, poisoners, true prophets, false doctors ; for it must necessarily occur that reason infuses into good kings as much hatred against tyrants, as nature imprints in dogs against wolves, for as the one lives by rapine and spoil, so the other is born or bred to redress and prevent all such outrages. It may be the flatterers of tyrants will cast a supercilious aspect on these lines ; but if they were not past all grace they would rather blush for shame. I very well know that the friends and faithful servants of kings will not only approve and lovingly entertain this discourse, but also, with their best abilities, defend the contents thereof. Accordingly as the reader shall find himself moved either with content or dislike in the reading hereof, let him know that by that he shall plainly discover either the affection or hatred that he bears to tyrants. Let us now enter into the matter.

Kings are made by the people

We have shewed before that it is God that does appoint kings, who chooses them, who gives the kingdom to them : now we say that the people establish kings, puts the sceptre into their hands, and who with their suffrages, approves the election. God would have it done in this manner, to the end that the kings should acknowledge, that after God they hold their power and sovereignty from the people, and that it might the rather induce them, to apply and address the utmost of their care and thoughts for the profit of the people, without being puffed with any vain imagination, that they were formed of any matter more excellent than other men, for which they were raised so high above others ; as if they were to command our flocks of sheep, or herds of cattle. But let them remember and know, that they are of the same mould and condition as others, raised from the earth by the voice and acclamations, now as it were upon the shoulders of the people unto their thrones, that they might afterwards bear on their own shoulders the greatest burdens of the commonwealth. Divers ages before that, the people of Israel demanded a king. God gave and appointed the law of royal government contained in the seventeenth chapter, verse fourteen of Deuteronomy, when, says Moses, " thou art come unto the land which the Lord thy God giveth thee, and shalt possess it, and shalt dwell therein, and shalt say, I will set a king over me like as all the nations that are about me, thou shalt in any wise set him whom the Lord thy God shall choose from amongst thy brethren, etc." You see here, that the election of the king is attributed to God, the establishment to the people : now when the practice of this law came in use, see in what manner they proceeded.

The elders of Israel, who presented the whole body of the people (under this name of elders are comprehended the captains, the centurions, commanders over fifties and tens, judges, provosts, but principally the chiefest of tribes) came to meet Samuel in Ramah, and not being willing longer to endure the government of the sons of Samuel, whose ill carriage had justly drawn on them the people's dislike, and withal persuading themselves that they had found the means to make their wars hereafter with more advantage, they demanded a king of Samuel, who asking counsel of the Lord, he made known that He had chosen Saul for the governor of His people. Then Samuel anointed Saul, and performed all those rights which belong to the election of a king required by the people. Now this might, perhaps, have seemed sufficient, if Samuel had presented to the people the king who was chosen by God, and had admonished them all to become good and obedient subjects. Notwithstanding, to the end that the king might know that he was established by the people, Samuel appointed the estates to meet at Mizpah, where being assembled as if the business were but then to begin, and nothing had already been done, to be brief, as if the election of Saul were then only to be treated of, the lot is cast and falls on the tribe of Benjamin, after on the family of Matri, and lastly on Saul, born of that family, who was the same whom God had chosen. Then by the consent of all the people Saul was declared king. Finally, that Saul nor any other might attribute the aforesaid business to chance or lot, after that Saul had made some proof of his valour in raising the siege of the Ammonites in Jabish Gilead, some of the people pressing the business, he was again confirmed king in a full assembly at Gilgal. Ye see that he whom God had chosen, and the lot had separated from all the rest, is established king by the suffrages of the people.

And for David, by the commandment of God, and in a manner more evident than the former, after the rejection of Saul, Samuel anointed for king over Israel, David, chosen by the Lord, which being done, the Spirit of the Lord presently left Saul, and wrought in a special manner in David. But David, notwithstanding, reigns not, but was compelled to save himself in deserts and rocks, oftentimes falling upon the very brim of destruction, and never reigned as king until after the death of Saul : for then by the suffrages of all the people of Judah he was first chosen king of Judah, and seven years after by the consent of all Israel, he was inaugurated king of Israel in Hebron. So, then, he is anointed first by the prophet at the commandment of God, as a token he was chosen. Secondly, by the commandment of the people when he was established king. And that to the end that kings may always remember that it is from God, but by the people, and for the people's sake that they do reign, and that in their glory they say not (as is their custom) they hold their kingdom only of God and their sword, but withal add that it was the people who first girt them with that sword. The same order offered in Solomon. Although he was the king's son, God had chosen Solomon to sit upon the throne of his kingdom, and by express words had promised David to be with him and assist him as a father his son. David had with his own mouth designed Solomon to be successor to his crown in the presence of some of the principal of his court.

But this was not enough, and therefore David assembled at Jerusalem the princes of Israel, the heads of the tribes, the captains of the soldiers, and ordinance officers of the kings, the centurions and other magistrates of towns, together with his sons, the noblemen and worthiest personages of the kingdom, to consult and resolve upon the election. In this assembly, after they had called upon the name of God, Solomon, by the consent of the whole congregation, was proclaimed and anointed for king, and sat (so says the text) upon the throne of Israel ; then, and not before, the princes, the noblemen, his brothers themselves do him homage, and take the oath of allegiance. And to the end, that it may not be said that that was only done to avoid occasion of difference, which might arise amongst the brothers and sons of David about the succession, we read that the other following kings have, in the same manner, been established in their places. It is said, that after the death of Solomon, the people assembled to create his son Rehoboam king. After that Amaziah was killed, Ozias, his only son, was chosen king by all the people, Ochosias after Joram, Joachim, the son of Josias, after the decease of his father, whose piety might well seem to require that without any other solemnity, notwithstanding, both he and the other were chosen and invested into the royal throne, by the suffrages of the people.

To which also belongs, that which Hushai said to Absolom : " Nay, but whom the Lord and His people, and all the men of Israel chose, his will I be, and with him will I abide " ; which is as much as to say, I will follow the king lawfully established, and according to the accustomed order ; wherefore, although that God had promised to His people a perpetual lamp, to wit, a king, and a continual successor of the line of David, and that the successor of the kings of this people were approved by the Word of God Himself : notwithstanding, since that, we see that the kings have not reigned before the people had ordained and installed them with requisite ceremonies. It may be collected from this, that the kingdom of Israel was not hereditary, if we consider David and the promise made to him, and that it was wholly elective, if we regard the particular persons. But to what purpose is this, but to make it apparent that the election is only mentioned, that the kings might have always in their remembrance that they were raised to their dignities by the people, and therefore they should never forget during life in what a strict bound of observance they are tied to those from whom they have received all their greatness. We read that the kings of the heathen have been established also by the people ; for as when they had either troubles at home, or wars abroad, someone, in whose ready valour and discreet integrity the people did principally rely and repose their greatest confidence, him they presently, with an universal consent, constituted king.

Cicero says, that amongst the Medes, Diocles, from a judge of private controversies, was, for his uprightness, by the whole people elected king, and in the same manner were the first kings chosen amongst the Romans. Insomuch, that after the death of Romulus, the interreign and government of the hundred senators being little acceptable to the Quirites, it was agreed that from thence forward the king should be chosen by the suffrages of the people, and the approbation of the senate. Tarquinius Superbus was therefore esteemed a tyrant, because being chosen neither by the people nor the senate, he intruded himself into the kingdom only by force and usurpation. Wherefore Julius Cæsar, long after, though he gained the empire by the sword, yet to the end he might add some shadow or pretence of right to his former intrusion, he caused himself to be declared, both by the people and senate, perpetual dictator. Augustus, his adopted son, would never take on him as inheritor of the empire, although he was declared so by the testaments of Cæsar, but always held it as of the people and senate. The same also did Tiberius, Caligula and Claudius, and the first that assumed the empire to himself, without any colour of right, was Nero, who also by the senate was condemned.

Briefly, for so much as none were ever born with crowns on their heads, and sceptres in their hands, and that no man can be a king by himself, nor reign without people, whereas on the contrary, the people may subsist of themselves, and were, long before they had any kings, it must of necessity follow, that kings were at the first constituted by the people ; and although the sons and dependants of such kings, inheriting their fathers' virtues, may in a sort seem to have rendered their kingdoms hereditary to their offsprings, and that in some kingdoms and countries, the right of free election seems in a sort buried ; yet, notwithstanding, in all well-ordered kingdoms, this custom is yet remaining. The sons do not succeed the fathers, before the people have first, as it were, anew established them by their new approbation : neither were they acknowledged in quality, as inheriting it from the dead ; but approved and accounted kings then only, when they were invested with the kingdom, by receiving the sceptre and diadem from the hands of those who represent the majesty of the people. One may see most evident marks of this in Christian kingdoms, which are at this day esteemed hereditary ; for the French king, he of Spain and England, and others, are commonly sacred, and, as it were, put into possession of their authority by the peers, lords of the kingdom, and officers of the crown, who represent the body of the people ; no more nor less than the emperors of Germany are chosen by the electors, and the kings of Polonia, by the yawodes and palatines of the kingdom, where the right of election is yet in force.

In like manner also, the cities give no royal reception, nor entries unto the king, but after their inauguration, and anciently they used not to count the times of their reign, but from the day of their coronation, the which was strictly observed in France. But lest the continued course of some successions should deceive us, we must take notice, that the estates of the kingdoms have often preferred the cousin before the son, the younger brother before the elder, as in France, Louis was preferred before his brother Robert, Earl of Eureux [Annales Gillii] ; in like manner Henry before Robert, nephew to Capet. Nay, which is more by authority of the people in the same kingdom, the crown has been transported (the lawful inheritors living) from one lineage to another, as from that of Merove to that of the Charlemains, and from that of the Charlemains, to that of Capets, the which has also been done in other kingdoms, as the best historians testify.

But not to wander from France, the long continuance and power of which kingdom may in some sort plead for a ruling authority, and where succession seems to have obtained most reputation. We read that Pharamond was chosen in the year 419, Pepin in the year 751, Charles the Great, and Charlemain, the son of Pepin, in the year 768, without having any respect to their fathers' former estate. Charlemain dying in the year 772, his portion fell not presently into the possession of his brother Charles the Great, as it ordinarily happens in the succession of inheritances, but by the ordinance of the people and the estates of the kingdom he is invested with it ; the same author witnesses, that in the year 812, Lewis the Courteous, although he was the son of Charles the Great, was also elected ; and in the testament of Charlemain, inserted into the history written by Nauclere, Charlemain does entreat the people to choose, by a general assembly of the estates of the kingdom, which of his grandchildren or nephews the people pleased, and commanding the uncles to observe and obey the ordinance of the people, by means whereof, Charles the Bold, nephew to Louis the Courteous and Judith, declares himself to be chosen king, as Aimonius the French historian recites.

To conclude in a word, all kings at the first were altogether elected, and those who at this day seem to have their crowns and royal authority by inheritance, have or should have, first and principally their confirmation from the people. Briefly, although the people of some countries have been accustomed to choose their kings of such a lineage, which for some notable merits have worthily deserved it, yet we must believe that they choose the stock itself, and not every branch that proceeds from it ; neither are they so tied to that election, as if the successor degenerate, they may not choose another more worthy, neither those who come and are the next of that stock, are born kings, but created such, nor called kings, but princes of the blood royal.

The whole body of the people is above the king

Now, seeing that the people choose and establish their kings, it follows that the whole body of the people is above the king ; for it is a thing most evident, that he who is established by another, is accounted under him who has established him, and he who receives his authority from another, is less than he from whom he derives his power. Potiphar the Egyptian sets Joseph over all his house ; Nebuchadnezar, Daniel over the province of Babylon ; Darius the six score governors over the kingdom. It is commonly said that masters establish their servants, kings their officers. In like manner, also, the people establish the king as administrator of the commonwealth. Good kings have not disdained this title ; yea, the bad ones themselves have affected it ; insomuch, as for the space of divers ages, no Roman emperor (if it were not some absolute tyrant, as Nero, Domitian, Caligula) would suffer himself to be called lord. Furthermore, it must necessarily be, that kings were instituted for the people's sake, neither can it be, that for the pleasure of some hundreds of men, and without doubt more foolish and worse than many of the other, all the rest were made, but much rather that these hundred were made for the use and service of all the other, and reason requires that he be preferred above the other, who was made only to and for his occasion : so it is, that for the ship's sail, the owner appoints a pilot over her, who sits at the helm, and looks that she keep her course, nor run not upon any dangerous shelf ; the pilot doing his duty, is obeyed by the mariners ; yea, and of himself who is owner of the vessel, notwithstanding, the pilot is a servant as well as the least in the ship, from whom he only differs in this, that he serves in a better place than they do.

In a commonwealth, commonly compared to a ship, the king holds the place of pilot, the people in general are owners of the vessel, obeying the pilot, whilst he is careful of the public good ; as though this pilot neither is nor ought to be esteemed other than servant to the public ; as a judge or general in war differs little from other officers, but that he is bound to bear greater burdens, and expose himself to more dangers. By the same reason also which the king gains by acquist of arms, be it that he possesses himself of frontier places in warring on the enemy, or that which he gets by escheats or confiscations, he gets it to the kingdom, and not to himself, to wit, to the people, of whom the kingdom is composed, no more nor less than the servant does for his master ; neither may one contract or oblige themselves to him, but by and with reference to the authority derived from the people. Furthermore, there is an infinite sort of people who live without a king, but we cannot imagine a king without people. And those who have been raised to the royal dignity were not advanced because they excelled other men in beauty and comeliness, nor in some excellency of nature to govern them as shepherds do their flocks, but rather being made out of the same mass with the rest of the people, they should acknowledge that for them, they, as it were, borrow their power and authority.

The ancient custom of the French represents that exceeding well, for they used to lift up on a buckler, and salute him king whom they had chosen. And wherefore is it said, " I pray you, that kings have an infinite number of eyes, a million of ears, with extreme long hands, and feet exceeding swift ? " Is it because they are like to Argos, Gerien, Midas, and divers others so celebrated by the poets ? No, truly, but it is said in regard of all the people, whom the business principally concerns, who lend to the king for the good of the commonwealth, their eyes, their ears, their means, their faculties. Let the people forsake the king, he presently falls to the ground, although before, his hearing and sight seemed most excellent, and that he was strong and in the best disposition that might be ; yea, that he seemed to triumph in all magnificence, yet in an instant he will become most vile and contemptible : to be brief, instead of those divine honours wherewith all men adore him, he shall be compelled to become a pedant, and whip children in the school at Corinth. Take away but the basis to this giant, and like the Rhodian Colossus, he presently tumbles on the ground and falls into pieces. Seeing then that the king is established in this degree by the people, and for their sake, and that he cannot subsist without them, who can think it strange, then, for us to conclude that the people are above the king ?

Now that which we speak of all the people universally, ought also to be understood, as has been delivered in the second question, of those who in every kingdom or town do lawfully represent the body of the people, and who ordinarily (or at least should be) called the officers of the kingdom, or of the crown, and not of the king ; for the officers of the king, it is he who places and displaces them at his pleasure, yea, after his death they have no more power, and are accounted as dead. On the contrary, the officers of the kingdom receive their authority from the people in the general assembly of the states (or, at the least were accustomed so anciently to have done) and cannot be disauthorized but by them, so then the one depends of the king, the other of the kingdom, those of the sovereign officer of the kingdom, who is the king himself, those of the sovereignty itself, that is of the people, of which sovereignty, both the king and all his officers of the kingdom ought to depend, the charge of the one has proper relation to the care of the king's person ; that of the other, to look that the commonwealth receive no damage ; the first ought to serve and assist the king, as all domestic servants are bound to do to their masters ; the other to preserve the rights and privileges of the people, and to carefully hinder the prince, that he neither omit the things that may advantage the state, nor commit anything that may endamage the public.

Briefly, the one are servants and domestics of the king, and received into their places to obey his person ; the other, on the contrary, are as associates to the king, in the administration of justice, participating of the royal power and authority, being bound to the utmost of their power to be assisting in the managing of the affairs of state, as well as the king, who is, as it were, president amongst them, and principal only in order and degree.

Therefore, as all the whole people is above the king, and likewise taken in one entire body, are in authority before him, yet being considered one by one, they are all of them under the king. It is easy to know how far the power of the first kings extended, in that Ephron, king of the Hittites, could not grant Abraham the sepulchre, but in the presence, and with the consent of the people : neither could Hemor the Hevite, king of Sichem, contract an alliance with Jacob without the people's assent and confirmation thereof ; because it was then the custom to refer the most important affairs to be dispensed and resolved in the general assemblies of the people. This might easily be practised in those kingdoms which were then almost confined within the circuit of one town.

But since the kings began to extend their limits, and that it was impossible for the people to assemble together all into one place because of their great numbers, which would have occasioned confusion, the officers of the kingdom were established, who should ordinarily preserve the rights of the people, in such sort notwithstanding, as when extraordinary occasion required, the people might be assembled, or at the least such an abridgment as might by the most principal members be a representation of the whole body. We see this order established in the kingdom of Israel, which (in the judgment of the wisest politicians) was excellently ordered. The king had his cupbearers, his carvers, his chamberlains and stewards. The kingdom had her officers, to wit, the seventy-one elders, and the heads and chief chosen out of all the tribes, who had the care of the public faith in peace and war.

Furthermore, the kingdom had in every town magistrates, who had the particular government of them, as the former were for the whole kingdom. At such times as affairs of consequence were to be treated of, they assembled together, but nothing that concerned the public state could receive any solid determination. David assembled the officers of his kingdom when he desired to invest his son Solomon with the royal dignity ; when he would have examined and approved that manner of policy, and managing of affairs, that he had revived and restored, and when there was no question of removing the ark of the covenant.

And because they represented the whole people, it is said in the history, that all the people assembled. These were the same officers who delivered Jonathan from death, condemned by the sentence of the king, by which it appears, that there might be an appeal from the king to the people.

After that the kingdom was divided through the pride of Rehoboam. The council at Jerusalem composed of seventy-one ancients, seems to have such authority, that they might judge the king as well as the king might judge every one of them in particular.

In this council was president the duke of the house of Judah, to wit, some principal man chosen out of that tribe ; as also, in the city of Jerusalem, there was a governor chosen out of the tribe of Benjamin residing there. This will appear more manifest by examples : Jeremy was sent by God to denounce to the Jews the destruction of Jerusalem, was therefore condemned first by the priests and prophets, in whose hands was the ecclesiastical jurisdiction, afterwards by all the people of the city ; that is, by the ordinary judges of Jerusalem, to wit, the milleniers, and the centurions. Finally, the matter being brought before the princes of Judah, who were the seventy-one elders assembled, and set near to the new gate of the temple, he was by them acquitted.

In this very assembly, they did discreetly condemn, in express terms, the wicked and cruel act of the king Jehoiakin, who a little before had caused the prophet Uriah to be slain, who also foretold the destruction of Jerusalem.

We read in another place, that Zedechias held in such reverence the authority of this council, that he was so far from delivering of Jeremy from the dungeon, whereunto the seventy-one had cast him, that he dare scarce remove him into a less rigorous prison. They persuading him to give his consent to the putting to death the prophet Jeremy, he answered, that he was in their hands, and that he might not oppose them in anything. The same king, fearing lest they might make information against him, to bring him to an account for certain speeches he had used to the Prophet Jeremy, was glad to feign an untrue excuse. It appears by this, that in the kingdom of Judah this council was above the king, in this kingdom, I say, not fashioned or established by Plato or Aristotle, but by the Lord God Himself, being author of all their order, and supreme moderator in that monarchy. Such were the seven magi or sages in the Persian empire, who had almost a paralleled dignity with the king, and were termed the ears and eyes of the king, who also never dissented from the judgment of those sages.

In the kingdom of Sparta there were the ephori, to whom an appeal lay from the judgment of the king, and who, as Aristotle says, had authority also to judge the kings themselves.

In Egypt the people were accustomed to choose and give officers to the king, to the end they might hinder and prevent any encroachment, or usurped authority, contrary to the laws. Now as Aristotle does ordinarily term those lawful kings, who have for their assistants such officers or counsellors, so also makes he no difficulty to say, that where they be wanting, there can be no true monarchy, but rather a tyranny absolutely barbarous, or at the least such a dominion, as does most nearly approach tyranny.

In the Roman commonwealth, such were the senators, and the magistrates created by the people, the tribune of those who were called Celeres, the prætor or provost of the city, and others, insomuch as there lay an appeal from the king to the people, as Seneca declares by divers testimonies drawn from Cicero's books of the commonwealth, and the history of Oratius sufficiently shews, who, being condemned by the judges for killing his sister, was acquitted by the people.

In the times of the emperors, there was the senate, the consuls, the prætors, the great provosts of the empire, the governors of provinces, attributed to the senate and the people, all which were called the magistrates and officers of the people of Rome. And therefore, when that by the decree of the senate, the emperor Maximus was declared enemy of the commonwealth, and that Maximus and Albinus were created emperors by the senate, the men of war were sworn to be faithful and obedient to the people of Rome, the senate, and the emperors. Now for the empires and public states of these times (except those of Turkey, Muscovy and such like, which are rather a rhapsody of robbers, and barbarous intruders, than any lawful empires), there is not one, which is not, or hath not heretofore been governed in the manner we have described. And if through the conveniency and sloth of the principal officers, the successors have found the business in a worse condition, those who have for the present the public authority in their hands, are notwithstanding bound as much as in them lies to reduce things into their primary estate and condition.

In the empire of Germany, which is conferred by election, there are the electors and the princes, both secular and ecclesiastical, the counts, barons, and deputies of the imperial cities, and as all these in their proper places are solicitors for the public good, likewise in the diets do they represent the majesty of the empire, being obliged to advise, and carefully foresee, that neither by the emperor's partiality, hate nor affection, the public state do suffer or be interested. And for this reason, the empire has its chancellor, as well as the emperor his, both the one and the other have their peculiar officers and treasurers apart. And it is a thing so notorious, that the empire is preferred before the emperor, that it is a common saying, " That emperor does homage to the empire."

In like manner, in the kingdom of Polonia, there are for officers of the crown, the bishops, the palatines, the castellains, the nobility, the deputies of towns and provinces assembled extraordinarily, before whom and with whose consent, and nowhere else, they make new laws, and determinations concerning wars. For the ordinary government there are the counsellors of the kingdom, the chancellor of the state, etc., although notwithstanding, the king has his stewards, chamberlains, servants, and domestics. Now if any man should demand in Polonia who were the greater, the king, or all the people of the kingdom, represented by the lords and magistrates, he should do as much, as if he asked at Venice, if the duke were above the seigniory. But what shall we say of kingdoms, which are said to go by hereditary succession ? We may indeed conclude the very same. The kingdom of France heretofore preferred before all other, both in regard of the excellency of their laws and majesty of their estate, may pass with most as a ruling case. Now, although that those who have the public commands in their hands do not discharge their duties as were to be desired, it follows not though that they are not bound to do it. The king has his high steward of his household, his chamberlains, his masters of his games, cup-bearers, and others, whose offices were wont so to depend on the person of the king : after that the death of their master, their offices were void. And indeed at the funeral of the king, the lord high steward in the presence of all the officers and servants of the household, breaks his staff of office, and says, " Our master is dead, let every one provide for himself." On the other side, the kingdom has her officers, to wit, the mayor of the palace, who since has been called the constable, the marshals, the admiral, the chancellor, or great referendary, the secretaries, the treasurers and others, who heretofore were created in the assembly of the three estates, the clergy, the nobility, and the people.

Since that the parliament of Paris was made sedentary, they are not thought to be established in their places before they have been first received and approved by that course of parliament, and may not be dismissed nor disposed, but by the authority and consent of the same. Now all these officers take their oath to the kingdom, which is as much as to say, to the people in the first place, then to the king who is protector of the kingdom, the which appears by the tenure of the oath. Above all, the constable, who, receiving the sword from the king, has it girded unto him with this charge, that he maintain and defend the commonwealth, as appears by the words that the king then pronounces.

Besides, the kingdom of France has the peers (so called either for that they are the king's companions, or because they are the fathers of the commonwealth) taking their denominations from the several provinces of the kingdom, in whose hands the king at his inauguration takes his oath as if all the people of the kingdom were in them present, which shews that these twelve peers are above the king. They on the other side swear, " That they will preserve not the king, but the crown, that they will assist the commonwealth with their counsel, and therefore will be present with their best abilities to counsel the prince both in peace and war," as appears plainly in the patentee of their peership.

And they therefore have the same right as the peers of the court, who, according to the law of the Lombards, were not only associates to the lord of the fee in the judgment of causes, but also did take an account, and judge the differences that happened between the lord and his vassals.

We may also know, that those peers of France did often discuss suits and differences between the king and his subjects. Insomuch, that when Charles the Sixth would have given sentence against the Duke of Brittany they opposed it, alleging that the discussing of that business belonged properly to the peers and not to the king, who might not in any sort derogate from their authority.

Therefore it is that yet at this day the parliament of Paris is called the court of peers, being in some sort constituted judge between the king and the people; yea, between the king and every private person, and is bound and ought to maintain the meanest in the kingdom against the king's attorney, if he undertake anything contrary to law.

Furthermore, if the king ordain anything in his council, if he treat any agreement with the princes his neighbours, if he begin a war, or make peace, as lately with Charles the Fifth the emperor, the parliament ought to interpose their authority, and all that which concerns the public state must be therein registered; neither is there anything firm and stable which the parliament does not first approve. And to the end that the counsellors of that parliament should not fear the king, formerly they attained not to that place, but by the nomination of the whole body of the court; neither could they be dismissed for any lawful cause, but by the authority of the said body.

Furthermore, if the letters of the king be not subsigned by a secretary of the kingdom, at this day called a secretary of state, and if the letters patent be not sealed by the chancellor, who has power also to cancel them, they are of no force or value. There are also dukes, marquesses, earls, viscounts, barons, seneschals, and, in the cities and good towns, mayors, bailiffs, lieutenants, capitols, consuls, syndics, sheriffs and others, who have special authority, through the circuit of some countries or towns to preserve the people of their jurisdiction. Time it is that at this day some of these dignities are become hereditary. Thus much concerning the ordinary magistrates.

The assembly of the three estates

Besides all this, anciently every year, and since less often, to wit, when some urgent necessity required it, the general or three estates were assembled, where all the provinces and towns of any worth, to wit, the burgesses, nobles and ecclesiastical persons, did all of them send their deputies, and there they did publicly deliberate and conclude of that which concerned the public state. Always the authority of this assembly was such that what was there determined, whether it were to treat peace, or make war, or create a regent in the kingdom, or impose some new tribute, it was ever held firm and inviolable ; nay, which is more by the authority of this assembly, the kings convinced of loose intemperance, or of insufficiency, for so great a charge or tyranny, were disthronized ; yea, their whole races were for ever excluded from their succession to the kingdom, no more nor less, as their progenitors were by the same authority formerly called to that administration of the same kingdom. Those whom the consent and approbation of the estates had formerly raised, were by the dissent and disallowing of the same afterwards cast down. Those who tracing in the virtuous steps of their ancestors, were called to that dignity, as if it had been their inheritance, were driven out and disinherited for their degenerate ingratitude, and for that being tainted with insupportable vices, they made themselves incapable and unworthy of such honour.

This shews that succession was tolerated to avoid practices, close and underhand canvassing, discontents of persons refused, contentions, interreigns, and other discommodities of elections. But on the other part, when successions brought other mischiefs more pernicious, when tyranny trampled on the kingdom, and when a tyrant possessed himself of the royal throne, the medicine proving much worse than the disease, then the estates of the kingdom lawfully assembled in the name of all the people, have ever maintained their authority, whether it were to drive out a tyrant, or other unworthy king, or to establish a good one in his place. The ancient French had learned that of the Gauls, as Cæsar shews in his commentaries. For Ambiorix, king of the Eburons, or Leigeons confesses, " That such were the condition of the Gaulish empire, that people lawfully assembled had no less power over the king, than the king had over the people." The which appears also in Vercingetorix, who gives an account of his actions before the assembly of the people.

In the kingdoms of Spain, especially Aragon, Valentia, and Catalonia, there is the very same. For that which is called the Justitia Major in Aragon has the sovereign authority in itself. And there, the lords who represent the people proceed so far, that both at the inauguration of the king, as also at the assembly of the estates, which is observed every third year, they say to the king in express words that which follows, " We who are as much worth as you, and have more power than you, choose you king upon these and these conditions, and there is one between you and us who commands over you, to wit, the Justitia Major of Aragon, who oftentimes refuses that which the king demands, and forbids that which the king enjoins."

In the kingdoms of England and Scotland the sovereignty seems to be in the parliament, which heretofore was held almost every year. They call parliaments the assembly of the estates of the kingdom, in the which the bishops, earls, barons, deputies of towns and provinces deliver their opinions, and resolve with a joint consent of the affairs of state. The authority of this assembly has been so sacred and inviolable, that the king dare not abrogate or alter that which had been there once decreed.

It was that which heretofore called and installed in their charges all the chief officers of the kingdom ; yea, and sometimes the ordinary councillors of that which they call the king's privy council. In some, the other Christian kingdoms, as Hungary, Bohemia, Denmark, Sweden, and the rest, they have their officers apart from the kings ; and histories, together with the examples that we have in these our times, sufficiently demonstrate that these officers and estates have known how to make use of their authority, even to the deposing and driving out of the tyrannous and unworthy kings.

We must not therefore esteem that this cuts too short the wings of royal authority, and that it is as much as to take the king's head from his shoulders.

We believe that God is almighty, neither think we it anything diminishes His power, because He cannot sin ; neither say we, " that His empire is less to be esteemed, because it cannot be neither shaken, nor cast down " : neither also must we judge a king to be too much abused, if he be withheld by others from falling into an error, to which he is over much inclined, or for that by the wisdom and discretion of some of his counsellors, his kingdom is preserved and kept entire and safe, which otherwise, haply by his weakness or wickedness, might have been ruined. Will you say that a man is less healthy because he is environed with discreet physicians, who counsel him to avoid all intemperance, and forbid him to eat such meats as are obnoxious to the stomach, and who purge him many times against his will ; and when he resists, who will prove his better friends, these physicians who are studiously careful of his health, or those sycophants who are ready at every turn to give him that which must of necessity hasten his end ? We must then always observe this distinction. The first are the friends of the king. The other are the friends of Francis who is king. The friends of Francis are those who serve him. The friends of the king are the officers and servants of the kingdom. For, seeing the king has this name, because of the kingdom, and that it is the people who give being and consistence to the kingdom, the which being lost or ruined, he must needs cease to be a king, or at the least not so truly a king, or else we must take a shadow for a substance.

Without question, those are most truly the king's friends, who are most industriously careful of the welfare of his kingdom, and those his worst enemies who neglect the good of the commonwealth, and seek to draw the king into the same lapse of error.

And, as it is impossible to separate the kingdom from the people, nor the king from the kingdom, in like manner, neither can the friends of the king be disjoined from the friends of the people, and the kingdom.

I say, further, that those who, with a true affection love Francis had rather see him a king than a subject. Now, seeing they cannot see him a king, it necessarily follows, that in loving Francis, they must also love the kingdom.

But those who would be esteemed more the friends of Francis, than of the kingdom and the people, are truly flatterers, and the most pernicious enemies of the king and public state.

Now, if they were true friends indeed, they would desire and endeavour that the king might become more powerful, and more assured in his estate according to that notable saying of Theopompus, king of Sparta, after the ephores or controllers of the kings were instituted. " The more " (said he) " are appointed by the people to watch over, and look to the affairs of the kingdom, the more those who govern shall have credit, and the more safe and happy shall be the state."

Whether prescription of time can take away the right of the people

But peradventure, some one will reply, you speak to us here of peers, of lords and officers of the crown. But I, for my part, see not any, but only some shows and shadows of antiquity as if they were to be represented on a stage. I see not for the present scarce any tract of that ancient liberty, and authority ; nay, which is worse, a great part, if not all, of those officers take care of nothing but their particular affairs, and almost, if not altogether, serve as flatterers about those kings who jointly toss the poor people like tennis balls : hardly is there one to be found who has compassion on, or will lend a helping hand to the miserable subjects, fleeced and scorched to the very bones, by their insolent and insupportable oppression. If any be but thought to have such a desire, they are presently condemned as rebels and seditious, and are constrained either to fly with much discommodity, or else must run hazard both of life and liberty. What can be answered to this ? The business goes thus. The outrageousness of kings, the ignorance of the party, together with the wicked connivance of the great ones of the kingdom, has been for the most part such throughout the world, that the licentious and unbridled power wherewith most kings are transported and which has made them insupportable, has in a manner, by the length of continuance, gained right of prescription, and the people, for want of using it, have intacitly quit, if not altogether lost, their just and ancient authority. So that it ordinarily happens that what all men's care ought to attend on, is for the most part neglected by every man ; for what is committed to the generality, no man thinks is commended to his custody. Notwithstanding, no such prescription nor prevarication can justly prejudice the right of the people. It is commonly said that the exchequers do admit no rule of prescription against it, much less against the whole body of the people, whose power transcends the king's, and in whose right the king assumes to himself that privilege ; for otherwise, wherefore is the prince only administrator, and the people true proprietor of the public exchequer, as we will prove here presently after.

Furthermore, it is not a thing resolved on by all, that no tyrannous intrusion or usurpation, and continuance in the same course, can by any length of time prescribe against lawful liberty. If it be objected that kings were enthronized, and received their authority from the people who lived five hundred years ago, and not by those now living, I answer that the commonwealth never dies, although kings be taken out of this life one after another : for as the continual running of the water gives the river a perpetual being, so the alternative revolution of birth and death renders the people (*quoad hunc mundum*) immortal.

And further, as we have at this day the same Seine and Tiber as was 1,000 years ago, in like manner also is there the same people of Germany, France, and Italy (excepting intermixing of colonies, or such like) ; neither can the lapse of time, nor changing of individuals, alter in any sort the right of those people. Furthermore, they say the king receives his kingdom from his father, and not from the people, and he from his grandfather, and so one from another upward.

I ask, could the grandfather or ancestor, transfer a greater right to his successor than he had himself ? If he could not

(as without doubt it must need be so) is it not plainly perspicuous, that what the successor further arrogates to himself, he may usurp with as safe a conscience as what a thief
gets by the highway side? The people, on the contrary,
have their right of eviction entire and whole. Although that
the officers of the crown have for a time lost or left their
ranks, this cannot in any true right prejudice the people,
but rather clear otherwise; as one would not grant audience,
or shew favour to a slave who had long since held his master
prisoner, and did not only vaunt himself to be free, but also
presumptuously assumed power over the life and death of
his master: neither would any man allow the excuses of
a thief, because he had continued in that trade thirty years,
or for that he had been bred in that course of life by his
father, if he presumed by his long continuance in that function to prescribe for the lawfulness; but rather the longer
he had continued in his wickedness, the more grievous
should be his punishment. In like manner, the prince is
altogether unsupportable, who, because he succeeds a tyrant,
or has kept the people (by whose suffrages he holds the
crown) in a long slavery, or has suppressed the officers of
the kingdom (who should be protectors of the public liberty),
that therefore presumes, that what he affects is lawful for
him to effect, and that his will is not to be restrained or
corrected by any positive law whatsoever. For prescription
in tyranny detracts nothing from the right of the people;
nay, it rather much aggravates the prince's outrages. But
what if the peers and principal officers of the kingdom make
themselves parts with the king? What if betraying the
public cause the yoke of tyranny upon the people's neck?
Shall it follow that by this prevarication and treason the
authority is devolved into the king? Does this detract anything from the right of the people's liberty, or does it add
any licentious power to the king? Let the people thank
themselves, say you, who relied on the disloyal loyalty of
such men.

But I answer, that these officers are indeed those protectors
whose principal care and study should be, that the people be
maintained in the free and absolute fruition of their goods and
liberty. And therefore, in the same manner as if a treacherous advocate for a sum of money should agree to betray
the cause of his client into the hands of his adversary, which

he ought to have defended, has not power for all that to alter the course of justice, nor of a bad cause to make a good one, although perhaps for a time he give some colour of it.

In like manner this conspiracy of the great ones combined to ruin the inferiors cannot disannul the right of the people. In the mean season, those great ones incur the punishment that the same allots against prevaricators, and for the people, the same law allows them to choose another advocate and afresh to pursue their cause, as if it were then only to begin.

For if the people of Rome condemned their captains and generals of their armies, because they capitulated with their enemies to their disadvantage (although they were drawn to it by necessity, being on the point to be all overthrown) and would not be bound to perform the soldiers' capitulation, much less shall a free people be tied up to bear the yoke of thraldom, which is cast on them by those who should and might have prevented it ; but being neither forced nor compelled, did, for their own particular gain, willingly betray those who had committed their liberty to their custody.

Wherefore kings were created

Now, seeing that kings have been ever established by the people, and that they have had associates joined with them, to contain them within the limits of their duties, the which associates considered in particular one by one, are under the king, and altogether in one entire body are above him : We must consequently see wherefore first kings were established, and what is principally their duty. We usually esteem a thing just and good when it attains to the proper end for which it is ordained.

In the first place every one consents, that men by nature loving liberty, and hating servitude, born rather to command, than obey, have not willingly admitted to be governed by another, and renounced as it were the privilege of nature, by submitting themselves to the commands of others, but for some special and great profit that they expected from it. For as Aesop says, " That the horse being before accustomed to wander at his pleasure, would never have received the bit into his mouth, nor the rider on his back, but that he hoped by that means to overmatch the bull. Neither let us imagine, that kings were chosen to apply to their own proper use the goods that are gotten by the sweat of their subjects ; for every man loves and cherishes his own. They have not received the power and authority of the people to make it serve as a pander to their pleasures : for ordinarily, the inferiors hate, or at least envy, their superiors.

Let us then conclude, that they are established in this place to maintain by justice, and to defend by force of arms, both the public state, and particular persons from all damages and outrages, wherefore Saint Augustine said, " Those are properly called lords and masters who provide for the good and profit of others, as the husband for the wife, fathers for their children." They must therefore obey them who provide for them ; although, indeed, to speak truly, those who govern in this manner may in a sort be said to serve those whom they command over.

For, as says the same doctor, they command not for the desire of dominion, but for the duty they owe to provide for the good of those who are subjected to them : not affecting any lord like domineering, but with charity and singular affection, desiring the welfare of those who are committed to them.

Seneca in the eighty-first epistle says, " That in the golden age, wise men only governed kingdoms : they kept themselves within the bounds of moderation, and preserved the meanest from the oppression of the greatest. They persuaded and dissuaded, according as it advantaged or disadvantaged, the public profit ; by their wisdom, they furnished the public with plenty of all necessaries, and by their discretion prevented scarcity, by their valour and courage they expelled dangers, by their many benefits they increased and enriched their subjects; they pleaded not their duty in making pompous shows, but in well governing their people. No man made trial what he was able to do against them, because every one received what he was capable of from them, " etc.

Therefore then, to govern is nothing else but to provide for. These proper ends of commanding, being for the people's commodity, the only duty of kings and emperors is to provide for the people's good. The kingly dignity to speak properly, is not a title of honour, but a weighty and burdensome office. It is not a discharge or vacation from affairs to run a licentious course of liberty, but a charge and vocation to all industrious employments, for the service of the commonwealth ; the which has some glimpse of honour with it, because in those first and golden ages, no man would have tasted of such continual troubles, if they had not been sweetened with some relish of honour ; insomuch as there was nothing more true than that which was commonly said in those times, " If every man knew with what turmoils and troubles the royal wreath was wrapt withal, no man would vouchsafe to take it up, although it lay at his feet."

When, therefore, that these words of mine and thine entered into the world, and that differences fell amongst fellow citizens, touching the propriety of goods, and wars amongst neighbouring people about the right of their confines, the people bethought themselves to have recourse to some one who both could and should take order that the poor were not oppressed by the rich, nor the patriots wronged by strangers.

Nor as wars and suits increased, they chose someone, in whose wisdom and valour they reposed most confidence. See, then, wherefore kings were created in the first ages ; to wit, to administer justice at home, and to be leaders in the wars abroad, and not only to repulse the incursions of the enemy, but also to repress and hinder the devastation and spoiling of the subjects and their goods at home ; but above all, to expel and drive away all devices and debauchments far from their dominions.

This may be proved by all histories, both divine and profane. For the people of God, they had at first no other king but God Himself, who dwelt in the midst of them, and gave answer from between the cherubims, appointed extra-ordinary judges and captains for the wars ; by means whereof the people thought they had no need of lieutenants, being honoured by the continual presence of their Sovereign King.

Now, when the people of God began to be a-weary of the injustice of the sons of Samuel, on whose old age they dare no longer rely, they demanded a king after the manner of other people, saying to Samuel, " Give us a king as other people have, that he may judge us." There is touched the first and principal point of the duty of a king, a little after they are both mentioned. " We will have " (said they) " a king over us like other nations. Our king shall judge us, and go in and out before us, and lead our armies." To do justice is always set in the first place, for so much as it is an ordinary and perpetual thing; but wars are extraordinary, and happen as it were casually.

Wherefore, Aristotle says, that in the time of Herold, all kings were judges and captains. For the Lacedemonian kings, they in his time also had sovereign authority only in the army, and that confined also to the commandments of the ephores.

In like manner the Medes, who were ever in perpetual quarrels amongst themselves, at the length chose Deolces for the judge, who had carried himself well in the deciding of some particular differences; presently after they made him king, and gave him officers and guards, that he might more easily suppress the powerful and insolent.

Cicero says, that anciently all kings were established to administer justice, and that their institution, and that of the laws, had one and the same end, which was, that equity and right might be duly rendered to all men; the which may be verified by the propriety of the words almost in all languages. Kings are called by the Latins, *Reges a regendo*, for that they must rule and govern the limits and bounds, both of the public and particulars. The names of emperors, princes, and dukes have relation to their conduct in the wars, and principal places in combats, and other places of command. Likewise the Greeks call them in their language, *Basiles*, *Archa*, *Hegomodes*, which is to say props of the people, princes, conductors. The Germans and other nations use all significant names, and which express that the duty of a king consists not in making glorious paradoes; but that it is an office of a weighty charge and continual care. But, in brief, the poet Homer calls kings the judges of cities, and in describing of Agamemnon, he calls him wise, strong, and valiant. As also, Ovid, speaking of Erechtheus, says, that it was hard to know, whether justice or valour were more transparent in him; in which these two poets seem exactly to have described the duties of kings and princes. You see what was the custom of the kings of the heathen nations; after whose examples, the Jews demanded and established their kings.

The Queen of Sheba said also to Solomon, that God had made him king over them to do judgment and justice.

And Solomon himself, speaking to God, said, " Thou hast chosen me to be a king over Thy people, and a judge of Thy sons and daughters."

For this cause also the good kings, as David, Josephat, and others, being not able in their own persons to determine all the suits and differences of their subjects (although in the causes of greatest importance they reserved an appeal always to themselves, as appears in Samuel), had ever above all things a special care, to establish in all places just and discreet judges, and principally still to have an eye to the right administration of justice ; knowing themselves to carry the sword, as well to chastise wicked and unjust subjects, as to repulse foreign enemies.

Briefly, as the apostle says, " The prince is ordained by God, for the good and profit of the people, being armed with the sword to defend the good from the violence of the wicked, and when he discharges his duty therein, all men owe him honour and obedience."

Seeing then that kings are ordained by God, and established by the people, to procure and provide for the good of those who are committed unto them, and that this good or profit be principally expressed in two things, to wit, in the administration of justice to their subjects, and in the managing of armies for the repulsing their enemies : certainly, we must infer and conclude from this, that the prince who applied himself to nothing but his peculiar profits and pleasures, or to those ends which most readily conduce thereunto, who contemns and perverts all laws, who uses his subjects more cruelly than the barbarous enemy would do, he may truly and really be called a tyrant, and that those who in this manner govern their kingdoms, be they of never so large an extent, are more properly unjust pillagers and free-booters, than lawful governors.

Whether kings be above the law

We must here yet proceed a little further : for it is demanded whether the king who presides in the administration of justice has power to resolve and determine business according to his own will and pleasure ? Must the kings be subject to the law, or does the law depend upon the king ? The law (says an ancient) is respected by those who otherways contemn virtue, for it enforces obedience, and ministers' conduct in warfaring, and gives vigour and lustre to justice and equity. Pausanias the Spartan will answer in a word, that it becomes laws to direct, and men to yield obedience to their authority. Agesilaus, king of Sparta, says that all commanders must obey the commandments of the laws. But it shall not be amiss to carry this matter a little higher. When people began to seek for justice to determine their differences, if they met with any private man that did justly appoint them, they were satisfied with it. Now for so much as such men were rarely and with much difficulty met withal, and for that the judgments of kings received as laws were oftentimes found contrary and difficult, then the magistrates and others of great wisdom invented laws, which might speak to all men in one and the same voice.

This being done, it was expressly enjoined to kings, that they should be the guardians and administrators, and sometimes also, for so much as the laws could not foresee the particularities of actions to resolve exactly, it was permitted the king to supply this defect, by the same natural equity by which the laws were drawn ; and for fear lest they should go against law, the people appointed them from time to time associates, counsellors, of whom we have formerly made mention, wherefore there is nothing which exempts the king from obedience which he owes to the law, which he ought to acknowledge as his lady and mistress, esteeming nothing can become him worse than that feminine of which Juvenal speaks : *Sic volo, sic jubeo, sic pro ratione voluntas.* I will, I command, my will shall serve instead of reason. Neither should they think their authority the less because they are

confined to laws, for seeing the law is a divine gift coming
from above, which human societies are happily governed
and addressed to their best and blessedest end ; those kings
are as ridiculous and worthy of contempt, who repute it a
dishonour to conform themselves to law, as those surveyors
who think themselves disgraced, by using of a rule, a compass, a chain or other instruments, which men understanding
the art of surveying are accustomed to do, or a pilot who
had rather fail, according to his fantasie and imagination,
than steer his course by his needle and sea-card. Who can
doubt, but that it is a thing more profitable and convenient
to obey the law, than the king who is but one man ? The law
is the soul of a good king, it gives him motion, sense and life.
The king is the organ and as it were the body by which the
law displays her forces, exercises her function, and expresses
her conceptions. Now it is a thing much more reasonable to
obey the soul, than the body ; the law is the wisdom of
diverse sages, recollected in few words, but many see more
clear and further than one alone. It is much better to follow
the law than any one man's opinion, be he never so acute.
The law is reason and wisdom itself, free from all perturba-
tion, not subject to be moved with choler, ambition, hate, or
acceptances of persons. Intreaties nor threats cannot make
to bow nor bend ; on the contrary, a man, though endued
with reason, suffers himself to be lead and transported with
anger, desire of revenge, and other passions which perplex
him in such sort, that he loses his understanding, because
being composed of reason and disordered affections, he cannot so contain himself, but sometimes his passions become
his master. Accordingly we see that Valentinian, a good
emperor, permits those of the empire to have two wives at
once, because he was misled by that impure affection. Because Cambises, the son of Cyrus, became enamoured of his
own sister, he would therefore have marriages between
brother and sister be approved and held lawful ; Cubades,
king of the Persians, prohibits the punishment of adulterers ;
we must look for such laws every day, if we will have the
law subject to the king. To come to our purpose, the
law is an understanding mind, or rather an obstacle of
many understandings : the mind being the seal of all
the intelligent faculties, is (if I may so term it) a parcel
of divinity ; in so much as he who obeys the law, seems

to obey God, and receive Him for arbitrator of the matters in controversy.

But, on the contrary, insomuch as man is composed of this divine understanding, and of a number of unruly passions ; so losing himself in that brutishness, as he becomes void of reason ; and, being in that condition, he is no longer a man, but a beast ; he then who desires rather to obey the king than the law, seems to prefer the commandment of a beast before that of God.

And furthermore, though Aristotle were the tutor of Alexander, yet he confesses that the Divinity cannot so properly be compared to anything of this life, as to the ancient laws of well-governed states. He who prefers the commonwealth, applies himself to God's ordinances : but he who leans to the king's fancies, instead of law, prefers brutish sensuality before well-ordered discretion. To which also the prophets seem to have respect, who, in some places describe these great empires, under the representation of ravening beasts. But to go on, is not he a very beast, who had rather have for his guide a blind and mad man, than he who sees both with the eyes of the body and mind, a beast rather than God. Whence it comes, that though kings, as says Aristotle, for a while, at the first, commanded without restraint of laws ; yet presently after, civilized people reduced them to a lawful condition, by binding them to keep and observe the laws : and for this unruly absolute authority, it remained only amongst those who commanded over barbarous nations.

He says afterwards, that this absolute power was the next degree to plain tyranny, and he had absolutely called it tyranny, had not these beasts, like barbarians, willingly subjected themselves unto it. But it will be replied, that it is unworthy the majesty of kings to have their wills bridled by laws. But I will say, that nothing is more royal than to have our unruly desires ruled by good laws.

It is much pity to be restrained from that which we would do ; it is much more worse to will that which we should not do, but it is the worst of all to do that which the laws forbid.

I hear, methinks, a certain furious tribune of the people who opposed the passing of a law that was made against the excess which then reigned in Rome, saying, " My masters,

you are bridled, you are idle and fettered with the rude
bonds of servitude; your liberty is lost, a law is laid
on you, that commands you to be moderate: to what
purpose is it to say you are free, since you may not live
in what excess of pleasure you like?" This is the very
complaint of many kings at this day, and of their minions
and flatterers.

The royal majesty is abolished, if they may not turn the
kingdom topsy-turvy at their pleasure. Kings may go and
shake their ears, if laws must be observed.

Peradventure, it is a miserable thing to live, if a madman
may not be suffered to kill himself when he will.

For what else do those things which violate and abolish
laws, without which, neither empires, no, nor the very
societies of free-booters can at all subsist?

Let us then reject these detestable, faithless, and impious
vanities of the court-marmosites, which make kings gods,
and receive their sayings as oracles; and which is worse, are
so shameless to persuade kings that nothing is just or equitable of itself, but takes its true form of justice or injustice,
according as it pleases the king to ordain: as if he were some
god, which could never err nor sin at all. Certainly, all
that which God wills is just, and therefore, suppose it is
God's will; but that must be just with the king's will,
before it is his will. For it is not just because the king has
appointed it; but that king is just, which appoints that to
be held for just, which is so of itself.

We will not then say as Anaxarchus did to Alexander,
much perplexed for the death of his friend Clitus, whom he
had killed with his own hands; to wit, that Themis, the
goddess of Justice, sits by kings' side, as she does by
Jupiter's, to approve and confirm whatsoever to them shall
seem good; but rather, she sits as president over kingdoms,
to severely chastise those kings who wrong or violate the
majesty of the laws. We can no ways approve that saying of
Thrasimacus the Chaldonian that the profit and pleasure
of princes is the rule by which all laws are defined: but
rather, that right must limit the profit of princes, and the
laws restrain their pleasures. And instead of approving that
which that villainous woman said to Caracalla, that whatsoever he desired was allowed him, we will maintain that
nothing is lawful but what the law permits.

And absolutely rejecting that detestable opinion of the same Caracalla, that princes give laws to others, but received none from any; we will say, that in all kingdoms well established, the king receives the laws from the people; the which he ought carefully to consider and maintain; and whatsoever, either by force or fraud he does, in prejudice of them, must always be reputed unjust.

Kings receive laws from the people

These may be sufficiently verified by examples. Before there was a king in Israel, God by Moses prescribed to him both sacred and civil ordinances, which he should have perpetually before his eyes; but after that Saul was elected and established by the people, Samuel delivered it to him written, to the end, he might carefully observe it; neither were the succeeding kings received before they had sworn to keep those ordinances.

The ceremony was this, that together with the setting of the crown on the king's head, they delivered into his hands the Book of the Testimony, which some understand to be the right of the people of the land, others, the law of God according to which he ought to govern the people. Cyrus, acknowledging himself conservator of his country's laws, obliges himself to oppose any man who would offer to infringe them; and at his inauguration, ties himself to observe them, although some flatterers tickled the ears of his son Cambises, that all things were lawful for him.

The kings of Sparta, whom Aristotle calls lawful princes, did every month renew their oaths, promising in the hands of the ephori, procures for the kingdom, to rule according to those laws which they had from Lycurgus.

Hereupon, it being asked Archidamus, the son of Zeuxidamus, who were the governors of Sparta, he answered, "The laws, and the lawful magistrates."

And lest the laws might grow into contempt, these people bragged that they received them from heaven; and that they were inspired from above, to the end that men might believe that their determinations were from God, and not from man. The kings of Egypt did in nothing vary from the tenor of the laws, and confessed that their principal felicity consisted in the obedience they yielded to them.   Romulus, at the institution of the Roman kingdom, made this agreement with senators : the people should make laws, and he would take both for himself and others, to see them observed and kept.   Antiochus, the third of that name, king of Asia, wrote unto all the cities of his kingdom, that if in the letters sent unto them in his name, there were anything found repugnant to the laws, they should believe they were no act of the king's, and therefore yield no obedience unto them.   Now, although some citizens say, that by decree of senate, the emperor Augustus was declared to be exempt from obedience to laws ; yet, notwithstanding, Theodosius, and all the other good and reasonable emperors, have professed that they were bound to the laws, lest what had been extorted by violence, might be acknowledged and received instead of law.   And for Augustus Cæsar, insomuch as the Roman commonwealth was enthralled by his power and violence ; she could say nothing freely, but that she had lost her freedom.   And because they dare not call Augustus a tyrant, the senate said he was exempt from all obedience to the laws, which was in effect as much as if they plainly should have said the emperor was an outlaw.   The same right has ever been of force in all well-governed states and kingdoms of Christendom.

For neither the emperor, the king of France, nor the kings of Spain, England, Polander, Hungary, and all other lawful princes ; as the archdukes of Austria, dukes of Brabante, earls of Flanders, and Holland, nor other princes, are not admitted to the government of their estates, before they have promised to the electors, peers, palatines, lords, barons, and governors, that they will render to every one right according to the laws of the country, yea, so strictly that they cannot alter or innovate anything contrary to the privileges of the countries, without the consent of the towns and provinces ; if they do it, they are no less guilty of rebellion against the laws than the people are in their kind, if they refuse obedience, when they command according to law. Briefly, lawful princes receive the laws from the people as well as the crown, in lieu of honour, and the sceptre, in lieu of power, which they are bound to keep and maintain and therein reposes their chiefest glory.

If the prince may make new laws

What then ? Shall it not be lawful for a prince to make new laws and abrogate the old ? seeing it belongs to the king, not only to advise that nothing be done neither against, nor to defraud the laws, but also that nothing be wanting to them, nor anything too much in them : briefly, that neither age nor lapse of time do abolish or entomb them ; if there be anything to abridge, to be added or taken away from them, it is his duty to assemble the estates, and to demand their advice and resolution, without presuming to publish anything before the whole have been, first, duly examined and approved by them, after the law is once enacted and published, there is no more dispute to be made about it, all men owe obedience to it, and the prince in the first place, to teach other men their duty, and for that all men are easier led by example than by precepts, the prince must necessarily express his willingness to observe the laws, or else by what equity can he require obedience in his subjects, to that which he himself contemns.

For the difference which is between kings and subjects ought not to consist in impunity, but in equity and justice. And therefore, although Augustus was esteemed to be exempt by the decree of the senate, notwithstanding, reproving of a young man who had broken the Julian law concerning adultery, he boldly replied to Augustus, that he himself had transgressed the same law which condemns adulterers. The emperor acknowledged his fault, and for grief forbore too late. So convenient a thing it is in nature, to practise by example that which we would teach by precept.

The lawgiver Solon was wont to compare laws to money, for they maintain human societies, as money preserves traffic ; neither improperly, then, if the king may not lawfully, or at the least heretofore could not, mannace or embase good money without the consent of the commonwealth, much more less can he have power to make and unmake laws, without the which, nor kings, nor subjects, can cohabit in security, but must be forced to live brutishly in caves and deserts like wild beasts, wherefore also the emperor of Germany, esteeming it

needful to make some law for the good of the empire, first
he demands the advice of the estates. If it be there approved,
the princes, barons, and deputies of the towns sign it, and
then the law is satisfied, for he solemnly swears to keep the
laws already made, and to introduce no new ones without
a general consent.

There is a law in Polonia, which has been renewed in
the year 1454, and also in the year 1538, and by this
it is decreed, that no new laws shall be made, but by
a common consent, nor nowhere else, but in the general
assembly of the estates.

For the kingdom of France, where the kings are thought
to have greater authority than in other places ; anciently all
laws were only made in the assembly of the estates, or in
the ambulatory parliament. But since this parliament has
been sedentary, the king's edicts are not received as authen-
tical, before the parliament has approved them.

Whereas on the contrary, the decrees of this parliament, where the law is defective, have commonly the
power and effect of law. In the kingdoms of England,
Spain, Hungary, and others, they yet enjoy in some sort
their ancient privileges.

For, if the welfare of the kingdom depends on the observation of the laws, and the laws are enthralled to the pleasure
of one man, is it not most certain, that there can be no
permanent stability in that government ? Must it not then
necessarily come to pass, that if the king (as some have been)
be infected with lunacy, either continually, or by intervals,
that the whole state fall inevitably to ruin ? But if the laws
be superior to the king, as we have already proved, and that
the king be tied in the same respect of obedience to the
laws as the servant is to his master, who will be so senseless,
who will not rather obey the law than the king or will
not readily yield his best assistance against those who seek
to violate or infringe them ? Now seeing that the king is
not lord over the laws, let us examine how far his power
may be justly extended in other things.

Whether the prince have power of life and death over his subjects

The minions of the court hold it for an undeniable maxim, that princes have the same power of life and death over their subjects as ancient masters had over their slaves, and with these false imaginations have so bewitched princes, that many, although they put not in use with much rigour this imaginary right, yet they imagine that they may lawfully do it, and in how much they desist from the practice thereof, insomuch that they quit and relinquish their right and due.

But we affirm on the contrary, that the prince is but as the minister and executor of the law, and may only unsheathe the sword against those whom the law has condemned ; and if he do otherwise, he is no more a king, but a tyrant ; no longer a judge, but a malefactor, and instead of that honourable title of conservator, he shall be justly branded with that foul term of violator of the law and equity.

We must here first of all take into our consideration the foundation on which this our disputation is built, which we have resolved into this head, that kings are ordained for the benefit and profit of the public state ; this being granted, the question is soon discussed. For who will believe that men sought and desired a king, who, upon any sudden motion, might at his pleasure cut their throats ; or which in choler or revenge, might, when he would, take their heads from their shoulders ?

Briefly, who (as the wise man says) carried death at his tongue's end, we must not think so idly.

There is no man so vain, who would willingly that his welfare should depend on another's pleasure. Nay, with much difficulty will any man trust his life in the hands of a friend or a brother, much less of a stranger, be he never so worthy. Seeing that envy, hate, rage, did so far transport Athanas and Ajax, beyond the bounds of reason, that the one killed his children, the other failing to effect his desire in the same kind against his friends and companions, turned his fury and murderous intent, and acted the same revenge upon himself. Now it being natural to every man to love himself, and to seek the preservation of his own life, in what assurance, I pray you, would any man rest, to have a sword continually hanging over his head by a small thread, with the point towards him? Would any mirth or jollity relish in such a continual affright? Can you possibly make choice of a more slender thread, than to expose your life and welfare into the hands and power of a man so mutable, who changes with every puff of wind. Briefly, who almost a thousand times a day, shakes off the restraint of reason and discretion, and yields himself slave to his own unruly and disordered passions.

Can there be hoped or imagined any profit or advantage so great or so worthy, which might equalize or counterpoise this fear, or this danger? Let us conclude then, that it is against delinquents only, whom the mouth of the law has condemned, that kings may draw forth the sword of their authority.

If the king may pardon those whom the law condemns

But, because life is a thing precious, and to be favoured, peradventure, it will be demanded, whether the king may not pardon and absolve those whom the law has condemned?

I answer, no. Otherwise this cruel pity would maintain thieves, robbers, murderers, ravishers, poisoners, sorcerers, and other plagues of mankind, as we may read tyrants have done heretofore in many places, and to our woeful experience, we may yet see at this present time; and therefore, the stopping of law in this kind will, by impunity, much increase the number of offenders.

So that he who received the sword of authority from the law, to pardon offences, will arm offenders therewith against the laws, and put himself the wolf into the fold, which he ought to have warranted from their ravenous outrage.

But for so much that it may chance in some occasions, that the law being mute, may have need of a speaking law, and that the king being in some cases the aptest expositor, taking for the rule of his actions, equity and reason, which as the soul of the soul may so clear the intention thereof, as where the offence is rather committed against the words than the intendment of the law, he may free the innocent offender from the guilt thereof because a just and equitable exposition of the law may in all good reason be taken for law itself, as nearest concurring with the intention of the law-makers.

Notwithstanding, lest passion should prepossess the place of reason, kings should in this fashion themselves to the ordinary practice of the emperor Severus, not to determine absolutely anything before it were maturely discussed by upright and discreet men in that faculty.

And so the king may rigorously punish the murderer ; and yet, notwithstanding, pardon him, which casually, and without any such purpose, killeth one. He may put to death the thief, and yet pardon that man, who, in his own defence killeth him that would have robbed him. Briefly, in all other occurrences, he may distinguish, as being established arbitrator and neuter, chance-medly from malice, fore-thought a good purpose from the rigour of the law, without favouring at any time malice or treason. Neither can the right omission of this duty gain to him any true esteem of merciful men : for certainly that shepherd is much more pitiful who kills the wolf, than he who lets him escape : the clemency of that king is more commendable who commits the malefactor to the hangman, than he who delivers him ; by putting to death the murderer, many innocents are delivered from danger : whereas by suffering him to escape, both he and others through hope of the like impunity, are made more audacious to perpetrate further mischief, so that the immediate act of saving one delinquent, arms many hands to murder divers innocents. There is, therefore, both truly mildness in putting to death some, and as certainly cruelty in pardoning of others. Therefore, as it is permitted the king, being as it were *custos* of the law, in some cases to interpret the words thereof, so in all well ordered kingdoms, it is enjoined the council of state, and their duty obliges them to examine the king's interpretation, and to moderate both his severity and facility. If, through the corruption and weakness of men, this have not been so really and thoroughly observed as it ought :

yet, notwithstanding, the right always remains entire, and there wants only integrity and courage in the parties to make it effectual.

But not to heap up too many examples in a matter so manifestly clear, it has been in this manner practised in the realm of France. For we have there oftentimes seen those put to death, to whom the king had granted his charter of pardon : and those pardoned, whom he commanded should be put to death : and sometimes offences committed in the king's presence remitted, because there was no other witness but himself. The which happened in the time of Henry II to a certain stranger, who was accused by the king himself of a grievous offence. If an offender by the intercession of friends have his pardon granted by the king, the chancellor upon sufficient cause may cancel it. If the chancellor connive, yet must the criminal present it before the judges, who ought not only carefully to consider whether the pardon were gotten by surreptitious or indirect means, but also if it be legal, and in due form. Neither can the delinquent who has obtained his charter of pardon make use of it, until first he appeal in public court bare-headed, and on his knees plead it, submitting himself prisoner until the judges have maturely weighed and considered the reasons that induced the king to grant him his pardon. If they be found insufficient, the offender must suffer the punishment of the law, as if the king had not granted him any pardon. But, if his pardon be allowed, he ought not so much to thank the king, as the equity of the law which saved his life. The manner of these proceedings was excellently ordained, both to contain the king within the limits of equity, lest being armed with public authority, he should seek to revenge his own particular spleen, or out of fancy or partiality remit the wrongs and outrages committed against the public safety : as partly also to restrain an opinion in the subject, that anything could be obtained of the king which might prejudice the laws. If these things have been ill observed in our times, notwithstanding that which we have formerly said remains always certain, that it is the laws which have power over the lives and deaths of the inhabitants of a kingdom, and not the king, who is but administrator and conservator of the laws.

Subjects are the king's brethren, and not his slaves

For truly neither are the subjects, as it is commonly said, the king's slaves, or bondmen : being neither prisoners taken in the wars, nor bought for money. But as considered in one entire body they are lords, as we have formerly proved ; so each of them in particular ought to be held as the king's brothers and kinsmen. And to the end that we think not this strange, let us hear what God Himself says when He prescribes a law to kings : That they lift not their heart above their brethren from amongst whom they were chosen. Whereupon Bartolus, a famous lawyer, who lived in an age that bred many tyrants, did yet draw this conclusion from that law, that subjects were to be held and used in the quality and condition of the king's brethren, and not of his slaves. Also king David was not ashamed to call his subjects his brethren. The ancient kings were called Abimelech, an Hebrew word which signifies, my father the king. The almighty and all good God, of whose great gentleness and mercy we are daily partakers, and very seldom feel His severity, although we justly deserve it, yet is it always mercifully mixed with compassion ; whereby He teacheth princes, His lieutenants, that subjects ought rather to be held in obedience by love, than by fear.

But, lest they should except against me, as if I sought to entrench too much upon the royal authority, I verily believe it is so much the greater, by how much it is likely to be of longer continuance. For, says one, servile fear is a bad guardian, for that authority we desire should continue ; for those in subjection hate them they fear, and whom we hate, we naturally wish their destruction. On the contrary, there is nothing more proper to maintain their authority than the affection of their subjects, on whose love they may safely and with most security lay the foundation of their greatness. And therefore that prince who governs his subjects as brethren, may confidently assure himself to live securely in the midst of dangers : whereas he who uses them like slaves, must needs live in much anxiety and fear, and may well be resembled to the condition of that master who remains alone in some desert in the midst of a great troop of slaves ; for look how many slaves any has, he must make account of so many enemies, which almost all tyrants who have been killed by their subjects have experienced. Whereas, on the contrary, the subjects of good kings are ever as solicitously careful of their safety, as of their own welfare.

To this may have reference that which is read in divers places of Aristotle, and was said by Agasicles, king of Sparta, That kings command as fathers over their children, and tyrants as masters over their slaves, which we must take in the same sense, that the civilian Martianus does, to wit, that paternal authority consists in piety, and not in rigour, for that which was practised amongst the men of the acorn age, that fathers might sell, and put to death their children at their pleasure, has no authority amongst Christians ; yea, the very pagans who had any humanity would not permit it to be practised on their slaves. Therefore, then, the father has no power over the son's life, before first the law have determined it, otherwise he offends the law : Cornelius against privy murderers, and by the law Pompeius against parricides, the father is no less guilty who kills the son, than the son who murders the father. For the same occasion the emperor Adrian banished into an island, which was the usual punishment for notorious offenders, a father who had slain his son, of whom he had entertained a jealous opinion for his mother-in-law. Concerning servants or slaves, we are admonished in holy writ to use them like brethren, and by human constitutions as hirelings, or mercenaries.

By the civil law of the Egyptians and Romans, and by the constitutions of the Antonines, the master is as well liable to punishment who has killed his own slave, as he who killed another man's. In like manner the law delivers from the power of the master, the slave, whom, in his sickness, he has altogether neglected, or has not afforded convenient food, and the enfranchised slave whose condition was somewhat better, might, for any apparent injury, bring his action against his patron. Now, seeing there is so great difference between slaves and lawful children, between lords and fathers, and, notwithstanding heretofore, it was not permitted amongst the heathen, to use their slaves cruelly, what shall we say, pray you, of that father of the people, who cries out tragically with Atreus, I will devour my children? In what esteem shall we hold that prince who takes such pleasure in the massacre of his subjects (condemned without being ever heard), that he despatched many thousand of them in one day, and yet is not glutted with blood? Briefly, who, after the example of Caligula (surnamed the Phaeton of the world) wishes that all his people had but one head that he might cut it off at one blow? Shall it not be lawful to implore the assistance of the law against such furious madness, and to pull from such a tyrant the sword which he received to maintain the law, and defend the good, when it is drawn by him only for rapine, and ruin?

Whether the goods of the people belong to the king

But to proceed, let us now see whether the king, whom we have already proved has not power over the lives of his subjects, is not at the least lord over their goods. In these days there is no language more common in the courts of princes, than of those who say all is the king's. Whereby it follows, that in exacting any thing from his subjects, he takes but his own, and in that which he leaves them, he expresses the care he has that they should not be altogether destitute of means to maintain themselves, and this opinion has gained so much power in the minds of some princes, that they are not ashamed to say that the pains, sweat and industry of their subjects is the proper revenue, as if their miserable subjects only kept beasts to till the earth for their insolent master's profit and luxury. And indeed, the practice at this day is just in this manner, although in all right and equity it ought to be contrary. Now we must always remember that kings were created for the good and profit of the people, and that these (as Aristotle says) who endeavour and seek the commodity of the people, are truly kings: whereas those who make their own private ends and pleasures the only butt and aim of their desires, are truly tyrants.

It being then so that every one loves that which is his own, yea, that many covet that which belongs to other men, is it anything probable that men should seek a master to give him frankly all that they had long laboured for, and

gained with the sweat of their brows ? May we not rather
imagine, that they chose such a man on whose integrity they
relied for the administering of justice equally both to the
poor and rich, and who would not assume all to himself, but
rather maintain every one in the fruition of his own goods ?
or who, like an unprofitable drone, should suck the fruit of
other men's labours, but rather preserve the house, for those
whose industry justly deserved it ? Briefly, who, instead of
extorting from the true owners their goods, would see them
defended from all ravening oppressors ? What, I pray you
matters it, says the poor country man, whether the king or
the enemy make havoc of my goods, since through the spoil
thereof I and my poor family die for hunger ? What imports
it whether a stranger or home-bred caterpillar ruin my
estate, and bring my poor fortune to extreme beggary ?
Whether a foreign soldier, or a sycophant courtier, by force
or fraud, make me alike miserable ? Why shall he be accounted a barbarous enemy, if thou be a friendly patriot ?
Why he a tyrant if thou be king ? Yea, certainly by how
much parricide is greater than manslaughter, by so much the
wickedness of a king exceeds in mischief the violence of an
enemy.

If then, therefore, in the creation of kings, men gave not
their own proper goods unto them, but only recommended
them to their protection ; by what other right then, but that
of freebooters, can they challenge the property of other men's
goods to themselves ? Wherefore the kings of Egypt were
not (according to law) at the first the lords of particular men's
estates, but only then when they were sold unto them for
corn, and yet may there well be question made of the validity
of that contract. Ahab, king of Israel, could not compel
Naboth to sell him his vineyard ; but rather if he had been
willing, the law of God would not permit it. The Roman
emperors who had an unreasonable power, could neither by
right have done it. At this day there is with much difficulty
any kingdom to be found, where the meanest subject may
not suit the king, and where many times the king is not cast
in the suit, which succeeding, he must as well as others
satisfy the judgment. And to this is not contrary, although
at the first view it seem so, that which some of their most
familiars have written of the emperors. That by the civil
law all things were the king's, and that Cæsar was absolute

lord of all things, they themselves expound this their opinion in this manner, that the dominion of all things belongs to the king, and the propriety to particular persons, in so much as the one possesses all by the right of commanding, the other by the law of inheritance. We know that it is a common saying amongst the civilians, that if any make claim to a house or a ship, it follows not therefore that he can extend his right to all the furniture or lading. And therefore, a king may challenge and gain right to the kingdom of Germany, France and England : and yet, notwithstanding, he may not lawfully take any honest man's estate from him, but by a manifest injustice, seeing that they are things diverse, and by law distinguished, to be possessors of the whole, and of all the particular parts.

Whether the king be the proper owner of the kingdom

But the king, is he not lord proprietor of the public revenue ? We must handle this point somewhat more exactly than we did the former. In the first place, we must consider that the revenue of the public exchequer is one thing, and the proper patrimony of the prince another ; of different nature are the goods of the emperor, king, or prince, to those of Antonius, Henry, or Phillip ; those are properly the king's, which he enjoys as king, those are Antonius' his which he possesses, as in the right of Antonius, the former he received from the people, the latter from those of his blood, as inheritor to them.

This distinction is frequent in the books of the civil law, where there is a difference ever made between the patrimony of the empire, and that of the emperor : the treasury of Cæsar is one thing, and the exchequer of the commonwealth another, and both the one and the other have their several procurers, there being diverse dispensers of the sacred and public distributions, and of the particular and private expenses, insomuch as he who as emperor is preferred before a private man in a grant by deed or charter, may also sometime as Antonius give place to an inferior person.

In like manner in the empire of Germany, the revenue of Ferdinand of Austria is one thing, and the revenue of the

Emperor Ferdinand is another : the empire, and the emperor
have their several treasures : as also there is difference in
the inheritances which the princes derive from the houses of
their ancestors, and those which are annexed to the electoral
dignities. Yea, amongst the Turks themselves, Selimus, his
gardens and patrimonial lands, are distinguished from those
of the public, the one serving for the provision of the Sultan's
table, the other employed only about the Turkish affairs of
state. There be, notwithstanding, kingdoms as the French
and English, and others in which the king has no particular
patrimony, but only the public which he received from the
people, there this former distinction has no place. For
the goods which belong to the prince as a private person
there is no question ; he is absolute owner of them as
other particular persons are, and may by the civil law sell,
engage, or dispose of them at his pleasure. But for the
goods of the kingdom, which in some places are commonly
called the demesnes, the kings may not be esteemed nor
called in any sort whatsoever, absolute lords proprietors of
them.

For what if a man for the flocks' sake have made thee
shepherd, does it follow that thou hast liberty to slay, pill,
sell, and transport the sheep at thy pleasure ? Although the
people have established thee judge or governor of a city, or
of some province, hast thou therefore power to alienate, sell,
or play away that city or province ? And seeing that in alienating or passing away a province, the people also are sold,
have they raised thee to that authority to the end thou
shouldest separate them from the rest, or that thou shouldest
prostitute and make them slaves to whom thou pleasest ?
Furthermore, I demand if the royal dignity be a patrimony,
or an office ? If it be an office, what community has it with
any propriety ? If it be a patrimony, is it not such a one that
at least the paramount propriety remains still in the people
who were the donors ? Briefly, if the revenue of the exchequer,
or the demesnes of the kingdom, be called the dowry of the
commonwealth, and by good right, and such a dowry whose
dismembering or wasting brings with it the ruin of the public
state, the kingdom and the king, by what law shall it be
lawful to alienate this dowry ? Let the emperor Wencislaus
be infatuated, the French King Charles the Sixth, lunatic,
and give or sell the kingdom, or part of it, to the English, let

Malcolm, King of the Scots, lavishly dissipate the demesnes and consume the public treasure, what follows for all this? Those who choose the king to withstand the invasions of foreign enemies, shall they through his madness and negligence be made the slaves of strangers: and those means and wealth, which would have secured them in the fruition of their own estates and fortunes, shall they, by the election of such a king, be exposed to the prey and rapine of all comers, and that which particular persons have saved from their own necessities, and from those under their tutorship and government (as it happened in Scotland) to endue the commonwealth with it, shall it be devoured by some pander or broker, for unclean pleasures?

But if, as we have often said, that kings were constituted for the people's use, what shall that use be, if it be perverted into abuse? What good can so much mischief and inconvenience bring, what profit can come of such eminent and irreparable damages and dangers? If (I say) in seeking to purchase my own liberty and welfare, I engage myself into an absolute thraldom, and willingly subject myself to another's yoke, and become a fettered slave to another man's unruly desires, therefore, as it is imprinted in all of us by nature, so also has it by a long custom been approved by all nations, that it is not lawful for the king by the counsel of his own fancy and pleasure, to diminish or waste the public revenue; and those who have run a contrary course, have even lost that happy name of a king, and stood branded with the infamous title of a tyrant.

I confess that when kings were instituted, there was of necessity means to be assigned for them, as well to maintain their royal dignity, as to furnish the expense of their train and officers. Civility, and the welfare of the public state, seem to require it, for it was the duty of a king to establish judges, in all places, who should receive no presents, nor sell justice: and also to have power ready to assist the execution of their ordinances, and to secure the ways from dangers, that commerce might be open, and free, etc. If there were likelihood of wars, to fortify and put garrisons into the frontier places, and to hold an army in the field, and to keep his magazines well stored with ammunition. It is commonly said, that peace cannot be well maintained without provision for wars, nor wars managed without men, nor men kept in discipline without pay, nor money got without subsidies and tributes.

To discharge therefore the burden of the state in time of peace was the demesne appointed, and in time of wars the tributes and imports, yet so as if any extraordinary necessity required it, money might be raised by subsidies or other fitting means. The final intendment of all was ever the public utility, in so much as he who converts any of these public revenues to his own private purposes, much more he who misspends them in any unworthy or loose occasions, no way merits the name of a king, for the prince (says the apostle) is the minister of God for the good of the people ; and for that cause is tribute paid unto them.

This is the true original cause of the customs and imposts of the Romans, that those rich merchandises which were brought from the Indies, Arabia, Ethiopia, might be secured in their passage by land from thieves and robbers, and in their transportation by sea from pirates, insomuch as for their security, the commonwealth maintained a navy at sea. In this rank we must put the custom which was paid in the Red Sea, and other imposts of gates, bridges, and passages, for the securing of the great roadways (therefore called the Pretorian Consular, and the king's highways) from the spoil of thieves and free-booters. The care also of the reparation of bridges was referred to commissaries deputed by the king, as appears by the ordinance of Lewis the Courteous, concerning the twelve bridges over the river Seine, commanding also boats to be in readiness, to ferry over passengers, etc.

For the tax laid upon salt there was none in use in those times, the most of the salt-pits being enjoyed by private persons, because it seemed that that which nature out of her own bounty presented unto men, ought no more to be enhanced by sale than either the light, the air, or the water. As a certain king called Lycurgus in the lesser Asia, began to lay some impositions upon the salt-pits there, nature, as it were, impatiently bearing such a restraint of her liberality, the springs are said to have dried up suddenly. Yet certain marmosets of the court would persuade us at this day (as Juvenal complained in his time) that the sea affords nothing of worth, or good, which falls not within the compass of the king's prerogative.

He who first brought this taxation into Rome, was the Censor Livius, who therefore gained the surname of Salter; neither was it done but in the commonwealth's extreme necessity. And in France King Philip the Long, for the same reason obtained of the estates the imposition upon salt for five years only. What turmoils and troubles the continuance thereof has bred every man knows. To be brief, all tributes were imposed and continued for the provision of means and stipends for the men of war: so as to make a province stipendiary or tributary, was esteemed the same with military.

Behold, wherefore Solomon exacted tributes, to wit, to fortify the towns, and to erect and furnish a public magazine, which, being accomplished, the people required of Rehoboam to be freed from that burden. The Turks call the tribute of the provinces, the sacred blood of the people, and account it a most wicked crime to employ it in anything but the defence of the people. Wherefore, by the same reason, all that which the king conquers in war belongs to the people, and not to the king, because the people bore the charges of the war, as that which is gained by a factor accrues to the account of his master. Yea, and what advantage he gains by marriage, if it belongs simply and absolutely to his wife, that is acquired also to the kingdom, for so much as it is to be presumed that he gained not that preferment in marriage in quality of Philip or Charles, but as he was king. On the contrary, in like manner, the queens have interest of endowment in the estates which their husbands gained and enjoyed before they attained the crown, and have no title to that which is gotten after they are created kings, because that is judged as the acquist of the common purse, and has no proper reference to the king's private estate, which was so determined in France, betwixt Philip of Valoys, and his wife Jean of Burgundy. But to the end that there be no money drawn from the people to be employed in private designs, and for particular ends and purposes, the emperor swears not to impose any taxes or tributes whatsoever, but by the authority of the estates of the empire. As much do the kings of Polonia, Hungary, and Denmark promise: the English in like manner enjoy the same unto this day, by the laws of Henry the Third, and Edward the First.

The French kings in former times imposed no taxes but in the assemblies, and with the consent of the three estates ; from thence sprung the law of Philip of Valoys, that the people should not have any tribute laid on them but in urgent necessity, and with the consent of the estates. Yea, and anciently, after these moneys were collected, they were locked in coffers through every diocese and recommended to the special care of selected men (who are the same who at this day are called esleus), to the end that they should pay the soldiers enrolled within the towns of their dioceses : the which was in use in other countries, as namely in Flanders and other neighbouring provinces. At this day, though many corruptions have crept in, yet without the consent and confirmation of the parliament, no exactions may be collected ; notwithstanding, there be some provinces which are not bound to anything without the approbation of the estates of the country, as Languedoke, Brittany, Province, Daulphiny, and some others. Finally, all the provinces of the low countries have the same privileges, lest the exchequer devour all, like the spleen which exhales the spirits from the other members of the body. In all places they have confined the exchequer within its proper bounds and limits.

Seeing then it is most certain that what has been ordinarily and extraordinarily assigned to kings, to wit, tributes, taxes, and all the demesnes which comprehend all customs, both importations and exportations, forfeitures, amercements, royal escheats, confiscations, and other dues of the same nature, were consigned into their hands for the maintenance and defence of the people and the state of the kingdom, insomuch as if the sinews be cut, the people must needs fall to decay, and in demolishing these foundations the kingdom will come to utter ruin : it necessarily follows, that he who lays impositions on the people only to oppress them, and by the public detriment seeks private profit, and with their own sword kills his subjects, he truly is unworthy the name of a king. Whereas contrarily, a true king, as he is a careful manager of the public affairs, so is he a ready protector of the common welfare, and not a lord in propriety of the commonwealth, having as little authority to alienate or dissipate the demesnes or public revenue, as the kingdom itself. And if he misgovern the state, seeing it imports the commonwealth that every one make use of his own talent, it is much more requisite for the public good, that he who has the managing of it, carry himself as he ought.

And therefore, if a prodigal lord by the authority of justice, be committed to the tuition of his kinsmen and friends, and compelled to suffer his revenues and means to be ordered and disposed of by others ; by much more reason may those who have interest in the affairs of state, and whose duty obliges them thereto, take all the administration and government of the state out of the hands of him who either negligently executes his place, or ruins the commonwealth, if after admonition he endeavours not to perform his duty. And for so much as it is easily to be proved, without searching into those elder times, that in all lawful dominions the king cannot be held lord in propriety of the demesnes ; whereof we have an apt representation in the person of Ephron king of the Hittites, who dare not sell the field to Abraham without the consent of the people. This right is at this day practised in public states : the emperor of Germany, before his coronation, solemnly swears that he will neither alienate, dismember, nor engage any of the rights or members of the empire. And, if he recover, or conquer anything with the arms and means of the public, it shall be gained to the empire, and not to himself. Wherefore when Charles the Fourth promised each of the electors an hundred thousand crowns to choose his son Wencislaus emperor, and, having not ready money to deliver them, he mortgaged customs, taxes, tributes, and certain towns unto them, which were the proper appurtenances of the empire : whereon followed much and vehement contestation, most men holding this engagement void. And questionless it had been so declared, but for the profit that those reaped thereby, who ought principally to have maintained and held entire the rights and dignities of the empire. And it followed also, that Wencislaus was justly held incapable of the government of the empire, chiefly because he suffered the rights of the empire over the duchy of Milan to be wrested from him.

There is a law very ancient in the kingdom of Polonia, which prohibits the alienating of any of the kingdom's lands ; the which also was renewed by King Lewis in the year 1375. In Hungary in A.D. 1221 there was a complaint made to Pope Honorius, that King Andrew had engaged the crown lands contrary to his oath. In England was the same by the law of King Edward in the year 1298. Likewise in Spain by the ordinance made under Alphonsus, and renewed in the year 1560, in the assembly of the estates at Toledo. These laws were then ratified, although long time before custom had obtained the vigour and effect of law.

Now, for the kingdom of France whereto I longer confine myself, because she may in a sort pass as a pattern to the rest, this right has ever remained there inviolable. It is one of the most ancient laws of the kingdom, and a right born with the kingdom itself, that the demesne may not be alienated: the which law in A.D. 1566 (although but ill deserved) was renewed. There are only two cases excepted, the portions or appanages of the children and brothers of the king, yet with this reservation, that the right of vassalage remains always to the crown in like manner if the condition of war require necessarily an alienation, yet it must be ever with power of redemption. Anciently neither the one nor the other were of validity, but by the commandment of the states : at this day since the parliament has been made sedentary, the parliament of Paris which is the court of the peers, and the chamber of accounts, and of the treasury, must first approve it : as the edicts of Charles the Sixth and Ninth do testify. This is a thing so certain, that if the ancient kings themselves would endow a church (although that was a work much favoured in those days), they were, notwithstanding, bound to have an allowance of the estates : witness King Childebert, who might not endow the Abbey of Saint Vincent at Paris before he had the French and Neustrians' consent. Clovis the Second, and other kings have observed the same. They might neither remit the regalities by granting enfranchisements, nor the nomination of prelates to any church. And if any of them have done it, as Lewis the Second, Philip the Fourth, and Philip surnamed Augustus, did in favour of the churches of Senis Auxera, and Nevers, the parliament has declared it void. When the king is anointed at Rheims, he swears to observe this law : and if he infringe it, that act has as much validity with it as if he contracted to sell the empires of the Great Turk, or Sophia of Persia. From this spring the constitutions or ordinances of Philip the Sixth, of John the Second, of Charles Fifth, Sixth, and Eighth, by which they revoke all alienations made by their predecessors.

In the assembly of the estates at Tours, where King Charles the Eighth was in person, divers alienations made by Lewis the Second were repealed, and annihilated, and there was taken away from the heirs of Tancred of Chastel his great minion, divers places which he had given him by his proper authority. This was finally ratified in the last assembly of the estates held at Orleans. Thus much concerning the kingdom's demesne. But to the end that we may yet more clearly perceive that the kingdom is preferred before the king, and that he cannot by his own proper authority diminish the majesty he has received from the people, nor enfranchise or release from his dominion any one of his subjects ; nor quit or relinquish the sovereignty of the least part of his kingdom. Charlemain in former times endeavoured to subject the kingdom of France to the German empire : the which the French did courageously oppose by the mouth of a prince of Glasconnie ; and if Charlemain had proceeded in that business, it had come to the trial of the sword. In like manner when any portion of the kingdom was granted to the English, the sovereignty was almost always reserved. And if sometimes they obtained it by force, as at the treaty of Bretigny, by the which King John quitted the sovereignty of Glasconnie and Poytou, that agreement was not kept, neither was he more bound to do it, than a tutor or guardian is being prisoner (as he was then), which for his own deliverance should engage the estate of his pupils.

By the power of the same law the parliament of Paris made void the treaty of Conlius, by the which Duke Charles of Burgundy had drawn from the king Amiens and other towns of Picardy. In our days the same parliament declared void the agreement made at Madrid, between Francis the First, then prisoner, and Charles the Fifth, concerning the Duchy of Burgundy. But the domain made by Charles the Sixth unto Henry King of England, of the kingdom of France, after his decease, is a sufficient testimony for this matter, and of his madness, if there had been no other proof. But to leave off producing any further testimonies, examples, or reasons, by what right can the king give or sell away the kingdom, or any part of it : seeing it consists of people, and not of earth or walls ? and of freemen there can be made no sale, nor traffic : yea, and the patrons themselves cannot compel the enfranchised servants to make their habitations in other places than themselves like. The which is the rather to be allowed, in that subjects are neither slaves nor enfranchised servants, but brothers : and not only the king's brethren taken one by one, but also considered in one body, they ought to be esteemed absolute lords and owners of the kingdom.

Whether the king be the usufructor of the kingdom?

But if the king be not lord in propriety, yet at the least we may esteem him usufructor of the kingdom, and of the demesne ; nay, truly we can allow him to have the usufruct for being usufructor, though the propriety remain in the people : yet may he absolutely dispose of the profits, and engage them at his pleasure. Now we have already proved that kings of their own authority cannot engage the revenues of the exchequer, or the demesne of the kingdom. The usufructor may dispose of the profits to whom, how, and when he pleases. Contrarily, the excessive gifts of princes are ever judged void, his unnecessary expenses are not allowed, his superfluous to be cut off, and that which is expended by him in any other occasion, but for the public utility, is justly esteemed to be unjustly extorted, and is no less liable to the law Cincea, than the meanest Roman citizen formerly was. In France, the king's gifts are never of force, until the chamber of accounts have confirmed them. From hence proceed the postils of the ordinary chamber, in giving up of the accounts in the reigns of prodigal kings, *Trop donne : soyt repele*, which is, excessive gifts must be recalled. The judges of this chamber solemnly swear to pass nothing which may prejudice the kingdom, or the public state, notwithstanding any letters the king shall write unto them ; but they are not always so mindful of this oath as were to be desired.

Furthermore, the law takes no care how a usufructor possesses and governs his revenues, but contrarywise, it prescribes unto the king, how and to what use he shall employ his. For the ancient kings of France were bound to divide their royal revenues into four parts. The first was implied in the maintaining of the ministers of the church, and providing for the poor : the second for the king's table :

the third for the wages of his officers and household servants; the last in repairing of bridges, castles, and the royal palaces. And what was remaining, was laid up in the treasury, to be bestowed on the necessities of the commonwealth. And histories do at large relate the troubles and tumults which happened about the year 1412 in the assembly of the estates at Paris, because Charles the Sixth had wasted all the money that was raised of the revenues and demesne, in his own and his minion's loose pleasures, and that the expenses of the king's household, which before exceeded not the sum of ninety-four thousand francs, did amount, in that miserable estate of the commonwealth, to five hundred and forty thousand francs. Now as the demesne was employed in the before-mentioned affairs, so the aids were only for the war, and the taxes assigned for the payment of the men at arms and for no other occasion. In other kingdoms the king has no greater authority, and in divers less, especially in the empire of Germany, and in Poland. But we have made choice of the kingdom of France, to the end it be not thought this has any special prerogative above others, because there perhaps, the commonwealth receives the most detriment. Briefly, as I have before said, the name of a king signifies not an inheritance, nor a propriety, nor a usufruct, but a charge, office, and procuration.

As a bishop is chosen to look to the welfare of the soul, so is the king established to take care of the body, so far forth as it concerns the public good; the one is dispenser of the heavenly treasure, the other of the secular, and what right the one has in the episcopal revenues, the same has the other, and no greater in the kingdom's demesne. If the bishop alien the goods of the bishopric without the consent of the chapter, this alienation is of no value; if the king alien the demesne without the approbation of the estates, that is also void; one portion of the ecclesiastical goods ought to be employed in the reparation of the churches; the second in relieving of the poor; the third, for the maintenance of the church men, and the fourth for the bishop himself. We have seen before, that the king ought to divide into four parts the revenues of the kingdom's demesne. The abuse of these times cannot infringe or annihilate the right, for, although some part of the bishops steal from the poor that which they profusely cast away on their panders, and ruin and destroy their lands and woods, the calling of the bishops is not for all that altered. Although that some emperors have assumed to themselves an absolute power, that cannot invest them with any further right, because no man can be judge in his own cause. What if some Caracalla vaunt he will not want money whilst the sword remains in his custody ? The Emperor Adrian will promise on the contrary, so to discharge his office of principality, that he will always remember that the commonwealth is not his, but the people's ; which one thing almost distinguishes a king from a tyrant. Neither can that act of Attalus King of Pergamus designing the Roman people for heirs to his kingdom, nor that of Alexander for Egypt, nor Ptolemy for the Cyrenians, bequeathing their kingdoms to the same people, nor Prasutagus King of the Icenians, who left his to Cæsar, draw any good consequence of right to those who usurp that which by no just title belongs to them, nay, by how much the intrusion is more violent, by so much the equity and justice of the cause is more perspicuous : for what the Romans assumed under the colour of right, they would have made no difficulty if that pretext had been wanting to have taken by force. We have seen almost in our days how the Venetians possessed themselves of the kingdom of Cyprus, under pretence of an imaginary adoption, which would have proved ridiculous, if it had not been seconded by power and arms. To which also may be not unfitly resembled the pretended donation of Constantine to Pope Silvester, for that straw of the decretist Gratian was long since consumed and turned to ashes ; neither is of more validity the grant which Lewis the Courteous made to Pope Paschal of the city of Rome, and part of Italy. Because he gave that which he possessed not, no man opposed it. But when his father Charlemain would have united and subjected the kingdom of France to the German empire, the French did lawfully oppose it : and if he had persisted in his purpose, they were resolved to have hindered him, and defended themselves by arms.

There can be, too, as little advantage alleged that act of Solomon's, whom we read to have delivered twenty towns to Hiram King of Tyre : for he did not give them to him but for the securing of the talents of gold which Hiram had lent him, and they were redeemed at the end of the term, as it appears by the text. Further, the soil was barren, and husbanded by the remaining Canaanites. But Solomon, having redeemed it out of the hands of Hiram, delivered it to the Israelites to be inhabited and tilled. Neither serves it to much more purpose, to allege that in some kingdoms there is no express agreement between the king and the people ; for suppose there be no mention made, yet the law of nature teacheth us, that kings were not ordained to ruin, but to govern the commonwealths, and that they may not by their proper authority alter or change the rights of the public state, and although they be lords, yet can they challenge it in no other quality, than as guardians do in the tuition of their pupils ; neither can we account him a lawful lord, who deprives the commonwealth of her liberty, and sells her as a slave. Briefly, neither can we also allege, that some kingdoms are the proper acquists of the king himself, insomuch as they were not conquered by their proper means and swords, but by the hands, and with the wealth of the public ; and there is nothing more agreeable to reason, than that which was gained with the joint difficulties and common danger of the public, should not be alienated or disposed of, without the consent of the states which represent the commonwealth : and the necessity of this law is such, that it is of force amongst robbers and free-booters themselves. He who follows a contrary course, must needs ruin human society. And although the French conquered by force of arms the countries of Germany and Gaule, yet this before-mentioned right remains still entire.

To conclude, we must needs resolve, that kings are neither proprietors nor usufructuaries of the royal patrimony, but only administrators. And being so, they can by no just right attribute to themselves the propriety, use, or profit of private men's estates, nor with as little reason the public revenues, which are in truth only the commonwealth's.

But before we pass any further, we must here resolve a doubt. The people of Israel having demanded a king, the Lord said to Samuel : hearken unto the voice of the people, notwithstanding, give them to understand what shall be the manner of the king who shall reign over them : " he will take your fields, your vineyards, your olive trees, to furnish his own occasions, and to enrich his servants," briefly, " he will make the people slaves." One would hardly believe in what estimation the courtiers of our times hold this text, when of all the rest of the Holy Scripture they make but a jest. In this place the almighty and all good God would manifest to the Israelites their levity, when that they had God Himself even present with them, who upon all occasions appointed them holy judges and worthy commanders for the wars, would, notwithstanding, rather subject themselves to the disordered commandments of a vain mutable man, than to the secure protection of the omnipotent and immutable God. He declares, then, unto them in what a slippery estate the king was placed, and how easily unruly authority fell into disordered violence, and kingly power was turned into tyrannous wilfulness. Seeing the king that he gave them would by preposterous violence draw the sword of authority against them, and subject the equity of the laws to his own unjust desires : and this mischief which they wilfully drew on themselves, they would happily repent of, when it would not be so easily remedied. Briefly, this text does not describe the rights of kings, but what right they are accustomed to attribute to themselves : not what by the privilege of their places they may justly do ; but what power for the satisfying of their own lusts, they unjustly usurp. This will manifestly appear from the seventeenth chapter of Deuteronomy, where God appoints a law for kings. Here says Samuel " the king will use his subjects like slaves." There God forbids the king " to lift his heart above his brethren," to wit, " over his subjects, whom he ought not to insult over, but to cherish as his kinsmen." " He will make chariots, levy horse-men, and take the goods of private men," says Samuel : on the contrary in Deuteronomy, he is exhorted " not to multiply horse-men, nor to heap up gold and silver, nor cause the people to return into Egypt," to wit, into bondage. In Samuel we see pictured to the life wicked Ahab, who by pernicious means gets Naboth's vineyard : there, David, who held it not lawful to drink that water which was purchased with the danger of his subjects' lives. Samuel foretells that the king demanded by the Israelites, instead of keeping the laws, would govern all according to his own fancy. On the contrary, God commands that His law should by the priests be delivered into the hands of the king, to copy it out, and to have it continually before his eyes. Therefore Samuel, being high priest, gave to Saul the royal law contained in the seventeenth of Deuteronomy, written into a book, which certainly had been a frivolous act if the king were permitted to break it at his pleasure. Briefly, it is as much as if Samuel had said : You have asked a king after the manner of other nations, the most of whom have tyrants for their governors : you desire a king to distribute justice equally amongst you : but many of them think all things lawful which their own appetites suggest unto them ; in the mean season you willingly shake off the Lord, whose only will is equity and justice in the abstract.

In Herodotus there is a history which plainly expresses how apt the royal government is to degenerate into tyranny, whereof Samuel so exactly forewarns the people. Deioces, much renowned for his justice, was first chosen judge amongst the Medes : presently after, to the end he might the better repress those who would oppose justice, he was chosen king, and invested with convenient authority; then he de-sired a guard, after, a citadel to be built in Ecbatana, the principal city of the kingdom, with colour to secure him from conspiracies and machinations of rebels ; which being effected, he presently applied himself to revenge the least displeasures which were offered him with the greatest punishments.

Finally, no man might presume to look this king in the face, and to laugh or cough in his presence was punished with grievous torments. So dangerous a thing it is, to put into the hands of a weak mind (as all men's are by nature) unlimited power. Samuel therefore teaches not in that place that the authority of a king is absolute ; on the contrary, he discreetly admonishes the people not to enthral their liberty under the unnecessary yoke of a weak and unruly master ; he does not absolutely exclude the royal authority, but would have it restrained within its own limits ; he does not amplify the king's right with an unbridled and licentious liberty ; but rather tacitly persuades to put a bit into his mouth. It seems that this advice of Samuel's was very beneficial to the Israel-ites, for that they circumspectly moderated the power of their kings, the which, most nations grown wise, either by the experience of their own, or their neighbour's harms, have carefully looked unto, as will plainly appear by that which follows.

We have shewed already, that in the establishing of the king, there were two alliances or covenants contracted : the first between God, the king, and the people, of which we have formerly treated ; the second, between the king and the people, of which we must now say somewhat. After that Saul was established king, the royal law was given him, according to which he ought to govern. David made a covenant in Hebron before the Lord, that is to say, taking God for witness, with all the ancients of Israel, who represented the whole body of the people, and even then he was made king. Joas also by the mouth of Johoiada the high priest, entered into covenant with the whole people of the land in the house of the Lord. And when the crown was set on his head, together with it was the law of the testimony put into his hand, which most expounds to be the law of God ; likewise Josias promises to observe and keep the commandments, testimonies, and statutes comprised in the book of the covenant : under which words are contained all which belongs to the duties both of the first and second table of the law of God. In all the before-remembered places of the holy story, it is ever said, " that a covenant was made with all the people, with all the multitude, with all the elders, with all the men of Judah " : to the end that we might know, as it is also fully expressed, that not only the principals of the tribes, but also all the milleniers, centurions, and subaltern magistrates should meet together, each of them in the name, and for their towns and communalties, to covenant and contract with the king. In this assembly was the creating of the king determined of, for it was the people who made the king, and not the king the people.

It is certain, then, that the people by way of stipulation, require a performance of covenants. The king promises it. Now the condition of a stipulator is in terms of law more worthy than of a promiser. The people ask the king, whether he will govern justly and according to the laws ? He promises he will. Then the people answer, and not before, that whilst he governs uprightly, they will obey faithfully. The king therefore promises simply and absolutely, the people upon condition : the which failing to be accomplished, the people rest according to equity and reason, quit from their promise.

In the first covenant or contract there is only an obligation to piety : in the second, to justice. In that the king promises to serve God religiously : in this, to rule the people justly.

By the one he is obliged with the utmost of his endeavours to procure the glory of God : by the other, the profit of the people. In the first, there is a condition expressed, " if thou keep my commandments " : in the second, " if thou distribute justice equally to every man." God is the proper revenger of deficiency in the former, and the whole people the lawful punisher of delinquency in the latter, or the estates, the representative body thereof, who have assumed to themselves the protection of the people. This has been always practised in all well-governed estates. Amongst the Persians, after the due performance of holy rites, they contracted with Cyrus in manner following :

" Thou, O Cyrus ! in the first place shalt promise, that if any make war against the Persians, or seek to infringe the liberty of the laws, thou wilt with the utmost of thy power defend and protect this country." Which, having promised, they presently add, " And we Persians promise to be aiding to keep all men in obedience, whilst thou defendest the country." Xenophon calls this agreement, " A Confederation," as also Isocrates calls that which he wrote of the duties of subjects towards their princes, " A Discourse of Confederation." The alliance or confederation was renewed every month between the kings and Ephores of Sparta, although those kings were descended from the line of Hercules. And as these kings did solemnly swear to govern according to the laws, so did the Ephores also to maintain them in their authority, whilst they performed their promise. Likewise in the Roman kingdom, there was an agreement between Romulus, the senate, and the people, in this manner : " That the people should make laws, and the king look they were kept : the people should decree war, and the king should manage it." Now, although many emperors, rather by force and ambition, than by any lawful right, were seized of the Roman empire, and by that which they call a royal law, attributed to themselves an absolute authority, notwithstanding, by the fragments which remain both in books and in Roman inscriptions of that law, it plainly appears, that power and authority were granted them to preserve and govern the commonwealth, not to ruin and oppress it by tyranny. Nay, all good emperors have ever professed, that they held themselves tied to the laws, and received the empire from the senate, to whose determination they always referred the most important affairs, and esteemed it a great error, without their advice, to resolve on the occasions of the public state.

If we take into our consideration the condition of the empires, kingdoms, and states of times, there is not any of them worthy of those names, where there is not some such covenant or confederacy between the people and the prince. It is not long since, that in the empire of Germany, the king of the Romans being ready to be crowned emperor, was bound to do homage, and make oath of fealty to the empire, no more nor less than as the vassal is bound to do to his lord when he is invested with his fee. Although the form of the words which he is to swear have been somewhat altered by the popes, yet, notwithstanding, the substance still remains the same. According to which we know that Charles the Fifth, of the house of Austria, was under certain conditions chosen emperor, as in the same manner his successors were, the sum of which was, that he should keep the laws already made, and make no new ones without the consent of the electors, that he should govern the public affairs by the advice of the general estates, nor engage anything that belongs to the empire, and other matters which are particularly recited by the historians. When the emperor is crowned at Aquisgrave, the Archbishop of Cologne requires of him in the first place : If he will maintain the church, if he will distribute justice, if he will defend the empire, and protect widows, orphans, and all others worthy of compassion. The which, after he has solemnly sworn before the altar, the princes also who represent the empire, are asked if they will not promise the same ; neither is the emperor anointed, nor receives the other ornaments of the empire, before he has first taken that solemn oath. Whereupon it follows, that the emperor is tied absolutely, and the princes of the empire, under condition. That the same is observed in the kingdom of Polonia, no man will make question, who had but seen or heard of the ceremonies and rites wherewith Henry of Anjou was lately chosen and crowned king of that country, and especially then when the condition of maintaining of the two religions, the reformed and the Roman, was demanded, the which the lords of the kingdom in express terms required of him three several times, and he as often made promise to perform. The same is observed in the kingdoms of Bohemia,

Hungary, and others ; the which we omit to relate particularly, to avoid prolixity.

Now this manner of stipulation is not only received in those kingdoms where the right of election is yet entirely observed ; but even in those also which are esteemed to be simply hereditary. When the king of France is crowned, the bishops of Laon and Beauvois, ecclesiastical peers, ask all the people there present, whether they desire and command, that he who is there before them, shall be their king ? Whereupon he is said even then in the style of the inauguration, to be chosen by the people : and when they have given the sign of consenting, then the king swears that he will maintain all the rights, privileges, and laws of France universally, that he will not alien the demesne, and the other articles, which have been yet so changed and accommodated to bad intentions, as they differ greatly from that copy which remains in the library of the chapter of Beauvois, according to which it is recorded, that King Philip, the first of that name, took his oath at his coronation ; yet, notwithstanding, they are not unfitly expressed. Neither is he girded with the sword, nor anointed, nor crowned by the peers (who at that time wore coronets on their heads), nor receives the sceptre and rod of justice, nor is proclaimed king, before first the people have commanded it : neither do the peers take their oaths of allegiance before he has first solemnly sworn to keep the laws carefully.

And those be, that he shall not waste the public revenue, that he shall not, of his own proper authority, impose any taxes, customs, or tributes, that he shall not make peace or war, nor determine of state affairs, without the advice of the council of state. Briefly, that he should leave to the parliament, to the states, and to the officers of the kingdom, their authority entire, and all things else which have been usually observed in the kingdom of France. And when he first enters any city or province, he is bound to confirm their privileges, and swears to maintain their laws and customs. This is straightly observed in the cities of Tholouse and Rochel, and in the countries of Daulpiny, Province and Brittany. The which towns and provinces have their particular and express covenants and agreements with the kings, which must needs be void, if the condition expressed in the contract be not of force, nor the kings tied to the performance.

There is the form of the oath of the ancient kings of Burgundy, yet extant in these words : " I will protect all men in their rights, according to law and justice."

In England, Scotland, Sweden, and Denmark, there is almost the same custom as in France ; but in no place there is used a more discreet care in their manner of proceeding, than in Spain. For in the kingdom of Arragon, after the finishing of many ceremonies, which are used between him, which represents the Justitia Major of Arragon, which comprehends the majesty of the commonwealth, seated in a higher seat, and the king, which is to be crowned, who swears fealty, and does his homage ; and having read the laws and conditions, to the accomplishment whereof he is sworn.

Finally, the lords of the kingdom use to the king these words in the vulgar language, as is before expressed, " We who are as much worth as you, and have more power than you, choose you king upon these and these conditions, and there is one between you and us, who commands over you." But, lest the king should think he swore only for fashion's sake, and to observe an old custom, every third year in full assembly of the estates, the very same words, and in the same manner are repeated unto him.

And, if under pretext of his royal dignity he become insolent, violating the laws, and neglect his public faith and promise given, then, by the privilege of the kingdom, he is judged, excommunicated, as execrable as Julian the apostate was by the primitive church : which excommunication is esteemed of that validity, that instead of praying for the king in their public orations, they pray against him, and the subjects are by the same right acquit from their oath of allegiance : as the vassal is exempted from obedience and obligation by oath to his lord who stands excommunicated ; the which hath been determined and confirmed both by act of council and decree of state in the kingdom of Arragon.

In like manner, in the kingdom of Castile in full assembly of the estates, the king, being ready to be crowned, is first in the presence of all advertised of his duty : and even then are read the articles discreetly composed for the good of the commonwealth ; the king swears he will observe and keep them carefully and faithfully, which, being done, then the constable takes his oath of allegiance, after the princes and deputies for the towns swear each of them in their order ; and the same is observed in the kingdoms of Portugal, Leon, and the rest of Spain. The lesser principalities have their institution grounded on the same right. The contracts which the Brabancers and the rest of the Netherlanders, together with those of Austria, Carinthia, and others, had with their princes, were always conditional. But especially the Brabancers, to take away all occasion of dispute, have this express condition : which is that in the receiving of their duke, there is read in his presence the ancient articles, wherein is comprised that which is requisite for the public good, and thereunto is also added, that if he do not exactly and precisely observe them, they may choose what other lord it shall seem good unto them ; the which they do in express words protest unto him. He having allowed and accepted of these articles, does in that public assembly promise and solemnly swear to keep them. The which was observed in the reception of Philip the Second, king of Spain. Briefly, there is not any man can deny, but that there is a contract mutually obligatory between the king and the subjects, which requires the people to obey faithfully, and the king to govern lawfully, for the performance whereof the king swears first, and after the people.

I would ask here, wherefore a man does swear, if it be not to declare that what he delivers he sincerely intends from his heart ? Can anything be judged more near to the law of nature, than to observe that which we approve ? Furthermore, what is the reason the king swears first, and at the instance, and required by the people, but to accept a condition either tacit or expressed ? Wherefore is there a condition opposed to the contract, if it be not that in failing to perform the condition, the contract, according to law, remains void ? And if for want of satisfying the condition by right, the contract is of no force, who shall dare to call that people perjured, which refuses to obey a king who makes no account of his promise, which he might and ought to have kept, and wilfully breaks those laws which he did swear to observe ? On the contrary, may we not rather esteem such a king perfidious, perjured, and unworthy of his place ? For if the law free the vassal from his lord, who dealt feloniously with him, although that to speak properly, the lord swears not fealty to his vassal, but he to him : if

the law of the twelve tables doth detest and hold in execration
the protector who defrauds him that is under his tuition :
if the civil law permit an enfranchised servant to bring his
action against his patron, for any grievous usage : if in such
cases the same law delivers the slave from the power of his
master, although the obligation be natural only, and not
civil : is it not much more reasonable that the people be
loosed from that oath of allegiance which they have taken,
if the king (who may be not unfitly resembled by an attorney,
sworn to look to his client's cause) first break his oath solemnly
taken ? And what if all these ceremonies, solemn oaths, nay,
sacramental promises, had never been taken ? Does not
nature herself sufficiently teach that kings were on this condition ordained by the people, that they should govern well ;
judges, that they should distribute justice uprightly ; captains in the war, that they should lead their armies against
their enemies ? If, on the contrary, they themselves forage
and spoil their subjects, and instead of governors become
enemies, as they leave indeed the true and essential qualities
of a king, so neither ought the people to acknowledge them
for lawful princes. But what if a people (you will reply)
subdued by force, be compelled by the king to take an oath
of servitude ? And what if a robber, pirate, or tyrant (I will
answer) with whom no bond of human society can be effectual,
holding his dagger to your throat, constrain you presently
to become bound in a great sum of money ? Is it not an
unquestionable maxim in law, that a promise exacted by
violence cannot bind, especially if anything be promised
against common reason, or the law of nature ? Is there anything more repugnant to nature and reason, than that a
people should manacle and fetter themselves ; and to be
obliged by promise to the prince, with their own hands and
weapons to be their own executioners ? There is, therefore,
a mutual obligation between the king and the people, which,
whether it be civil or natural only, whether tacit or expressed
in words, it cannot by any means be annihilated, or by any
law be abrogated, much less by force made void. And this
obligation is of such power that the prince who wilfully
violates it, is a tyrant. And the people who purposely break
it, may be justly termed seditious.

Hitherto we have treated of a king. It now rests we do
somewhat more fully describe a tyrant. We have shewed

that he is a king who lawfully governs a kingdom, either derived to him by succession, or committed to him by election. It follows, therefore, that he is reputed a tyrant, which, as opposite to a king, either gains a kingdom by violence or indirect means, or being invested therewith by lawful election or succession, governs it not according to law and equity, or neglects those contracts and agreements, to the observation whereof he was strictly obliged at his reception. All which may very well occur in one and the same person. The first is commonly called a tyrant without title : the second a tyrant by practice. Now, it may well so come to pass, that he who possesses himself of a kingdom by force, to govern justly, and he on whom it descends by a lawful title, to rule unjustly. But for so much as a kingdom is rather a right than an inheritance, and an office than a possession, he seems rather worthy the name of a tyrant, who unworthily acquits himself of his charge, than he who entered into his place by a wrong door. In the same sense is the pope called an intruder who entered by indirect means into the papacy : and he an abuser who governs ill in it.

Pythagoras says " that a worthy stranger is to be preferred before an unworthy citizen, yea, though he be a kinsman." Let it be lawful also for us to say, that a prince who gained his principality by indirect courses, provided he govern according to law, and administer justice equally, is much to be preferred before him, who carries himself tyrannously, although he were legally invested into his government with all the ceremonies and rites thereunto appertaining.

For seeing that kings were instituted to feed, to judge, to cure the diseases of the people : Certainly I had rather that a thief should feed me, than a shepherd devour me : I had rather receive justice from a robber, than outrage from a judge : I had better be healed by an empiric, than poisoned by a doctor in physic. It were much more profitable for me to have my estate carefully managed by an intruding guardian, than to have it wasted and dissipated by one legally appointed.

And although it may be that ambition was his first solicitor to enter violently into the government, yet may it perhaps appear he affected it rather to give testimony of his equity and moderation in governing ; witness Cyrus, Alexander, and the Romans, who ordinarily accorded to those people they subdued, permission to govern themselves according to their own laws, customs, and privileges, yea, sometimes incorporated them into the body of their own state : on the contrary, the tyrant by practice seems to extend the privilege of his legal succession, the better to execute violence and extortion, as may be seen in these days, not only by the examples of the Turks and Muscovites, but also in divers Christian princes. Therefore the act of one who at the first was ill, is in some reasonable time rectified by justice : whereas the other like an inveterate disease, the older it grows, the worse it affects the patient.

Now, if according to the saying of Saint Augustine, " those kingdoms where justice hath no place, are but a rhapsody of free-booters," they are in that, both the tyrant without title, and he by practice alike, for that they are both thieves, both robbers, and both unjust possessors, as he certainly is no less an unjust detainer who takes another man's goods against the owner's will, than he who employs it ill when it was taken before.

But the fault is without comparison, much more greater of him who possesses an estate for to ruin it, than of the other who made himself master of it to preserve it.

Briefly, the tyrant by practice vainly colouring his unjust extortions with the justice of his title, is much more blameable than the tyrant without title, who recompenses the violence of his first intrusion in a continued course of a legal and upright government.

But to proceed, there may be observed some difference amongst tyrants without title : for there are some who ambitiously invade their neighbour's countries to enlarge their own, as Nimrod, Minus, and the Canaanites have done. Although such are termed kings by their own people, yet to those on whose confines they have encroached without any just right or occasion, they will be accounted tyrants.

There be others, who having attained to the government of an elective kingdom, that endeavour by deceitful means, by corruption, by presents, and other bad practices, to make it become hereditary. For witness whereof, we need not make search into older times ; these are worse than the former, for so much as secret fraud, as Cicero says, " is ever more odious than open force."

There be also others who are so horribly wicked, that they seek to enthral their own native country like the viperous

brood which gnaws through the entrails of their mother : as
be those generals of armies created by the people, who afterwards, by the means of those forces, make themselves masters
of the stage, as Cæsar at Rome under pretence of the dictator-
ship, and divers princes of Italy.

There be women also who intrude themselves into the
government of those kingdoms which the laws only permit
to the males, and make themselves queens and regents, as
Athalia did in Judah, Semiramis in Assyria, Agrippina in the
Roman empire in the reign of her son Nero, Mammea in
the time of Alexander Severus, Semiamira in Heliogabalus's ;
and certain Bruniehildes in the kingdom of France, who so
educated their sons (as the queens of the house of Medicis
in these latter times) during their minority, that attaining to
more maturity, their only care was to glut themselves in
pleasures and delights, so that the whole management of
affairs remained in the hands of their mothers, or of their
minions, servants and officers.   Those also are tyrants without title, who, taking advantage of the sloth, weakness, and
dissolute courses of those princes who are otherwise lawfully
instituted, and seeking to enwrap them in a sleepy dream of
voluptuous idleness (as under the French kings, especially
those of the Merovingian line, some of the mayors of the
palace have been advanced to that dignity for such egregious
services), transferring into their own command all the royal
authority, and leaving the king only the bare name.   All
which tyrants are certainly of this condition, that if for the
manner of their government they are not blameable.   Yet for
so much as they entered into that jurisdiction by tyrannous
intrusion, they may justly be termed tyrants without title.

Concerning tyrants by practice, it is not so easy to describe
them as true kings.   For reason rules the one, and selfwill
the other : the first prescribes bounds to his affections, the
second confines his desires within no limits.   What is the
proper rights of kings may be easily declared, but the outrageous insolences of tyrants cannot without much difficulty
be expressed.   And as a right angle is uniform, and like to
itself one and the same, so an oblique diversifies itself into
various and sundry species.   In like manner is justice and
equity simple, and may be deciphered in few words : but
injustice and injury are divers, and for their sundry accidents
not to be so easily defined ; but that more will be omitted

than expressed. Now, although there be certain rules by which these tyrants may be represented (though not absolutely to the life), yet, notwithstanding, there is not any more certain rule than by conferring and comparing a tyrant's fraudulent slights with a king's virtuous actions.

A tyrant lops off those ears which grow higher than the rest of the corn, especially where virtue makes them most conspicuously eminent; oppresses by calumnies and fraudulent practices the principal officers of the state; gives out reports of intended conspiracies against himself, that he might have some colourable pretext to cut them off; witness Tiberius, Maximinius, and others, who spared not their own kinsmen, cousins, and brothers.

The king, on the contrary, does not only acknowledge his brothers to be as it were consorts unto him in the empire, but also holds in the place of brothers all the principal officers of the kingdom, and is not ashamed to confess that of them (in quality as deputed from the general estates) he holds the crown.

The tyrant advances above and in opposition to the ancient and worthy nobility, mean and unworthy persons; to the end that these base fellows, being absolutely his creatures, might applaud and apply themselves to the fulfilling of all his loose and unruly desires. The king maintains every man in his rank, honours and respects the grandees as the kingdom's friends, desiring their good as well as his own.

The tyrant hates and suspects discreet and wise men, and fears no opposition more than virtue, as being conscious of his own vicious courses, and esteeming his own security to consist principally in a general corruption of all estates, introduces multiplicity of taverns, gaming houses, masks, stage plays, brothel houses, and all other licentious superfluities that might effeminate and bastardise noble spirits, as Cyrus did, to weaken and subdue the Sardiens. The king, on the contrary, allures from all places honest and able men, and encourages them by pensions and honours; and for seminaries of virtue, erects schools and universities in all convenient places.

A tyrant as much as in him lies, prohibits or avoids all public assemblies, fears parliaments, diets and meetings of the general estates, flies the light, affecting (like the bat) to converse only in darkness; yea, he is jealous of the very gesture, countenance, and discourse of his subjects. The king, because he converses always as in the presence of men and angels, glories in the multitude and sufficiency of his counsellors, esteeming nothing well done which is ordered without their advice, and is so far from doubting or distasting the public meeting of the general estates, as he honours and respects those assemblies with much favour and affection.

A tyrant nourishes and feeds factions and dissentions amongst his subjects, ruins one by the help of another, that he may the easier vanquish the remainder, advantaging himself by this division, like those dishonest surgeons who lengthen out their cures. Briefly, after the manner of that abominable Vitellius, he is not ashamed to say that the carcass of a dead enemy, especially a subject's, yields a good savour. On the contrary, a good king endeavours always to keep peace amongst his subjects, as a father amongst his children, choke the seeds of troubles, and quickly heals the scar ; the execution, even of justice upon rebels, drawing tears from his compassionate eyes ; yea, those whom a good king maintains and defends against a foreign enemy, a tyrant (the enemy of nature) compels them to turn the points of their swords into their own proper entrails. A tyrant fills his garrisons with strange soldiers, builds citadels against his subjects, disarms the people, throws down their forts, makes himself formidable with guards of strangers, or men only fit for pillage and spoil, gives pensions out of the public treasury to spies and calumniating informers, dispersed through all cities and provinces. Contrariwise, a king reposes more his safety in the love of his subjects than in the strength of his fortresses against his enemies, taking no care to enroll soldiers, but accounts every subject as a man-at-arms to guard him, and builds forts to restrain the irruptions of foreign enemies, and not to constrain his subjects to obedience, in whose fidelity he puts his greatest confidence. Therefore, it is that tyrants, although they have such numberless guards about them to drive off throngs of people from approaching them, yet cannot all those numbers secure them from doubts, jealousies and distrusts, which continually afflict and terrify their timorous consciences : yea, in the midst of their greatest strength, the tyrannizer of tyrants, fear, makes prize of their souls, and there triumphs in their affliction.

A good king, in the greatest concourse of people, is freest from doubts or fears, nor troubled with solicitous distrusts in his solitary retirements : all places are equally secure unto him, his own conscience being his best guard. If a tyrant wants civil broils to exercise his cruel disposition in, he makes wars abroad ; erects idle and needless trophies to continually employ his tributaries, that they might not have leisure to think on other things, as Pharaoh did the Jews, and Policrates the Samians ; therefore he always prepares for, or threatens war, or, at least, seems so to do, and so still rather draws mischief on, than puts it further off. A king never makes war, but compelled unto it, and for the preservation of the public, he never desires to purchase advantage by treason ; he never enters into any war that exposes the commonwealth to more danger than it affords probable hope of commodity.

A tyrant leaves no design unattempted by which he may fleece his subjects of their substance, and turn it to his proper benefit, that being continually troubled in gaining means to live, they may have no leisure, no hope, how to regain their liberty. On the contrary, the king knows that every good subject's purse will be ready to supply the commonwealth occasion, and therefore believes he is possessed of no small treasure, whilst through his good government his subjects flow in all abundance.

A tyrant extorts unjustly from many to cast prodigally upon two or three minions, and those unworthy ; he imposes on all, and exacts from all, to furnish their superfluous and riotous expenses : he builds his own, and followers' fortunes on the ruins of the public : he draws out the people's blood by the veins of their means, and gives it presently to carouse to his court-leeches. But a king cuts off from his ordinary expenses to ease the people's necessities, neglects his private state, and furnishes with all magnificence the public occasions ; briefly is prodigal of his own blood, to defend and maintain the people committed to his care.

If a tyrant, as heretofore Tiberius, Nero, Commodus and others, did suffer his subjects to have some breathing time from unreasonable exactions, and like sponges to gather some moisture, it is but to squeeze them out afterwards to his own use : on the contrary, if a king do sometimes open a vein, and draw some blood, it is for the people's good, and not to be expended at his own pleasure in any dissolute courses.

And therefore, as the Holy Scripture compares the one to a shepherd, so does it also resemble the other to a roaring lion, to whom, notwithstanding, the fox is oftentimes coupled. For a tyrant, as says Cicero, " is culpable in effect of the greatest injustice that may be imagined, and yet he carries it so cunningly, that when he most deceives, it is then that he makes greatest appearance to deal sincerely." And therefore does he artificially counterfeit religion and devotion, wherein saith Aristotle, " he expresses one of the most absolute subtleties that tyrants can possibly practise : he does so compose his countenance to piety, by that means to terrify the people from conspiring against him ; who they may well imagine to be especially favoured of God, expressing in all appearance so reverently to serve Him." He feigns also to be exceedingly affected to the public good ; not so much for the love of it, as for fear of his own safety.

Furthermore, he desires much to be esteemed just and loyal in some affairs, purposely to deceive and betray more easily in matters of greater consequence : much like those thieves who maintain themselves by thefts and robberies, yet cannot long subsist in their trade without exercising some parcel of justice in their proceedings. He also counterfeits the merciful, but it is in pardoning of such malefactors, in punishing whereof he might more truly gain the reputation of a pitiful prince.

To speak in a word, that which the true king is, the tyrant would seem to be, and knowing that men are wonderfully attracted with, and enamoured of virtue, he endeavours with much subtlety to make his vices appear yet masked with some shadow of virtue : but let him counterfeit never so cunningly, still the fox will be known by his tail : and although he fawn and flatter like a spaniel, yet his snarling and grinning will ever betray his currish kind.

Furthermore, as a well-ordered monarchy partakes of the principal commodities of all other governments, so, on the contrary, where tyranny prevails, there all the discommodities of confusion are frequent.

A monarchy has in this conformity with an aristocracy, that the most able and discreet are called to consultations. Tyranny and oligarchy accord in this, that their councils are composed of the worst and most corrupted. And as in the council royal, there may in a sort seem many kings to have interests in the government, so, in the other, on the contrary, a multitude of tyrants always domineers.

The monarchy borrows of the popular government the assemblies of the estates, whither are sent for deputies the most sufficient of cities and provinces, to deliberate on, and determine matters of state : the tyranny takes this of the ochlocracy, that if she be not able to hinder the convocation of the estates, yet will she endeavour by factious subtleties and pernicious practices, that the greatest enemies of order and reformation of the state be sent to those assemblies, the which we have known practised in our times. In this manner assumes the tyrant the countenance of a king, and tyranny the semblance of a kingdom, and the continuance succeeds commonly according to the dexterity wherewith it is managed ; yet, as Aristotle says, " we shall hardly read of any tyranny that has outlasted a hundred years " : briefly, the king principally regards the public utility, and a tyrant's chiefest care is for his private commodity.

But, seeing the condition of men is such, that a king is with much difficulty to be found, that in all his actions he only agrees at the public good, and yet cannot long subsist without expression of some special care thereof, we will conclude that where the commonwealth's advantage is most preferred, there is both a lawful king and kingdom ; and where particular designs and private ends prevail against the public profit, there questionless is a tyrant and tyranny.

Thus much concerning tyrants by practice, in the examining whereof we have not altogether fixed our discourse on the loose disorders of their wicked and licentious lives, which some say is the character of a bad man, but not always of a bad prince. If therefore, the reader be not satisfied with this description, besides the more exact representations of tyrants which he shall find in histories, he may in these our days behold an absolute model of many living and breathing tyrants : whereof Aristotle in his time did much complain. Now, at the last we are come as it were by degrees to the chief and principal point of the question. We have seen how that kings have been chosen by God, either with relation to their families or their persons only, and after installed by the people. In like manner what is the duty of the king, and of the officers of the kingdom, how far the authority, power, and duty both of the one and the other extends, and what and how sacred are the covenants and contracts which are made at the inauguration of kings, and what conditions are intermixed, both tacit and expressed ; finally, who is a tyrant without title, and who by practice, seeing it is a thing unquestionable that we are bound to obey a lawful king, which both to God and people carries himself according to those covenants whereunto he stands obliged, as it were to God Himself, seeing in a sort he represents his divine Majesty ? It now follows that we treat, how, and by whom a tyrant may be lawfully resisted, and who are the persons who ought to be chiefly actors therein, and what course is to be held, that the action may be managed according to right and reason.   We must first speak of him who is commonly called a tyrant without title.   Let us suppose then that some Ninus, having neither received outrage nor offence, invades a people over whom he has no colour of pretension : that Cæsar seeks to oppress his country, and the Roman commonwealth : that Popiclus endeavours by murders and treasons to make the elective kingdom of Polonia to become hereditary to him and his posterity : or some Bruniehilde draws to herself and her Protadius the absolute government of France, or Ebronius, taking advantage of Theoderick's weakness and idleness, gains the entire administration of the state, and oppresses the people, what shall be our lawful refuge herein ?

First, the law of nature teaches and commands us to maintain and defend our lives and liberties, without which life is scant worth the enjoying, against all injury and violence.   Nature has imprinted this by instinct in dogs against wolves, in bulls against lions, betwixt pigeons and sparrowhawks, betwixt pullen and kites, and yet much more in man against man himself, if man become a beast : and therefore he who questions the lawfulness of defending oneself, does, as much as in him lies, question the law of nature.   To this must be added the law of nations, which distinguishes possessions and dominions, fixes limits, and makes out confines, which every man is bound to defend against all invaders. And, therefore, it is no less lawful to resist Alexander the Great, if without any right or being justly provoked, he invades a country with a mighty navy, as well as Diomedes the pirate who scours the seas in a small vessel.   For in this case Alexander's right is no more than Diomedes' but only he has more power to do wrong, and not so easily to be compelled to reason as the other. Briefly, one may as well oppose Alexander in pillaging a country, as a thief in purloining a cloak; as well him when he seeks to batter down the walls of a city, as a robber who offers to break into a private house.

There is, besides this, the civil law, or municipal laws of several countries which governs the societies of men, by certain rules, some in one manner, some in another; some submit themselves to the government of one man, some to more; others are ruled by a whole commonalty, some absolutely exclude women from the royal throne, others admit them; these here choose their king descended of such a family, those there make election of whom they please, besides other customs practised amongst several nations. If, therefore, any offer either by fraud or force to violate this law, we are all bound to resist him, because he wrongs that society to which we owe all that we have, and would ruin our country, to the preservation whereof all men by nature, by law and by solemn oath, are strictly obliged: insomuch that fear or negligence, or bad purposes, make us omit this duty, we may justly be accounted breakers of the laws, betrayers of our country, and contemners of religion. Now as the laws of nature, of nations, and the Civil commands us to take arms against such tyrants; so, is there not any manner of reason that should persuade us to the contrary; neither is there any oath, covenant, or obligation, public or private, of power justly to restrain us; therefore the meanest private man may resist and lawfully oppose such an intruding tyrant. The law Julia, which condemns to death those who raise rebellion against their country or prince, has here no place; for he is no prince, who, without any lawful title invades the commonwealth or confines of another; nor he a rebel, who by arms defends his country; but rather to this had relation the oath which all the youth of Athens were accustomed to take in the temple of Aglaura, " I will fight for religion, for the laws, for the altars, and for our possessions, either alone, or with others; and will do the utmost of my endeavour to leave to posterity our country, at the least, in as good estate as I found it." To as little purpose can the laws made against seditious persons be alleged here; for he is seditious who undertakes to defend the people, in opposition of order and public discipline ; but he is no raiser, but a suppressor of sedition, who restrains within the limits of reason the subverter of his country's welfare, and public discipline.

On the contrary, to this has proper relation the law of tyrannicide, which honours the living with great and memorable recompenses, and the dead with worthy epitaphs, and glorious statues, that have been their country's liberators from tyrants ; as Harmodius and Aristogiton at Athens, Brutus and Cassius in Rome, and Aratus of Sycione. To these by a public decree were erected statues, because they delivered their countries from the tyrannies of Pisistratus, of Cæsar, and of Nicocles. The which was of such respect amongst the ancients, that Xerxes having made himself master of the city of Athens, caused to be transported into Persia the statues of Harmodius and Aristogiton ; afterwards Seleucus caused them to be returned into their former place : and as in their passage they came by Rhodes, those famous citizens entertained them with public and stupendous solemnities, and during their abode there, they placed them in the choicest sacresties of their gods. But the law made against forsakers and traitors, takes absolutely hold on those who are negligent and careless to deliver their country oppressed with tyranny, and condemns them to the same punishment as those cowardly soldiers, who, when they should fight, either counterfeit sickness, or cast off their arms and run away. Every one, therefore, both in general and particular, ought to yield their best assistance unto this : as in a public fire, to bring both hooks, and buckets, and water ; we must not ceremoniously expect that the captain of the watch be first called, nor till the governor of the town be come into the streets ; but let every man draw water and climb to the house-top ; it is necessary for all men that the fire be quenched. For if whilst the Gaules with much silence and vigilancy seek to scale and surprise the capital, the soldiers be drowsy with their former pains, the watch buried in sleep, the dogs fail to bark, then must the geese play the sentinels, and with their cackling noise, give an alarm. And the soldiers and watch shall be degraded, yea, and put to death. The geese for perpetual remembrance of this deliverance, shall be always fed in the capital, and much esteemed.

This, of which we have spoken, is to be understood of a tyranny not yet firmly rooted, to wit, whilst a tyrant conspires, machinates, and lays his plots and practices. But if he be once so possessed of the state, and that the people, being subdued, promise and swear obedience ; the commonwealth being oppressed, resign their authority into their hands ; and that the kingdom in some formal manner consent to the changing of their laws ; for so much certainty as then, he has gained a title which before he wanted and seems to be as well a legal as actual possessor thereof, although this yoke were laid on the people's neck by compulsion, yet must they quietly and peaceably rest in the will of the Almighty, who, at His pleasure transfers kingdoms from one nation to another ; otherways there should be no kingdom, whose jurisdiction might not be disputed. And it may well chance, that he who before was a tyrant without title, having obtained the title of a king, may free himself from any tyrannous imputation, by governing those under him with equity and moderation. Therefore then, as the people of Jurie, under the authority of King Ezechias, did lawfully resist the invasion of Senacherib the Assyrian ; so, on the contrary was Zedechias and all his subjects worthily punished, because that without any just occasion, after they had done homage and sworn fealty to Nebuchadnezar, they rose in rebellion against him. For, after promise of performance, it is too late to repent. And, as in battles every one ought to give testimony of his valour, but, being taken prisoner, must faithfully observe covenants, so it is requisite, that the people maintain their rights by all possible means ; but, if it chance that they be brought into the subjection of another's will, they must then patiently support the dominion of the victor. So did Pompey, Cato, and Cicero and others, perform the parts of good patriots then when they took arms against Cæsar, seeking to alter the government of the state ; neither can those be justly excused, whose base fear hindered the happy success of Pompey and his partakers' noble designs. Augustus himself is said to have reproved one who railed on Cato, affirming that he carried himself worthily and exceedingly affected to the greatness of his country, in courageously opposing the alteration which his contraries sought to introduce in the government of the state, seeing all innovations of that nature are ever authors of much trouble and confusion.

Furthermore, no man can justly reprehend Brutus, Cassius, and the rest who killed Cæsar before his tyrannical authority had taken any firm rooting. And so there were statues of brass erected in honour of them by public decree at Athens, and placed by those of Harmodius and Aristogiton, then when, after the despatching of Cæsar, they retired from Rome, to avoid Marc Antonie and Augustus their revenge. But Cinna was certainly guilty of sedition, who, after a legal transferring of the people's power into the hands of Augustus, is said to have conspired against him. Likewise, when the Pepins sought to take the crown of France from the Merovingians ; as also when those of the line of Capet endeavoured to supplant the Pepins, any might lawfully resist them without incurring the crime of sedition. But when, by public counsel and the authority of the estates, the kingdom was transferred from one family to another, it was then unlawful to oppose it. The same may be said, if a woman possess herself of the kingdom, which the Salic law absolutely prohibits, or if one seek to make a kingdom merely elective, hereditary to his offspring, while those laws stand in force, and are unrepealed by the authority of the general estates, who represent the body of the people. Neither is it necessary in this respect, to have regard whether faction is the greater, more powerful or more illustrious. Always those are the greater number who are led by passion, than those who are ruled by reason, and therefore tyranny has more servants than the commonwealth. But Rome is there, according to the saying of Pompey, where the senate is, and the senate is where there is obedience to the laws, love of liberty, and studious carefulness for the country's preservation. And therefore, though Brennus may seem to be master of Rome, yet, notwithstanding, is Rome at Veii with Camillus, who prepares to deliver Rome from bondage. It behoves, therefore, all true Romans to repair to Camillus, and assist his enterprise with the utmost of their power and endeavours. Although Themistocles, and all his able and worthiest companions leave Athens, and put to sea with a navy of two hundred galleys, notwithstanding, it cannot be said that any of these men are banished Athens, but rather, as Themistocles answered, " These two hundred galleys are more useful for us, than the greatest city of all Greece ; for that they are armed, and prepared for the defence of those who endeavour to maintain and uphold the public state."

But to come to other examples : it follows not that the church of God must needs be always in that place where the ark of the covenant is ; for the Philistines may carry the ark into the temples of their idols. It is no good argument, that because we see the Roman eagles waving in ensigns, and hear their legions named, that therefore presently we conclude that the army of the Roman commonwealth is there present ; for there is only and properly the power of the state where they are assembled to maintain the liberty of the country against the ravenous oppression of tyrants, to enfranchise the people from servitude, and to suppress the impudency of insulting flatterers, who abuse the prince's weakness by oppressing his subjects for the advantage of their own fortunes, and contain ambitious minds from enlarging their desires beyond the limits of equity and moderation. Thus much concerning tyrants without title.

But for tyrants by practice, whether they at first gained their authority by the sword, or were legally invested therewith by a general consent, it behoves us to examine this point with much wary circumspection. In the first place we must remember that all princes are born men, and therefore reason and passion are as hardly to be separated in them, as the soul is from the body whilst the man lives. We must not then expect princes absolute in perfection, but rather repute ourselves happy if those who govern us be indifferently good. And therefore, although the prince observe not exact mediocrity in state affairs ; if sometimes passion overrule his reason, if some careless omission make him neglect the public utility ; or if he do not always carefully execute justice with equality, or repulse not with ready valour an invading enemy ; he must not therefore be presently declared a tyrant. And certainly, seeing he rules not as a god over men, nor as men over beasts, but is a man composed of the same matter, and of the same nature with the rest : as we would questionless judge that prince unreasonably insolent, who should insult over and abuse his subjects, as if they were brute beasts ; so those people are doubtless as much void of reason, who imagine a prince should be complete in perfection, or expect divine abilities in a nature so frail and subject to imperfections. But if a

prince purposely ruin the commonwealth, if he presumptuously pervert and resist legal proceedings or lawful rights,
if he make no reckoning of faith, covenants, justice nor piety,
if he prosecute his subjects as enemies ; briefly, if he express
all or the chiefest of those wicked practices we have formerly
spoken of ; then we may certainly declare him a tyrant, who
is as much an enemy both to God and men. We do not
therefore speak of a prince less good, but of one absolutely
bad ; not of one less wise, but of one malicious and treacherous ; not of one less able judiciously to discuss legal differences, but of one perversely bent to pervert justice and
equity ; not of an unwarlike, but of one furiously disposed
to ruin the people, and ransack the state.

For the wisdom of a senate, the integrity of a judge, the
valour of a captain, may peradventure enable a weak prince
to govern well. But a tyrant could be content that all the
nobility, the counsellors of state, the commanders for the
wars, had but one head that he might take it off at one blow :
those being the proper objects of his distrust and fear, and
by consequence the principal subjects on whom he desires
to execute his malice and cruelty. A foolish prince, although
(to speak according to right and equity) he ought to be deposed, yet may he perhaps in some sort be borne withal.
But a tyrant the more he is tolerated, the more he becomes
intolerable.

Furthermore, as the princes pleasure is not always law,
so many times it is not expedient that the people do all that
which may lawfully be done ; for it may oftentimes chance
that the medicine proves more dangerous than the disease.
Therefore it becomes wise men to try all ways before they
come to blows, to use all other remedies before they suffer
the sword to decide the controversy. If then, those who
represent the body of the people, foresee any innovation or
machination against the state, or that it be already embarked
into a course of perdition ; their duty is, first to admonish
the prince, and not to attend, that the disease by accession
of time and accidents becomes unrecoverable. For tyranny
may be properly resembled unto a fever hectic, the which
at the first is easy to be cured, but with much difficulty to
be known ; but after it is sufficiently known, it becomes
incurable. Therefore small beginnings are to be carefully
observed, and by those whom it concerns diligently prevented.

If the prince therefore persist in his violent courses, and contemn frequent admonitions, addressing his designs only to that end, that he may oppress at his pleasure, and effect his own desires without fear or restraint ; he then doubtless makes himself liable to that detested crime of tyranny : and whatsoever either the law, or lawful authority permits against a tyrant, may be lawfully practised against him. Tyranny is not only a will, but the chief, and as it were the complement and abstract of vices. A tyrant subverts the state, pillages the people, lays stratagems to entrap their lives, breaks promise with all, scoffs at the sacred obligations of a solemn oath, and therefore is he so much more vile than the vilest of usual malefactors. By how much offences committed against a generality, are worthy of greater punishment than those which concern only particular and private persons. If thieves and those who commit sacrilege be declared infamous ; nay, if they justly suffer corporal punishment by death, can we invent any that may be worthily equivalent for so outrageous a crime ?

Furthermore, we have already proved, that all kings receive their royal authority from the people, that the whole people considered in one body is above and greater than the king ; and that the king and emperor are only the prime and supreme governors and ministers of the kingdom and empire ; but the people the absolute lord and owner thereof. It therefore necessarily follows, that a tyrant is in the same manner guilty of rebellion against the majesty of the people, as the lord of a fee, who feloniously transgresses the conditions of his investitures, and is liable to the same punishment, yea, and certainly deserves much more greater than the equity of those laws inflicts on the delinquents. Therefore as Bartolus says, " He may either be deposed by those who are lords in sovereignty over him, or else justly punished according to the law Julia, which condemns those who offer violence to the public." The body of the people must needs be the sovereign of those who represent it, which in some places are the electors, palatines, peers ; in other, the assembly of the general estates. And, if the tyranny have gotten such sure footing, as there is no other means but force to remove him, then it is lawful for them to call the people to arms, to enroll and raise forces, and to employ the utmost of their power, and use against him all advantages and stratagems of war, as against the enemy of the commonwealth, and the disturber of the public peace. Briefly, the same sentence may be justly pronounced against him, as was against Manlius Capitolinus at Rome. " Thou wast to me, Manlius, when thou didst tumble down the Gaules that scaled the capital : but since thou art now become an enemy, like one of them, thou shalt be precipitated down from the same place from whence thou formerly tumbled those enemies."

The officers of the kingdom cannot for this be rightly taxed of sedition ; for in a sedition there must necessarily concur but two parts, or sides, the which peremptorily contest together, so that it is necessary that the one be in the right, and the other in the wrong. That part undoubtedly has the right on their side, which defends the laws, and strives to advance the public profit of the kingdom. And those, on the contrary, are questionless in the wrong, who break the laws, and protect those who violate justice, and oppress the commonwealth. Those are certainly in the right way, as said Bartolus, " who endeavour to suppress tyrannical government, and those in the wrong, who oppose lawful authority." And that must ever be accounted just, which is intended only for the public benefit, and that unjust, which aims chiefly at private commodity. Wherefore Thomas Aquinas says, " That a tyrannical rule, having no proper address for the public welfare, but only to satisfy a private will, with increase of particular profit to the ruler, cannot in any reasonable construction be accounted lawful, and therefore the disturbance of such a government cannot be esteemed seditious, much less traitorous " ; for that offence has proper relation only to a lawful prince, who, indeed, is an inanimated or speaking law ; therefore, seeing that he who employs the utmost of his means and power to annihilate the laws, and quell their virtue and vigour, can no ways be justly intituled therewith. So neither, likewise, can those who oppose and take arms against him, be branded with so notorious a crime. Also this offence is committed against the commonwealth ; but for so much as the commonwealth is there only where the laws are in force, and not where a tyrant devours the state at his own pleasure and liking, he certainly is quit of that crime which ruins the majesty of the public state, and those questionless are worthily protectors and preservers of the commonwealth, who, confident in the

lawfulness of their authority, and summoned thereunto by
their duty, do courageously resist the unjust proceedings of
the tyrant.

And in this their action, we must not esteem them as
private men and subjects, but as the representative body of
the people, yea, and as the sovereignty itself, which demands
of his minister an account of his administration. Neither
can we in any good reason account the officers of the kingdom disloyal, who in this manner acquit themselves of their
charge.

There is ever, and in all places, a mutual and reciprocal
obligation between the people and the prince ; the one
promises to be a good and wise prince, the other to obey
faithfully, provided he govern justly. The people therefore
are obliged to the prince under condition, the prince to
the people simply and purely. Therefore, if the prince fail
in his promise, the people are exempt from obedience, the
contract is made void, the right of obligation of no force.
Then the king if he govern unjustly is perjured, and the
people likewise forsworn if they obey not his lawful commands. But that people are truly acquit from all perfidious-
ness, who publicly renounce the unjust dominion of a tyrant,
or he, striving unjustly by strong hand to continue the possession, do constantly endeavour to expulse him by force of
arms.

It is therefore permitted the officers of a kingdom, either
all, or some good number of them, to suppress a tyrant ;
and it is not only lawful for them to do it, but their duty
expressly requires it ; and, if they do it not, they can by no
excuse colour their baseness. For the electors, palatines,
peers, and other officers of state, must not think they were
established only to make pompous paradoes and shows, when
they are at the coronation of the king, habited in their robes
of state, as if there were some masque or interlude to be
represented ; or as if they were that day to act the parts of
Roland, Oliver, or Renaldo, and such other personages on
a stage, or to counterfeit and revive the memory of the
knights of the round table ; and after the dismissing of
that day's assembly, to suppose they have sufficiently acquitted themselves of their duty, until a recess of the like
solemnity. Those solemn rites and ceremonies were not
instituted for vain ostentation, nor to pass, as in a dumb

show, to please the spectators, nor in children's sports, as it is with Horace, to create a king in jest ; but those grandees must know, that as well for office and duty, as for honour, they are called to the performance of those rites, and that in them, the commonwealth is committed and recommended to the king, as to her supreme and principal tutor and protector, and to them as co-adjutors and assistants to him : and therefore, as the tutors or guardians (yea, even those who are appointed by way of honour) are chosen to have care of and observe the actions and importments of him who holds the principal rank in the tutorship, and to look how he carries himself in the administration of the goods of his pupil. So likewise are the former ordained to have an eye to the courses of the king, for, with an equivalent authority, as the others for the pupil, so are they to hinder and prevent the damage and detriment of the people, the king being properly reputed as the prime guardian, and they his co-adjutors.

In like manner, as the faults of the principal tutor who manages the affairs are justly imputed to the co-adjoints in the tutorship, if when they ought and might, they did not discover his errors, and cause him to be despoiled, especially failing in the main points of his charge, to wit, in not communicating unto them the affairs of his administration, in dealing unfaithfully in his place, in doing anything to the dishonour or detriment of his pupil, in embezzling of his goods or estate, or if he be an enemy to his pupil : briefly, if either in regard of the worthlessness of his person, or weakness of his judgment, he be unable well to discharge so weighty a charge, so also, are the peers and principal officers of the kingdom accountable for the government thereof, and must both prevent, and if occasion require, suppress the tyranny of the prince, as also supply with their care and diligence, his inability and weakness.

Finally, if a tutor omitting or neglecting to do all that for his pupil, which a discreet father of a family would and might conveniently perform, cannot well be excused, and the better acquitting himself of his charge, has others as concealers and associates, joined with him to oversee his actions ; with much more reason may and ought the officers of the crown to restrain the violent irruptions of that prince, who, instead of a father, becomes an enemy to his people ;

seeing, to speak properly, they are as well accountable for his actions wherein the public has interests, as for their own.

Those officers must also remember, that the king holds truly the first place in the administration of the state, but they the second, and so following according to their ranks ; not that they should follow his courses, if he transgress the laws of equity and justice ; not that if he oppress the commonwealth, they should connive to his wickedness. For the commonwealth was as well committed to their care as to his, so that it is not sufficient for them to discharge their own duty in particular, but it behoves them also to contain the prince within the limits of reason ; briefly, they have both jointly and severally promised with solemn oaths, to advance and procure the profit of a commonwealth, although then that he forswore himself ; yet may not they imagine that they are quit of their promise, no more than the bishops and patriarchs, if they suffer an heretical pope to ruin the church ; yea, they should esteem themselves so much the more obliged to the observing their oath, by how much they find him wilfully disposed to rush on in his perfidious courses. But, if there be collusion betwixt him and them, they are prevaricators ; if they dissemble, they may justly be called forsakers and traitors ; if they deliver not the commonwealth from tyranny, they may be truly ranked in the number of tyrants ; as on the contrary they are protectors, tutors, and in a sort kings, if they keep and maintain the state safe and entire, which is also recommended to their care and custody.

Although these things are sufficiently certain of themselves, yet may they be in some sort confirmed by examples. The kings of Canaan who pressed the people of Israel with a hard, both corporal and spiritual, servitude (prohibiting them all meetings and use of arms) were certainly tyrants by practice, although they had some pretext of title. For Eglon and Jabin had peaceably reigned almost the space of twenty years. God stirred up extraordinarily Ehud, who, by a politic stratagem killed Eglon, and Deborah who overthrew the army of Jabin, and by his service delivered the people from the servitude of tyrants, not that it was unlawful for the ordinary magistrates, the princes of the tribes, and such other officers to have performed it, for Deborah does reprove the sluggish idleness of some, and flatly detests the disloyalty of others, for that they failed to perform their duty herein.

But it pleased God, taking commiseration of the distress of his people, in this manner to supply the defects of the ordinary magistrates.

Rehoboam, the son of Solomon, refused to disburden the people of some unnecessary imposts and burdens ; and being petitioned by the people in the general assembly of the states, he grew insolent, and relying on the counsel of his minions, arrogantly threatens to lay heavier burdens on them hereafter. No man can doubt, but that according to the tenure of the contract, first passed between the king and the people, the prime and principal officers of the kingdom had authority to repress such insolence. They were only blame-able in this, that they did that by faction and division, which should more properly have been done in the general assembly of the states ; in like manner, in that they transferred the sceptre from Judah (which was by God only confined to that tribe) into another lineage ; and also (as it chances in other affairs) for that they did ill and disorderly manage a just and lawful cause. Profane histories are full of such examples in other kingdoms.

Brutus, general of the soldiers, and Lucretius, governor of the city of Rome, assembled the people against Tarquinius Superbus, and by their authority thrust him from the royal throne : nay, which is more, his goods were confiscated ; whereby it appears that if Tarquinius had been apprehended, undoubtedly he should have been according to the public laws, corporally punished.

The true causes why Tarquinius was deposed, were be-cause he altered the custom, whereby the king was obliged to advise with the senate on all weighty affairs ; that he made war and peace according to his own fancy ; that he treated confederacies without demanding counsel and consent from the people or senate ; that he violated the laws whereof he was made guardian ; briefly that he made no reckoning to observe the contracts agreed between the former kings, and the nobility and people of Rome. For the Roman emperors, I am sure you remember the sentence pronounced by the senate against Nero, wherein he was judged an enemy to the commonwealth, and his body condemned to be ignomin-iously cast on the dung hill. And that other pronounced against Vitellius, which adjudged him to be shamefully dis-membered, and in that miserable estate trailed through the city, and at last put to death. Another against Maximinius, who was despoiled of the empire ; and Maximus and Albinus established in his place by the senate. There might also be added many others drawn from unquestionable historians.

The Emperor Trajan held not himself exempt from laws, neither desired he to be spared if he became a tyrant ; for in delivering the sword unto the great provost of the empire, he says unto him : " If I command as I should, use this sword for me : but if I do otherways, unsheathe it against me." In like manner the French by the authority of the states, and solicited thereunto by the officers of the kingdom, deposed Childerick the First, Sigisbert, Theodorick, and Childerick the Third for their tyrannies, and chose others of another family to sit on the royal throne. Yea, they deposed some because of their idleness and want of judgment, who exposed the state in prey to panders, courtesans, flatterers, and such other unworthy mushrooms of the court, who governed all things at their pleasure ; taking from such rash phaetons the bridle of government, lest the whole body of the state and people should be consumed through their unadvised folly.

Amongst others, Theodoret was degraded because of Ebroinus, Dagobert for Plectude and Thibaud his pander, with some others : the estates esteeming the command of an effeminate prince, as insupportable as that of a woman, and as unwillingly supporting the yoke of tyrannous ministers managing affairs in the name of a loose and unworthy prince, as the burden of a tyrant alone. To be brief, no more suffering themselves to be governed by one possessed by a devil, than they would by the devil himself. It is not very long since the estates compelled Lewis the Eleventh (a prince as subtle and it may be as wilful as any) to receive thirty-six overseers, by whose advice he was bound to govern the affairs of state. The descendants from Charlemaine substituted in the place of the Merovingians for the government of the kingdom, or those of Capet, supplanting the Charlemains by order of the estates, and reigning at this day, have no other nor better right to the crown, than what we have formerly described ; and it has ever been according to law permitted the whole body of the people, represented by the council of the kingdom, which are commonly called the assembly of the states, to depose and establish princes, according to the necessities of the commonwealth. According to the same rule we read that Adolph was removed from the Empire of Germany A.D. 1296, because for covetousness without any just occasion, he invaded the kingdom of France, in favour of the English, and Wenceslaus was also deposed in the year of our Lord 1400. Yet were not these princes exceeding bad ones, but of the number of those who are accounted less ill. Isabella, the wife of Edward the Second, King of England, assembled the Parliament against her husband, who was there deposed, both because he tyrannized in general over his subjects ; as also for that he cut off the heads of many noble men, without any just or legal proceeding. It is not long since Christian lost the crown of Denmark, Henry that of Sweden, Mary Stuart that of Scotland, for the same or near resembling occasions. And the most worthy histories relate divers alterations and changes which have happened in like manner, in the kingdoms of Polonia, Hungary, Spain, Portugal, Bohemia, and others.

But what shall we say of the pope himself ? It is generally held that the cardinals, because they do elect him, or if they fail in their duty, the patriarchs who are next in rank to them, may upon certain occasions maugre the pope, call a council, yea, and in it judge him ; as when by some notorious offence he scandalizes the universal church. If he be incorrigible, if reformation be as necessary in the head as the members, if contrary to his oath he refuse to call a general council. And we read for certain, that divers popes have been deposed by general councils. But if they obstinately abuse their authority, there must (saith Baldus) first be used verbal admonitions ; secondly, herbal medicaments or remedies ; thirdly, stones or compulsion ; for where virtue and fair means have not power to persuade, there force and terror must be put in use to compel. Now, if according to the opinions of most of the learned, by decrees of councils, and by custom in like occasions, it plainly appears, that the council may depose the pope, who, notwithstanding, vaunts himself to be the king of kings, and as much in dignity above the emperor, as the sun is above the moon, assuming to himself power to depose kings and emperors when he pleases : who will make any doubt or question, that the general assembly of the estates of any kingdom, who are the representative body thereof, may not only degrade and disthronize

a tyrant ; but also, even disauthorize and depose a king,
whose weakness or folly is hurtful or pernicious to the
state.

But let us suppose, that in this our ship of state, the pilot
is drunk, the most of his associates are asleep, or after large
and unreasonable tippling together, they regard their eminent
danger in approaching a rock with idle and negligent jollity ;
the ship in the mean season instead of following her right
course, that might serve for the best advantage of the owners'
profit, is ready rather to split herself. What should then a
master's mate, or some other under officer do, who is vigilant
and careful to perform his duty ? Shall it be thought sufficient
for him to pinch or punch them who are asleep, without
daring in the meantime to put his helping hand to preserve
the vessel which runs on a course to destruction, lest he
should .be thought to intermeddle with that which he has
no authority nor warrant to do ? What mad discretion, nay,
rather notorious impiety were this ? Seeing then that tyranny,
as Plato says, " is a drunken frenzy or frantic drunkenness,"
if the prince endeavour to ruin the commonwealth, and the
principal officers concur with him in his bad purposes, or at
the least are lulled in a dull and drowsy dream of security,
and the people (being indeed the true and absolute owner
and lord of the state) be, through the pernicious negligence
and fraudulent connivency of those officers, brought to the
very brim of danger and destruction, and that there be, notwithstanding, amongst those unworthy ministers of state,
some one who does studiously observe the deceitful and
dangerous encroachments of tyranny, and from his soul
detests it, what opposition do we suppose best befits such
a one to make against it ? Shall he consent himself to admonish his associates of their duty, who to their utmost
ability endeavour the contrary ? Besides, that such an
advertisement is commonly accompanied with too much
danger, and the condition of the times considered, the very
soliciting of reformation will be held as a capital crime : so
that in so doing he may be not unfitly resembled to one,
who, being in the midst of a desert, environed with thieves,
should neglect all means of defence, and after he had cast
away his arms, in an eloquent and learned discourse commend justice, and extol the worth and dignity of the laws.
This would be truly according to the proverb, " To run mad

with reason." What then ? Shall he be dull and deaf to
the groans and cries of the people ? Shall he stand still and
be silent when he sees the thieves enter ? Shall he only hold
his hands in his bosom, and with a demure countenance,
idly bewail the miserable condition of the times ? If the
laws worthily condemn a soldier, who, for fear of the enemies,
counterfeits sickness, because in so doing he expresses both
disloyalty and treachery, what punishment can we invent
sufficient for him, who either maliciously or basely betrays
those whose protection and defence he has absolutely undertaken and sworn ? Nay, rather than let such a one cheerfully
call one and command the mariners to the performance of
their duty : let him carefully and constantly take order that
the commonwealth be not endamaged, and if need so require, even in despite of the king, preserve the kingdom,
without which the kingly title were idle and frivolous, and
if by no other means it can be affected, let him take the
king and bind him hand and foot, that so he may be more
conveniently cured of his frenzy and madness.

For as we have already said, all the administration of the
kingdom is not by the people absolutely resigned into the
hands of the king ; as neither the bishopric nor care of the
universal church, is totally committed to the pope : but also
to the care and custody of all the principal officers of the
kingdom. Now, for the preserving of peace and concord
amongst those who govern, and for the preventing of jealousies, factions, and distrusts amongst men of equal rank and
dignity, the king was created prime and principal super-
intendent in the government of the commonwealth. The
king swears that his most special care shall be for the welfare
of the kingdom ; and the officers of the crown take all the
same oath. If then the king, or divers of them falsifying
their faith, ruin the commonwealth, or abandon her in her
greatest necessity, must the rest also fashion themselves to
their base courses, and quit all care of the state's safety ; as
if the bad example of their companions absolved them from
their oath of fidelity ? Nay, rather on the contrary, in seeing
them neglect their promise, they shall best advantage the
commonwealth in carefully observing theirs : chiefly because for this reason they were instituted, as in the steads of
ephori, or public controllers, and for that every thing gains
the better estimation of just and right in that it is mainly

and principally addressed to that end for which it was first ordained.

Furthermore, if divers have jointly vowed one and the same thing, is the obligation of the one annihilated by the perjury of the other ? If many become bound for one and the same sum, can the bankrupting of one of the obligees quit the rest of their engagement ? If divers tutors administer ill the goods of their pupil, and that there be one amongst them who makes conscience of his actions, can the bad dealing of his companions acquit him ? Nay, rather on the contrary, he cannot free himself from the infamy of perjury, if to the utmost of his power he do not truly discharge his trust, and perform his promise : neither can the others' deficiency be excused, in the bad managing of the tutorship, if they likewise accuse not the rest who were joined with them in the administration, for it is not only the principal tutor who may call to an account those who are suspected to have unjustly or indiscreetly ordered the affairs of their pupil, but even those who were formerly removed may also upon just occasion discharge and remove the delinquents therein. Therefore those who are obliged to serve a whole empire and kingdom, as the constables, marshals, peers and others, or those who have particular obligations to some provinces or cities, which make a part or portion of the kingdom, as dukes, marquises, earls, sheriffs, mayors, and the rest, are bound by the duty of their place, to succour the commonwealth, and to free it from the burden of tyrants, according to the rank and place which they hold of the people next after the king. The first ought to deliver the whole kingdom from tyrannous oppression ; the other, as tutors, that part of the kingdom whose protection they have undertaken ; the duty of the former is to suppress the tyrant, that of the latter, to drive him from their confines. Wherefore Mattathias, being a principal man in the state, when some basely connived, others perniciously consorted with Antiochus, the tyrannous oppressor of the Jewish kingdom, he courageously opposing the manifest oppression both of church and state, encourages the people to the taking of arms, with these words, " Let us restore the decayed estate of our people, and let us fight for our people, and for the sanctuary." Whereby it plainly appears, that not for religion only, but even for our country and our possessions, we may fight and take arms against a tyrant, as this Antiochus was. For the Machabites are not by any questioned, or reprehended for conquering the kingdom, and expelling the tyrant, but in that they attributed to themselves the royal dignity, which only belongs by God's special appointment, to the tribe of Judah.

Humane histories are frequently stored with examples of this kind. Arbactus, governor of the Medes, killed effeminate Sardanapalus, spinning amongst women, and sportingly distributing all the treasures of the kingdom amongst those his loose companions. Vindex and Galba quit the party of Nero, yea, though the senate connived, and in a sort supported his tyranny, and drew with them Gallia and Spain, being the provinces whereof they were governors.

But amongst all, the decree of the senate of Sparta is most notable, and ought to pass as an undeniable maxim amongst all nations. The Spartans being lords of the city Byzantium, sent Olearchus thither for governor and commander for the wars ; who took corn from the citizens, and distributed it to his soldiers. In the meantime the families of the citizens died for hunger, Anaxilaus, a principal man of the city, disdaining that tyrannous usage, entered into treaty with Alcibiades to deliver up the town, who shortly after was received into it. Anaxilaus, being accused at Sparta for the delivery of Byzantium, pleaded his cause himself, and was there acquit by the judges ; for (said they) " Wars are to be made with families, and not with nature, nothing being more repugnant to nature, than that those who are bound to defend a city, should be more cruel to the inhabitants, than their enemies who besiege them."

This was the opinion of the Lacedemonians, certainly just rulers. Neither can he be accounted a just king, who approves not this sentence of absolution ; for those who desire to govern according to the due proportion of equity and reason, take into consideration, as well what the law inflicts on tyrants, as also, what are the proper rights and bounds, both of the patrician and plebeian orders. But we must yet proceed a little further. There is not so mean a mariner, but must be ready to prevent the shipwreck of the vessel, when either the negligence or wilfulness of the pilot casts it into danger. Every magistrate is bound to relieve, and as much as in him lies, to redress the miseries of the commonwealth, if he shall see the prince, or the principal officers of state, his associates, by their weakness or wickedness, to hazard the ruin thereof ; briefly, he must either free the whole kingdom, or at least that portion especially recommended to his care, from their imminent and encroaching tyranny. But has this duty proper relation to every one ? Shall it be permitted to Hendonius Sabinus, to Ennus Suranus, or to the fencer Spartanus ; or to be brief, to a mere private person to present the bonnet to slaves, put arms into the hands of subjects, or to join battle with the prince, although he oppress the people with tyranny ? No, certainly, the commonwealth was not given in charge to particular persons, considered one by one ; but, on the contrary, particulars even as papists are recommended to the care of the principal officers and magistrates ; and therefore they are not bound to defend the commonwealth, which cannot defend themselves. God nor the people have not put the sword into the hands of particular persons ; therefore, if without commandment they draw the sword, they are seditious, although the cause seem never so just.

Furthermore, the prince is not established by private and particular persons, but by all in general considered in one entire body ; whereupon it follows, that they are bound to attend the commandment of all, to wit, of those who are the representative body of a kingdom, or of a province, or of a city, or at the least of some one of them, before they undertake anything against the prince.

For, as a pupil cannot bring an action, but, being avowed in the name of his tutor, although the pupil be indeed the true proprietor of the estate, and the tutor only owner with reference to the charge committed unto him ; so likewise the people may not enterprise actions of such nature, but by the command of those into whose hands they have resigned their power and authority, whether they be ordinary magistrates, or extraordinary, created in the assembly of the estates ; whom, if I may so say, for that purpose, they have girded with their sword, and invested with authority, both to govern and defend them, established in the same kind as the pretor at Rome, who determined all differences between masters and their servants, to the end that if any controversy happened between the king and the subjects, they should be judges and preservers of the right, lest the subjects should assume power to themselves to be judges in their own causes. And therefore if they were oppressed with tributes and unreasonable imposts ; if anything were attempted contrary to covenant and oath, and no magistrate opposed those unjust proceedings ; they must rest quiet, and suppose that many times the best physicians, both to prevent and cure some grievous disease, do appoint both letting blood, evacuation of humours, and lancing of the flesh ; and that the affairs of this world are of that nature, that with much difficulty, one evil cannot be remedied without the adventuring, if not the suffering of another ; nor any good be achieved without great pains.

They have the example of the people of Israel, who, during the reign of Solomon, refused not to pay those excessive taxes imposed on them, both for the building of the temple, and fortifying of the kingdom, because by a general consent they were granted for the promulgation of the glory of God, and for an ornament and defence of the public state.

They have also the example of our Lord and Saviour Jesus Christ, who, though he were King of Kings, notwithstanding, because he conversed in this world in another quality, to wit, of a private and particular man, paid willingly tribute. If the magistrates themselves manifestly favour the tyranny, or at the least do not formally oppose it ; let private men remember the saying of Job, " That for the sins of the people God permits hypocrites to reign," whom it is impossible either to convert or subvert, if men repent not of their ways, to walk in obedience to God's commandments ; so that there are no other weapons to be used, but bended knees and humble hearts. Briefly, let them bear with bad princes, and pray for better, persuading themselves that an outragious tyranny is to be supported as patiently, as some exceeding damage done by the violence of tempests, or some excessive overflowing waters, or some such natural accidents unto the fruits of the earth, if they like not better to change their habitations, by retiring themselves into some other countries. So David fled into the mountains, and attempted nothing against the tyrant Saul, because the people had not declared him any public magistrate of the kingdom.

Jesus Christ, whose kingdom was not of this world, fled into Egypt, and so freed himself from the paws of the tyrant. Saint Paul, teaching of the duty of particular Christian men, and not of magistrates, teaches that Nero must be obeyed. But if all the principal officers of state, or divers of them, or but one, endeavour to suppress a manifest tyranny, or if a magistrate seek to free that province, or portion of the kingdom from oppression, which is committed to his care and custody, provided under colour of freedom he bring not in a new tyranny, then must all men with joint courage and alacrity run to arms, and take part with him or them, and assist with body and goods, as if God Himself from heaven had proclaimed wars, and meant to join battle against tyrants, and by all ways and means endeavour to deliver their country and commonwealth from their tyrannous oppression. For as God does oftentimes chastise a people by the cruelty of tyrants, so also does He many times punish tyrants by the hands of the people. It being a most true saying, verified in all ages : " For the iniquities, violences, and wickedness of princes, kingdoms are translated from one nation to another ; but tyranny was never of any durable continuance."

The centurions and men at arms did freely and courageously execute the commandments of the high priest Jehoiada, in suppressing the tyranny of Athalia. In like manner all the faithful and generous Israelites took part and joined with the Machabites, as well to re-establish the true service of God, as also to free and deliver the state from the wicked and unjust oppression of Antiochus, and God blessed with happy success their just and commendable enterprise. What then, cannot God when He pleases stir up particular and private persons, to ruin a mighty and powerful tyranny ? He that gives power and ability to some even out of the dust, without any title or colourable pretext of lawful authority, to rise to the height of rule and dominion, and in it tyrannize and afflict the people for their transgressions ; cannot He also even from the meanest multitude raise a liberator ? He who enthralled and subjected the people of Israel to Jabin, and to Eglon, did he not deliver and enfranchise them by the hand of Ehud, Barack and Deborah, whilst the magistrates and officers were dead in a dull and negligent ecstasy of security ? What then shall hinder ? You may say the same God, who in these days sends us tyrants to correct us, that he may not also extraordinarily send correctors of tyrants to deliver us ? What if Ahab cut off good men, if Jezebel suborn false witnesses against Naboth, may not a

Jehu be raised to exterminate the whole line of Ahab, to revenge the death of Naboth, and to cast the body of Jezebel to be torn and devoured of dogs ? Certainly, as I have formerly answered, the Almighty is ever mindful of His justice, and maintains it as inviolably as His mercy.

But for as much as in these latter times, those miraculous testimonies by which God was wont to confirm the extraordinary vocation of those famous worthies, are now wanting for the most part : let the people be advised, that in seeking to cross the sea dry foot, they take not some impostor for their guide, who may lead them headlong to destruction (as we may read happened to the Jews) ; and that in seeking freedom from tyranny, he who was the principal instrument to disenthral them, become not himself a more insupportable tyrant than the former. Briefly, lest endeavouring to advantage the commonwealth, they introduce not a common misery upon all the undertakers participating therein with divers States of Italy, who, seeking to suppress the present evil, added an accession of greater and more intolerable servitude.

Finally, that we may come to some period of this third question ; princes are chosen by God, and established by the people. As all particulars considered one by one, are inferior to the prince ; so the whole body of the people and officers of state, who represent that body, are the princes' superiors. In the receiving and inauguration of a prince, there are covenants and contracts passed between him and the people, which are tacit and expressed, natural or civil ; to wit, to obey him faithfully whilst he commands justly, that he serving the commonwealth, all men shall serve him, that whilst he governs according to law, all shall be submitted to his government, etc. The officers of the kingdom are the guardians and protectors of these covenants and contracts. He who maliciously or wilfully violates these conditions, is questionless a tyrant by practice. And therefore the officers of state may judge him according to the laws. And if he support his tyranny by strong hands, their duty binds them, when by no other means it can be effected by force of arms to suppress him.

Of these officers there be two kinds, those who have generally undertaken the protection of the kingdom ; as the constable, marshals, peers, palatines, and the rest, every one of whom, although all the rest do either connive or consort with the tyranny, are bound to oppose and repress the tyrant ; and those who have undertaken the government of any province, city, or part of the kingdom, as dukes, marquesses, earls, consuls, mayors, sheriffs, etc., they may according to right, expel and drive tyranny and tyrants from their cities, confines, and governments.

But particular and private persons may not unsheathe the sword against tyrants by practice, because they were not established by particulars, but by the whole body of the people. But for tyrants, who, without title intrude themselves for so much as there is no contract or agreement between them and the people, it is indifferently permitted all to oppose and depose them ; and in this rank of tyrants may those be ranged, who, abusing the weakness and sloth of a lawful prince, tyrannously insult over his subjects. Thus much for this, to which for a more full resolution may be added that which has been formerly discoursed in the second question.

THE FOURTH QUESTION

Whether neighbour princes may, or are bound by law to aid the subjects of other princes, persecuted for true religion, or oppressed by manifest tyranny.

We have yet one other question to treat of, in the discussing whereof, there is more use of an equitable judgment than of a nimble apprehension ; and if charity were but in any reasonable proportion prevalent amongst the men of this age, the disputation thereof was altogether frivolous ; but, seeing nothing in these days is more rare, nor less esteemed than charity, we will speak somewhat of this our question. We have already sufficiently proved, that all tyrants, whether those who seek to captivate the minds and souls of the people with an erroneous and superstitious opinion in matter of religion, or, those who would enthral their bodies and estates with miserable servitude and excessive impositions, may justly by the people, be both suppressed and expulsed ? But, for so much as tyrants are for the most part so cunning, and subjects seldom so cautelous, that the disease is hardly known, or, at the least, not carefully observed before the remedy prove almost desperate, nor think of their own defence before they are brought to those straits, that they are unable to defend themselves, but compelled to implore the assistance of others : Our demand therefore is, if Christian princes lawfully may, and ought to succour those subjects who are afflicted for true religion, or oppressed by unjust servitude, and whose sufferings are either for the kingdom of Christ, or for the liberty of their own state ? There are many, who, hoping to advance their own ends, and encroach on others' rights, will readily embrace the part of the afflicted, and proclaim the lawfulness of it ; but the hope of gain is the certain and only aim of their purposes. And in this manner the Romans, Alexander the Great, and divers others, pretending to suppress tyrants, have oftentimes enlarged their own limits.

It is not long since we saw King Henry the Second make wars on the Emperor Charles the Fifth, under colour of defending and delivering the Protestant princes. As also Henry the Eighth, King of England, was in like manner ready to assist the Germans, if the Emperor Charles should molest them. But if there be some appearance of danger, and little expectance of profit, then it is that most princes do vehemently dispute the lawfulness of the action. And as the former cover their ambition and avarice with the veil of charity and piety, so, on the contrary do the others call their fear and cowardly baseness integrity and justice; although that piety (which is ever careful of another's good) have no part in the counsels of the first, nor justice (which affectionately desires the easing of a neighbour's grief) in cooling the charitable intendments of the latter. Therefore, without leaning either to the one side or the other, let us follow those rules which piety and justice trace us out in matter of religion.

First, all accord in this, that there is only one Church, whereof Jesus Christ is the head, the members whereof are so united and conjoined together, that if the least of them be offended or wronged, they all participate both in the harm and sorrow, as throughout Holy Scripture plainly appears: wherefore the church is compared to a body. Now, it oftentimes happens, that the body is not only overthrown by a wound in the arm or thigh, but even also much endangered, yea, sometimes killed by a small hurt in the little finger. Vainly, therefore, does any man vaunt that this body is recommended to his care and custody, if he suffer that to be dismembered and pulled in pieces which he might have preserved whole and entire. The church is compared to an edifice: on which side soever the building is undermined, it many times chances that the whole tumbles down, and on what rafter or piece of timber soever the flame takes hold, it endangers the whole house of burning; he must needs be therefore worthy of scorn, who should defer to quench the fire which had caught his house top, because he dwells most in the cellar. Would not all hold him for a madman who should neglect by countermining to frustrate a mine, because it was intended to overthrow that wall there, and not this here.

Again, the church is resembled to a ship, which, as it sails together, so does it sink together; in so much that in a tempest, those who be in the forecastle, or in the keel, are no more secure than those who remain at the stern or on the deck : so that the proverb commonly says, " When men run the like hazard in matter of danger, that they venture both in one bottom." This being granted questionless, whosoever has not a fellow-feeling in commiserating the trouble, danger, and distress of the church, is no member of that body, nor domestic in the family of Jesus Christ, nor hath any place in the ark of the covenant of grace. He who has any sense of religion in his heart, ought no more to doubt whether he be obliged to aid the afflicted members of the church, than he would be assisting to himself in the like distress; for the union of the church unites us all into one body, and therefore every one in his calling must be ready to assist the needy, and so much the more willingly, by how much the Almighty has bestowed a greater portion of his blessings on us, which were not conferred that we should be made possessors of them, but that we should be dispensers thereof according to the necessity of his saints.

As this church is one, so is she recommended and given in charge to all Christian princes in general, and to every one of them in particular; for so much as it was dangerous to leave the care to one alone, and the unity of it would not by any means permit that she should be divided into pieces, and every portion assigned unto one particular; God has committed it all entire to particulars, and all the parts of it to all in general, not only to preserve and defend it, but also to amplify and increase it as much as might be. Insomuch that if a prince who has undertaken the care of a portion of the church, as that of Germany and England, and, notwithstanding, neglect and forsake another part that is oppressed, and which he might succour, he doubtless abandons the church, Christ having but one only spouse, which the prince is so bound to preserve and defend, that she be not violated or corrupted in any part, if it be possible. And in the same manner, as every private person is bound by his humble and ardent prayers to God, to desire the restoring of the church, so likewise are the magistrates tied diligently to procure the same, with the utmost of their power and means which God has put into their hands. For the church of Ephesus is no other than that of Colossus, but these two are portions of the universal church, which is the kingdom of Christ, the increase and prosperity whereof ought to be the continual subject of all private men's prayers and desires ; but it is the duty of all kings, princes, and magistrates, not only to amplify and extend the limits and bounds of the church in all places, but only to preserve and defend it against all men whatsoever. Wherefore there was but one temple in Judea built by Solomon, which represented the unity of the church ; and therefore ridiculous and worthy of punishment was that churchwarden, who had care only of some small part of the church, and suffered all the rest to be spoiled with rain and weather. In like manner, all Christian kings, when they receive the sword on the day of their coronation, solemnly swear to maintain the catholic or universal church, and the ceremony then used doth fully express it, for holding the sword in their hands, they turn to the east, west, north, and south, and brandish it, to the end that it may be known that no part of the world is excepted. As by this ceremony they assume the protection of the church, it must be questionless understood of the true church, and not of the false ; therefore ought they to employ the utmost of their ability to reform, and wholly to restore that which they hold to be the pure and truly Christian church, to wit, ordered and governed according to the direction of the Word of God. That this was the practice of godly princes, we have their examples to instruct us.

In the time of Ezechias, King of Judah, the kingdom of Israel had been a long time before in subjection to the Assyrians, to wit, ever since the King Hosea, his time ; and therefore if the church of Judah only, and not the whole universal church had been committed to the custody of Ezechias ; and if in the preservation of the church, the same course were to be held, as in the dividing of lands, and imposing of tributes, then questionably Ezechias would have contained himself within his own limits, especially then when the exorbitant power of the Assyrians lorded it everywhere. Now, we read that he sent express messengers throughout Israel, to wit, to the subjects of the King of Assyria, to invite them to come to Jerusalem to celebrate the Paschal Feast ; yea, and he aided the faithful Israelites of the tribes of Ephraim and Manasses, and others the subjects of the Assyrians, to ruin the high places which were in their quarters.

We read also, that the good king Josias expelled idolatry, not only out of his own kingdom, but also even out of the kingdom of Israel, which was then wholly in subjection to the King of Assyria, and no marvel, for where the glory of God and the kingdom of Christ are in question, there no bounds or limits can confine the zeal and fervent affection of pious and godly princes. Though the opposition be great, and the power of the opposers greater, yet the more they fear God, the less they will fear men. These generous examples of divers godly princes, have since been imitated by sundry Christian kings, by whose means the church (which was heretofore restrained within the narrow limits of Palestine) has since been dilated throughout the universal world. Constantine and Licinius governed the empire together, the one in the Orient, the other in the Occident. They were associates of equal power and authority. And amongst equals, as the proverb is, " There is no command."

Notwithstanding, because Licinius does everywhere banish, torment, and put to death the Christians, and amongst them divers of the nobility, and that for and under pretence of religion, Constantine makes war against him, and by force compels him to give free liberty of religion to the Christians ; and because he broke his faith, and relapsed into his former cruelties, he caused him to be apprehended and put to death in the city of Thessalonica. This emperor's piety was with so great an applause celebrated by the divines of those times, that they suppose that saying in the prophet Isaiah to be meant by him : " That kings shall be pastors and nursing fathers of the church." After his death, the Roman empire was divided equally between his sons, without advantaging the one more than the other. Constans favoured the orthodox Christians, Constantus, being the elder, leaned to the Arrians, and for that cause banished the learned Athanasius from Alexandria ; the greatest professed adversary of the Arrians. Certainly, if any consideration in matter of confines be absolutely requisite, it must needs be amongst brethren ; and notwithstanding, Constans threatened to war on his brother if he restore not Athanasius, and had without doubt performed it, if the other had long deferred the accomplishment of his desire. And if he proceeded so far for the restitution of one bishop, had it not been much more likely and reasonable for him to have assisted a good part of the people, if they implored his aid against the tyranny of those who refused them the exercise of their religion, under the authority of their magistrates and governors ? So at the persuasion of Atticus the bishop, Theodosius made war on Chosroes, King of Persia, to deliver the Christians of his kingdom from persecution, although they were but particular and private persons ; which certainly those most just princes, who instituted so many worthy laws, and had so great and special care of justice, would not have done, if by that fact they had supposed anything were usurped on another man's right, or the law of nations violated. But to what end were so many expeditions undertaken by Christian princes into the Holy Land against the Saracens ? Wherefore were demanded and raised so many of those Saladine tenths ? To what purpose were so many confederacies made, and crusades proclaimed against the Turks, if it were not lawful for Christian princes, yea, those furthest remote, to deliver the church of God from the oppression of tyrants, and to free captive Christians from under the yoke of bondage ? What were the motives that led them to those wars ? What were the reasons that urged them to undergo those dangers ? But only in regard of the churches' union, Christ summoned every man from all parts with a unanimous consent, to undertake the defence thereof ? For all men are bound to repulse common dangers with a joint and common opposition, all which have a natural consent and relation with this we now treat of. If this were lawful for them against Mahomet, and not only lawful, but that the backward and negligent were ever made liable to all infamous contempt, and the forward and ready undertakers always recompensed with all honourable respect and reward, according to the merit of their virtues ; wherefore not now against the enemy of Christ and his saints ? If it be a lawful war to fight against the Greeks (that I may use that phrase) when they assail our Troy ; wherefore is it unlawful to pursue and prevent that incendiary Sinon ? Finally, if it have been esteemed an heroical act to deliver Christians from corporal servitude (for the Turks enforce none in point of religion), is it not a thing yet much more noble to enfranchise and set at liberty souls imprisoned in the mists of error ?

These examples of so many religious princes, might well have the directive power of law. But let us hear what God Himself pronounces in many places of His Word by the mouth of His prophets, against those who advance not the building up of His church, or who make no reckoning of her afflictions. The Gadites, the Reubenites, and half the tribe of Manasses desire of Moses that he would allot them their portion on the other side of Jordon. Moses grants their request, but with this proviso and condition, that they should not only assist their other brethren the Israelites to conquer the land of Canaan ; but also that they should march the first, and serve as vanguard to the rest, because they had their portions first set them forth, and if they fail to perform this duty, he with an anathema, destines them to destruction, and compares them to those who were adjudged rebels at Cadisbarnea. And what, says he, " your brethren shall fight, and you in the mean season rest quiet at home ? " Nay, on the contrary, you also shall pass Jordan, and not return into their houses, before first the Lord have driven his enemies out from before his face, and granted place to your brethren as well as you, then shall you be innocent before the Lord and His people Israel. He shews by this, that those who God first blessed with so great a benefit, if they help not their brethren, if they make not themselves sharers in their labours, companions in their travels, and leaders in their dangers, they must questionless expect a heavy punishment to fall upon them.

Likewise when under the conduct of Deborah, the Nephtalites and Zabulonites took arms against the tyrant Jabin ; and that in the mean season the Reubenites, who should have been first in the field, took their ease and played on their pipes, whilst their flocks and herds fed at liberty ; the Gadites held themselves secured with the rampire of the river ; the Danites gloried in their command at sea ; and Ashur, to be brief, was confident in the difficult access of their mountains. The Spirit of the Lord speaking by the prophetess, does in express terms condemn them all : " Curse ye Meros " (said the Angel of the Lord), " curse ye bitterly the inhabitants thereof, because they came not to the help of the Lord, to the help of the Lord against the mighty.

But blessed above women shall Jael the wife of Heber the Kenite be " ; who, though she might have alleged the alliance which her husband had with the Canaanites, did, notwithstanding, kill Sisera, the general of the enemies' army. And therefore Uriah spoke religiously, and like a true patriarch, when he said : " The ark of the Lord, and Israel, and Judah abide in tents, and my Lord Joab, and the servants of my Lord are encamped in the open fields ; shall I then go into mine house, to eat and to drink and to lie with my wife ? As thou livest, and as thy soul liveth, I will not do this thing." But, on the contrary, impious and wicked were the Princes of Israel, who, supposing themselves secured by the craggy mountains of Samaria, and strong fortification of Sion, took liberty to loose themselves in luxurious feasts, loose delights, drinking delicious wines, and sleeping in perfumed beds of ivory, despising in the mean season poor Joseph ; to wit, the Lord's flock tormented and miserably vexed on all sides, nor have any compassion on their affliction. " The Lord God hath sworn by Himself, saith the Lord God of Hosts, I abhor the excellency of Jacob, and hate his palaces, therefore will I deliver up the city, with all that is therein, and those that wallow thus in pleasures, shall be the first that shall go into captivity." Wickedly, therefore, did those Ephraimnes, who, instead of congratulating and applauding the famous and notable victories of Gideon and Jephta, did envy and traduce them, whom, notwithstanding, they had forsaken in dangers.

As much may be said of the Israelites, who, seeing David overcome the difficulty of his affairs, and remain a peaceable king, say aloud, " We are thy flesh and thy bones." And some years after, seeing him embroiled again in troubles, cried out, " We have no part in David, neither have we inheritance in the son of Jesse." Let us rank also with these, all those Christians in name only, who will communicate at the holy table, and yet refuse to take the cup of affliction with their brethren, who look for salvation in the church, and care not for the safety and preservation of the church and the members thereof. Briefly, who adore one and the same God the Father, acknowledge and avow themselves of the same household of faith, and profess to be one and the same body in Jesus Christ, and, notwithstanding, yield no succour nor assistance to their Saviour, afflicted in his members ;

what vengeance do you think will God inflict on such impiety ? Moses compares those who abandon their brethren to the rebels of Cadisbarnea. Now, none of those by the decree of the Almighty, entered into the land of Canaan. Let not those then pretend any interest in the heavenly Canaan, who will not succour Christ when He is crucified, and suffering a thousand times a day in his members ; and, as it were, begging their alms from door to door. The Son of God with his own mouth condemns them to everlasting fire, that when he was hungry gave Him no meat ; when He was thirsty gave Him no drink ; when He was a stranger, lodged Him not ; naked, and clothed Him not ; sick, and in prison, and visited Him not. And, therefore, let those expect punishments without end, who lend a deaf ear to the complaints and groans of our Saviour Jesus Christ, suffering all these things daily in his members ; although otherwise they may appear both to others and themselves, to be jolly Christians, yet shall their condition be much more miserable than that of many infidels. For why ? were they the Jews only, and Scribes and Pharisees, to speak properly, that crucified Christ ? or were they Ethnicks, Turks, or some certain pernicious sects of Christians, which crucify, torment, and persecute him in his members ? No, certainly, the Jews hold Him as impostor, the Ethnicks a malefactor, the Turks an infidel, the others an heretic, insomuch as if we consider the intention of these men, as the censoring of all offences ought to have principal relation thereunto, we cannot conclude that it is properly Christ that they persecute with such hatred, but some criminal person, who, in their opinion deserves this usage. But they do truly and properly persecute and crucify Christ Jesus, who profess to acknowledge Him for the Messiah, God and Redeemer of the world ; and which, notwithstanding, fail to free Him from persecution and vexation in His members, when it is in their power to do it. Briefly, he who omits to deliver his neighbour from the hands of the murderer, when he sees him in evident danger of his life, is questionless guilty of the murder, as well as the murderer. For seeing he neglected when he had means to preserve his life, it must needs necessarily follow that he desired his death. And in all crimes the will and intendment ought principally to be regarded. But questionless, these Christian princes, who do not relieve and assist the true professors, who suffer for true religion, are much more guilty of murder than any other, because they might deliver from danger an infinite number of people, who for want of timely succour, suffer death and torments under the cruel hands of their persecutors. And to this may be added, That to suffer one's brother to be murdered, is a greater offence than if he were a stranger. Nay, I say further, These forsakers of their brethren in their time of danger and distress, are more vile, and more to be abhorred than the tyrants themselves who persecute them. For it is much more wicked, and worthy of greater punishment, to kill an honest man who is innocent and fearing God (as those who consent with them in the faith, must of necessity know the true professors to be), than a thief, an impostor, a magician, or an heretic, as those who persecute the true Christians do commonly believe them to be. It is a greater offence by many degrees to strive with God, than man. Briefly, in one and the same action it is a much more grievous crime, perfidiously to betray, than ignorantly to offend. But may the same also be said of them who refuse to assist those who are oppressed by tyranny, or defend the liberty of the commonwealth against the oppression of tyrants ? For in this case the conjunction or confederacy seems not to be of so strict a condition between the one and the other ; here we speak of the commonwealth diversely governed according to the customs of the countries, and particularly recommended to these here, or those there ; and not of the church of God, which is composed of all, and recommended to all in general, and to every one in particular.

The Jew says, our Saviour Christ is not only neighbour to the Jew, but also to the Samaritan, and to every other man. But we ought to love our neighbour as ourselves ; and therefore an Israelite is not only bound to deliver an Israelite from the hands of thieves, if it be in his power, but every stranger also ; yea, though unknown, if he will rightly discharge his duty. Neither let him dispute whether it be lawful to defend another, who believes he may justly defend himself. For it is much more just, if we truly consider the concomitants, to deliver from danger and outrage another than one's self ; seeing that what is done for pure charity, is more right and allowable, than that which is executed for colour, or desire of revenge, or by any other transport of passion : in revenging our own wrongs we never keep a mean ; whereas in other men's, though much greater, the most intemperate will easily observe moderation. Furthermore, the heathens themselves may teach us what humane society, and what the law of nature requires of us in this business ; wherefore Cicero says, " That nature being the common mother of mankind, prescribes and ordains, that every man endeavour and procure the good of another, whatsoever he be, only because he is a man ; otherwise all bonds of society, yea, and mankind itself, must needs go to ruin."

And therefore, justice is built on these two bases or pillars ; first, that none be wronged ; secondly, that good be done to all, if it be possible. So also are there two sorts of injustice ; the first, in those who offer injury to their neighbours ; the second, in them who, when they have means to deliver the oppressed, do, notwithstanding, suffer them to sink under the burden of their wrongs. For whosoever does wrong to another, either moved thereunto by anger, or any other passion, he may in a sort be truly said to lay violent hands on his companion ; but he that hath means, and defends not the afflicted, or to his power, wards not the blows that are struck at him, is as much faulty, as if he forsook his parents, or his friends, or his country in their distress. That which was done by the first may well be attributed to choler which is a short madness ; the fault committed by the other discovers a bad mind and a wicked purpose, which are the perpetual tormentors and tyrants of the conscience. The fury of the first may be in some sort excused, but the malice of the second admits no colour of defence. Peradventure you will say, I fear in aiding the one I shall do wrong to the other. And I answer, you seek a cloak of justice wherewith to cover your base remissness. And, if you lay your hand on your heart, you will presently confess, that it is somewhat else, and not justice, that withholds you from performing your duty. For, as the same Cicero says in another place, " Either thou wilt not make the wrongdoer thine enemy, or not take pains, or not be at so much charge, or else negligence, sloth or the hindering of thine own occasions, or the crossing of other purposes, takes thee off from the defence of those who otherwise thou art bound to relieve. Now in saying thou only attend thine own affairs, fearing to wrong another, thou fallest into another kind of injustice : for thou abandoneth human society, in that thou wilt not afford any endeavour either of mind, body, or goods, for the necessary preservation thereof." Read the directions of the heathen philosophers and politicians who have written more divinely herein, than many Christians in these days. From hence also proceeds, that the Roman law designs punishment to that neighbour who will not deliver the slave from the outrageous fury of his master.

Amongst the Egyptians, if any man had seen another assailed and distressed by thieves and robbers, and did not according to his power presently aid him, he was adjudged worthy of death, if at the least he discovered or delivered not the delinquents into the hand of the magistrate. If he were negligent in performing this duty for the first mulct, he was to receive a certain number of blows on his body, and to fast for three days together. If the neighbour be so firmly obliged in this mutual duty of succour to his neighbour, yea, to an unknown person in case he be assailed by thieves : shall it not be lawful for a good prince to assist, not slaves to an imperious master, or children against a furious father, but a kingdom against a tyrant, the commonwealth against the private spleen of one, the people (who are indeed the true owners of the state) against a ministering servant to the public. And, if he carelessly or wilfully omit this duty, deserves he not himself to be esteemed a tyrant, and punished accordingly, as well as the other a robber, who neglected to assist his neighbour in that danger ? Thucydides upon this matter says, " That those are not only tyrants which make other men slaves, but much more those who, having means to suppress and prevent such oppression, take no care to perform it "; and amongst others, those who assumed the title of protectors of Greece, and defenders of the country, and yet stir not to deliver their country from oppression of strangers. And truly indeed ; for a tyrant is in some sort compelled to hold a straight and tyrannous hand over those who, by violence and tyranny, he hath constrained to obey him, because, as Tiberius said, " he holds the wolf by the ears, whom he can neither hold without pain and force, nor let go without danger and death."

To the end then that he may blot out one sin with another sin, he fills up one wickedness to another, and is forced to do injuries to others, lest he should prove by remissness injurious to himself. But the prince who, with a negligent and idle regard, looks on the outrageousness of a tyrant, and the massacring of innocents that he might have preserved, like the barbarous spectacles of the Roman sword-plays is so much more guilty than the tyrant himself, by how much the cruel and homicidious directors and appointers of these bloody sports were more justly punishable by all good laws than the poor and constrained actors in those murdering tragedies. And as he questionless deserves greater punishment who, out of insolent jollity, murders one, than he who unwillingly for fear of a further harm kills a man ; if any object that is it against reason and good order to meddle in the affairs of another, I answer with the old man in Terence " I am a man, and I believe that all duties of humanity are fit and convenient for me. If others seeking to cover their base negligence, and careless unwillingness, allege that bounds and jurisdictions are distinguished one from another, and that it is not lawful to thrust one's sickle into another's harvest," neither am I also of that opinion, that upon any such colour or pretence, it is lawful for a prince to encroach upon another's jurisdiction or right, or upon that occasion to usurp another's country, and so carry another man's corn into his barn, as divers have taken such shadows to mask their bad intentions. I will not say that after the manner of those arbitrators whom Cicero speaks of, thou adjudge the things in controversy to thyself. But I require that you repress the prince who invades the kingdom of Christ, that you contain the tyrant within his own limits, that you stretch forth your hand of compassion to the people afflicted, that you raise up the commonwealth lying grovelling on the ground, and that you so carry yourself in the ordering and managing of this, that all men may see your principal aim and end was the public benefit of human society, and not any private profit or advantage of your own. For seeing that justice respects only the public, and that which is without, and injustice fixes a man wholly on himself, it doubtless becomes a man truly honest to dispose his actions, that every private interest give place, and yield to public commodity.

Briefly, to epitomize what has been formerly said, if a prince outrageously overpass the bounds of piety and justice, a neighbour prince may justly and religiously leave his own country, not to invade and usurp another's, but to contain the other within the limits of justice and equity. And if he neglect or omit his duty herein, he shews himself a wicked and unworthy magistrate. If a prince tyrannize over the people, a neighbour prince ought to yield succour as freely and willingly to the people, as he would do to the prince his brother if the people mutinied against him : yea, he should so much the more readily succour the people, by how much there is more just cause of pity to see many afflicted, than one alone. If Porsenna brought Tarquinius Superbus back to Rome, much more justly might Constantine, requested by the senate, and Roman people, expel Maxentius the tyrant from Rome. Briefly, if man become a wolf to man, who hinders that man (according to the proverb), may not be instead of God to the needy ? And therefore the ancients have ranked Hercules amongst the gods, because he punished and tamed Procrustes, Busiris, and other tyrants, the plagues of mankind, and monsters of the earth. So whilst the Roman empire retained her freedom, she was truly accounted the safeguard of all the world against the violence of tyrants, because the senate was the port and refuge of kings, people, and nations. In like manner Constantine, called by the Romans against Maxentius, had God Almighty for the leader of his army. And the whole church does with exceeding commendations celebrate his enterprise, although that Maxentius had the same authority in the West, as Constantine had in the East. Also Charlemaine undertook war against the Lombards, being requested to assist the nobility of Italy : although the kingdom of the Lombards had been of a long continuance, and he had no just pretence of right over them. In like manner when Charles the Bold, King of France, had tyrannously put to death the governor of the country between the rivers of Seine and Loire, with the Duke Lambert, and another nobleman called Jametius, and that other great men of the kingdom were retired unto Lewis King of Germany, brother (but by another mother) unto Charles, to request aid against him, and his mother called Judith, one of the most pernicious women in the world, Lewis gave them audience in a full assembly of the German princes, by whose joint advice it was decreed, that wars should be made against Charles for the re-establishing in their goods, honours, and estates, those whom he had unjustly dispossessed.

Finally, as there have ever been tyrants distressed here and there, so also all histories testify that there have been neighbouring princes to oppose tyranny, and maintain the people in their right. The princes of these times by imitating so worthy examples, should suppress the tyrants both of bodies and souls, and restrain the oppressors both of the commonwealth, and of the church of Christ : otherwise, they themselves may most deservedly be branded with that infamous title of tyrant.

And to conclude this discourse in a word, piety commands that the law and church of God be maintained. Justice requires that tyrants and destroyers of the commonwealth be compelled to reason. Charity challenges the right of relieving and restoring the oppressed. Those who make no account of these things, do as much as in them lies to drive piety, justice, and charity out of this world, that they may never more be heard of.

FINIS